THE SOCIALLY DISADVANTAGED:
Physiological and Psychological Aspects of Deprivation

VOLUME II

Edited by
Earl J. Ogletree
Chicago State University

MSS Information Corporation
655 Madison Avenue, New York, N. Y. 10021

This is a custom-made book of readings prepared for the courses taught by the editor, as well as for related courses and for college and university libraries. For information about our program, please write to:

MSS INFORMATION CORPORATION
655 Madison Avenue
New York, New York 10021

MSS wishes to express its appreciation to the authors of the articles in this collection for their cooperation in making their work available in this format.

Library of Congress Cataloging in Publication Data

Ogletree, Earl J   comp.
    The socially disadvantaged.

    1. Socially handicapped children — Education — United States. 2. Socially handicapped — Education — United States. I. Title. [DNLM: 1. Cultural deprivation — Collected works. 2. Education, Special — Collected works. LC4065.D4 035s   1973]
LC4091.034   1973   371.9'67   73-17001
ISBN 0-8422-5156-1
ISBN 0-8422-0380-X (pbk.)

11/2/79 Berhart Tyler 18.00

CONTENTS

TEACHING THE DISADVANTAGED

ISSUES IN URBAN EDUCATION

PREFACE: VOLUME II

Volume II covers four major topics which are a continuous dialog of the topics discussed in Volume I. This volume is concerned with self-concept development, cognitive readiness and the effects of early schooling, teaching strategies, trends and programs for the disadvantaged, and urban education issues.

Section V, *Self-Concept Development* explores the cumulative effects of poor environment, school failure and the subsequent personality disorders resulting in a distorted concept of self. Not only is the disadvantaged child's self-concept affected by the conditions of poverty, language difficulties, and migration, it is influenced by the actions of teachers. A negative self-concept is reinforced by the high rates of failure in school, school dropouts, unemployment, delinquency and the feeling of powerlessness. This low self-image is further perpetuated by the "self-fulfilling prophecy" in which the stereotyping of a group predicts its future hence creating the condition or situation for the perpetuation of the prediction. The schools are sometimes guilty of this practice. A difference in language and cultural backgrounds can create low self-concepts in foreign-speaking children. Children from bilingual backgrounds often lack basic communication skills, which adversely affects their achievement and success in school. Bilingual students are, in many cases, culturally different from monolingual students and the community in general both in values and life style. The cultural background of the bilingual students may not permit them to value certain personality characteristics, such as aggressiveness and competitiveness, that contribute to academic success. Bilingual/bicultural programs have helped to increase school achievement and positive self-concepts of children with different languages and cultures.

There are ways that teachers can help children develop self-esteem:

1. Provide a warm, supportive classroom atmosphere, where children feel accepted.
2. Establish realistic classroom goals that are clear and definite.
3. Emphasize competition with self rather than with other children.
4. Make constructive criticisms prefaced and followed by encouragement and praise.
5. Stretch each child's abilities.
6. Show genuine interest and personal concern.

Section VI, *Psychological Implications for Schooling* examines the effects of forced learning — premature schooling and school readiness — based on the cognitive theories of Piaget, Jensen, and Ogletree. The articles in this section explicate the developmental and educational problems of the disadvantaged. The O'Neil article, "Reading Disabilities: A Product of the Age," underlines the present mania for early reading in the American schools and the disastrous effects on children, particularly on those from lower socioeconomic backgrounds. O'Neil offers a solution and a method of teaching reading. The article by Beck, "Pressure in the Nursery School," Moore, Moon and Moore's article, "The California Report: Early Schooling for All" and Ogletree's article, "The Socially Disadvantaged: A Rationale and New Concept of Human Development," vividly demonstrate the cataclysmic effects and implications of premature academic learning on cognitive and emotional development and later success in school. Although not all the research on school readiness is in, the present data are formidably against early schooling and anything that smacks of intellectual learning for immature learners.

Ogletree's article, "The Socially Disadvantaged: A Rationale and New Concept of Human Development," develops a rationale of human development for school readiness, the effects of premature academic learning, and the effects of deprivation on human development based on the new concept of bioplasmic forces in organic growth. It is a theory known by acupuncturists for thousands of years and recently rediscovered by Russian scientists, and it provides a model explicating the relationship between physical and mental development and the basis of Piaget's stages of cognition.

Section VII, *Teaching the Disadvantaged* examines teaching methods, strategies and programs for the disadvantaged. The strengths as well as the weaknesses of the disadvantaged learner are discussed. Some of the characteristic strengths of the disadvantaged that can be capitalized on by teachers are:

1. The visual and physical orientation to learning.

2. Reliance on concrete rather than abstract experiences.

3. Orientation to collective or group values rather than individual values.

4. Less conditioned by a particular learning set or style.

5. Acceptance of responsibility at an early age.

6. Problem solving oriented rather than symbolic or abstract.

7. Oriented toward concrete application of content learned.

Some of the learning characteristics that need to be and can be strengthened by the teachers are:

1. Disorientation to standardized tests, which he confronts with a defeatist attitude.

2. Oriented towards the physical and visual rather than towards the aural.

3. Weak perceptual discrimination skills.

4. Limited concentration and attention span.

5. Gaps in experience, knowledge and skills essential for school success.

6. Orientation to present fulfillment rather than the nebulous perspective of the future.

7. Unfamiliarity with middle-class standards and values.

8. Achievement is highly motivated by a personal relationship with and high expectations of the teacher.

9. Inclined to communicate through actions rather than words.

10. Thinking is inductive rather than deductive.

Present day curricula in inner-city schools are not designed for socially disadvantaged children. Learning environments should be tailored to the special needs of minority children to build on their strengths and help them surmount their weaknesses.

Section VIII, *Issues in Urban Education* surveys controversial issues still unresolved. Levin in "Why Ghetto Schools Fail" examines critically the problems of federal funding, the failure of compensatory programs, and the historical and present inflexibility of urban schools to adjust to the educational needs of the disadvantaged. Harvey and Holmes in "Busing and School Desegregation" and St. John in "Desegregation and Minority Group Performance" research past, present and future implications of desegregation as a vehicle for increasing school achievement of inner-city children. Ogletree and Ujlaki examine another form of segregation — ability grouping — and its effects on the self-concept of children placed in different ability group levels. Miller in "Theoretical Issues in Poverty Research" surveys the culture of poverty manifested in high rates of unemployment, chronic economic insecurity, extremely crowded and low quality living conditions, the disproportionate number of broken homes, segregation by race, ethnic group and social class, and continual suppression by varying degrees of prejudice and discrimination.

SELF-CONCEPT DEVELOPMENT

The Relationship Between Self-Concept and Underachievement

By D. EUGENE MEYER

For many years, educators have been concerned with the problem of accurately predicting the academic achievement of students. Through years of teaching, they have noticed that in many cases there is a wide discrepancy between intelligence and ability predictors and actual school performance. Some teachers have sensed a significant relationship between a student's concept of himself and his performance in school. They believed that students who viewed themselves in a positive light were the ones most likely to succeed. Conversely, it appeared that students who viewed themselves and their abilities in a negative fashion usually failed to achieve good grades.

Through the use of available research, this study seeks to either verify or refute the hypothesis that a positive relationship exists between self-concept and underachievement. In order to clarify the problem and facilitate research, general definitions for three key terms were decided upon.

— Academic Achievement: Academic achievement is the teacher's measurement of the student's performance. The traditional unit of measure is the student's grades.

— Self-concept: Self-concept is "the person's total appraisal of his appearance, background and origins, abilities and resources, attitudes and feelings which culminate as a directing force in behavior."[1]

— Underachievement: Underachievement is defined as performing below the level of learning predicted by either intelligence or ability tests.

ILLINOIS JOURNAL OF EDUCATION, 1972, Vol. 63, pp. 63-68. Permission to reprint "The Relationship Between Self-Concept and Underachievement" has been given by the author and the *Illinois Journal of Education*, Office of the Superintendent of Public Instruction, State of Illinois.

The study of the problem is limited to available research on the relationship between self-concept and underachievement. Although family and peer relationships affect the formation of the self-concept, primary importance is given to the teacher's influence on the self-concept. These limitations were imposed with the intent that a thorough examination of the teacher's influence would be of more value to the educator than a broad attempt at defining and analyzing all influences.

Early research concerning the prediction of academic achievement centered on intelligence and ability factors. Although these factors were considered to be the best *single* type of predictor, they still could not accurately predict achievement. Numerous studies on academic prediction showed that the average relationship between aptitude and academic performance ranged between $+.50$ and $-.75$. The realization that there were other variables led educators to inquire into the possibility of a relationship between "nonintellectual" or personality characteristics and achievement. The areas first explored were motivation, study habits, attitude, emotional adjustment, and socialization.

One area, regarding the prediction of academic performance, which received great attention and research beginning in 1950 was the self-concept. The first half of this century had evidenced a decline in the interest in the self-concept. During this time many psychologists ascribed to the theory of behaviorism. They concerned themselves with observable stimuli and response, believing that the inner life or "self" was beyond the scope of psychologists. A growing number of psychologists, though, became discontent with behaviorism. They based their objections on the belief that the theory was too narrow and passive to account for most human behavior.

The writings and research of perceptual psychologists, such as K. Lewin, C. Rogers, P. Lecky, and A. Combs, were instrumental in bringing attention to the concept of self. Instead of emphasizing objective reality as the behaviorists did or the unconscious as psychoanalyst did, they emphasized the individual's perceptions of his world. The main tenet of these psychologists is that a person's perception of his environment is an active agent in determining his conduct. They defined the self-concept as "the person's total appraisal of his appearance, background and origins, abilities and resources, attitudes and feelings which culminate as a directing force in his behavior."[2] Beginning the first year of life, the theorists believed that the self-concept developed through interaction and communication with others in the environment.

METHODS OF MEASURING

THE SELF-CONCEPT

The psychological principle that the self-concept is a function of the individual's own perceptions of his environment presents some difficulty in its assessment. If it cannot be directly observed, how can it be measured? In answering the question of measuring the self-concept, educators have usually relied on at least one of the following techniques.

— Introspective self-reflections in personal, family, and social or work settings.
— Congruence or discrepancy between description of current self-concept and ideal self-concept.
— Congruence or discrepancy between subjective self-reports and actions and the objective reports of clinically trained observers.
— Nonintrospective inferences derived from projective techniques and clinical interviews

The limitation in measuring self-concept is that it is dependent upon the individual's desire and ability to reveal his attitudes and beliefs. Some subjects may not be able to give accurate evaluations of themselves because of emotional blocks or defenses. Results may also be affected by mood fluctuations or by conditions at the time of testing. In understanding the limitations in measurement, the educator must avoid overgeneralization and exercise caution in his interpretations.

Numerous studies have been conducted to determine if a relationship exists between self-concept and underachievement. In 1954, Torrance observed little relationship between self-estimate and achievement standings among a given group of entering college freshmen. Fiedler et al. (1958) reported that there was no relationship between the self-esteem of students and their grade point average. Likewise, Turner and Vanderlippe (1958) obtained nonsignificant trends toward high grade point average among students with high self-ideal congruence.

In contrast, considerable evidence exists that there is a positive relationship between self-concept and underachievement. Studies by Brookover (1959), Rogers (1959), and Lecky (1961) have shown a significant relationship between patterns of achievement and self-perception. M. B. Fink (1962) studied two groups of ninth grade students paired for achievement and underachievement. On the basis of instruments used to measure self-concept, Fink had three psychologists determine whether the individual's self-concept was adequate or inadequate. In his study, he concluded that achievers were rated by the psychologists as being far more adequate in their concept of self. In 1964, D. L. Haarer working with ninth grade students found that the reported self-concept of ability was better than intelligence quotient as a predictor of the achievement of both public school male students and institutionalized delinquent boys involved in his experiment. M. Gill (1969) conducted a study involving 1,424 male and female students in the City of Toronto Schools. To determine if there was any relationship between self-concept and achievement, he divided the students into four ability levels according to their intelligence quotient. He found that no important difference existed in self-concept among students of different ability levels. The significant difference in self-concept was found to exist between different achievement levels. Those students who were underachievers exhibited negative self-concepts as compared to achievers. Shaw, Edson, and Bell (1960) concerned themselves with a study of the self-concept of bright underachieving high school students. Although their study involved both sexes, the results had more consequences for the male underachiever. Through the use of an adjective check list, they found that male underachievers view themselves more negatively than do male achievers.

SELF-CONCEPT OF THE UNDERACHIEVER

In determining the relationship between self-concept and underachievement, a further study as to the nature of the underachiever's self-concept seems warranted. Taylor (1961) found underachievers to be more derogatory, more unrealistic in self-attitudes, and experiencing more conflicts in dealing with others than high achievers. Educational psychologist, T. Ringness (1963, 1965), studying eighth and ninth grade boys, concluded that low achievers had less feelings of personal worth and less sense of well-being than high achievers. Further reasearch led Ringness to conclude that underachievers are less able to manage their anxieties than achievers. The underachiever fears failure and employs defense mechanisms such as denial of inadequacy, rejection of school achievement norms, and compensation through other activities to reduce his anxiety. More time and effort is concentrated on reducing anxiety than achieving.

Studies have shown that males are considered to be underachievers three to four times more than females. In the previously cited study by Shaw, Edson, and Bell, male underachievers were characterized by negative feelings of self, while females were characterized by ambivalent attitudes toward self. Shaw hypothesized in a later study that the difference may be due to the female's self-concept being influenced to a greater extent by her perceptions of how others see her.

Utimately, education is concerned with the development of the individual student's potential. Since available research has tended to support a positive relationship between self-concept and underachievement, the educational process should concern itself with the development of positive self-concepts in students.

DEVELOPMENT OF THE SELF

The self-concept of an individual is a learned phenomenon evolving out of interpersonal relationships with others deemed to be significant in the individual's life. The general rule that behavior is motivated by a desire to maintain and enhance self has special import in determining the individual's experiences and resulting self-concept. E. C. Kelley seems to have established best the interrelationship between self-concept and experience in the following statement:

"The self 'looks out' upon the surrounding scene largely in terms of its own enhancement or defense. It tends to extend in the direction of that which promises to make it better off. It withdraws from that which seems likely to

14

endanger it."[3]

Therefore, the self-concept determines the kind and quality of experiences perceived. The person with a weak self-concept is more likely to have a narrowed perceptual field. Past experiences which have affected him negatively have taught him to limit his experiences to nonthreatening confrontations. He devotes his behavior to maintaining his present self-concept. Conversely, the person with a positive self-concept is concerned more with enhancement than maintenance of the self. He devotes his energies to exploration and discovery of his environment and self.

Relating self-concept theory to the underachiever seems to provide reason for the observance that underachievement is a chronic problem which increases with age. The underachiever's inability to learn becomes a self-fulfilling prophecy. A circular relationship evolves in which the student's poor self-concept affects his school performance which, in turn, reinforces his existing self-concept. The underachiever begins to develop defensive behavior causing him to avoid experiences in learning which may alter his notions about himself.

The developmental stages of the self-concept have special significance concerning the underachieving grade student. Although the self-concept is modified through life's experiences, adolescence represents its final formative phase. This period is crucial in determining an individual's adjustment and maturity in later life. If defensive behaviors are reinforced by the learning experience, he will probably not be able to fully realize his potential.

EDUCATIONAL IMPLICATIONS

Next to the home, the school is the single most important force in shaping a child's self-concept. In order to be effective in this role, the school's curriculum must take social-emotional factors into account. Since nonintellective factors have been shown to be susceptible to modification, an emphasis in education on positive changes in self-concept may help to provide a more conducive psychological environment for learning. This may, in turn, improve an individual's scholastic performance.

Educators must give more consideration to understanding the meaning of behavior and ways of modifying it. Although the self-concept of the underachiever by nature resists change, it can be changed if a favorable atmosphere exists. In order for change, the student must view the educational process as a meaningful, self-enhancing, and non-threatening experience.

The importance of developing a positive self-concept in the underachiever has already received considerable attention. In the schools, the individual who is usually in the best position to influence the developing self-concept is the teacher. This is especially applicable to a number of junior high schools where a separate position of guidance counselor does not exist. The homeroom teacher, in many cases, then assumes this role. The purpose of the following chapter is to suggest methods and behavior the teacher can employ in fostering a positive self-concept in the underachiever.

IDENTIFICATION OF THE UNDERACHIEVER

A universal problem in teaching, which becomes more acute when the student progresses from a self-contained classroom to departmental scheduling, is the lack of available time for the teacher to spend with each student. In the junior high school, the teacher's identification of the underachiever is dependent to a certain extent on his desire and willingness to provide for individual differences and the school's resources.

The teacher's first step in remediation of underachievement would be to examine carefully, by the use of standardized tests given in the school and direct observation, the accomplishments of all pupils to discover if they are in line with the student's measured ability. Such an examination would allow the teacher to identify those students who are achieving below their ability.

A number of tests, such as the Self-Concept Inventory, have been constructed by educational psychologists to determine an individual's self-concept. If the tests are available in the school district, the teacher could administer the testing instrument to better define the individual's concept of self. From observing the behavior of students in the classroom, the teacher may also be able to make certain inferences regarding the student's self-concept. Many teachers can recite examples of classroom behavior in which a student's conception of his abilities was far below their actual level. The underachiever may insist that he cannot do a task, before he has had any opportunity to examine the nature of the task. Also, his manner of answering a question may provide clues to his self-concept. If he tends to offer an apology for his answer or discount his information as probably being wrong, this may indicate a poor self-concept.

DEVELOPMENT OF TRUST

Children's feelings about themselves stem from the important and significant people around them. In studying the relationship between teachers' attitudes and student achievement William Purkey has stated:

"The almost unavoidable conclusion is that the teacher's attitudes and opinion regarding his students have a significant influence on their success in school. In other words, when the teacher believes that his students can achieve, the student appears to be more successful; when the teacher believes that the student cannot achieve, then it influences their performance negatively."[4]

In order for the teacher to be in a position to influence the self-concept of the achiever, his attitude toward the student must reflect acceptance of the student as he is and a faith in his abilities. The teacher must respect the individual differences of his students. Through this feeling of acceptance, the underachiever will gain confidence in the teacher's ability to help him. After the relationship has been established, the teacher is then in a position to initiate change.

In discussing the self-concept, A. Combs has written, ". . . a positive view is learned from the ways people treat the learner. People learn that they are able, not from failure, but from success."[5] If individual differences are not taken into account in selection of learning experiences for the underachiever, conditions are ripe for the student to experience further feelings of inadequacy.

The teacher should select learning experiences for the underachiever that provide an opportunity for success. Studies in achievement motivation have shown that when a task is seen as virtually impossible, there is no shame in failure. When the assignment is viewed as ridiculously easy, there is no desire to perform. Therefore, the teacher must present tasks which are adequate in terms of incentive and satisfaction, yet still provide an opportunity for success. If a history of success is developed, the student will be both encouraged and inspired to try other tasks.

Since the underachiever usually performs below the class average, a method of evaluation should be chosen which will encourage him to perform better and not reinforce his feeling of inadequacy. One method would be to have the teacher plan learning goals with the student. This method will also give the underachiever a feeling of responsibility in achieving the goals he has helped to construct. When the time for student evaluation comes, the teacher could let the individual participate in his own assessment. If the student is able to help in the evaluation, he will have a more realistic understanding of his progress.

The teacher should be honest in his evaluation of the student's progress. Encouragement in the learning situation cannot be given in the form of false praise for a poor performance. Although the underachiever may want to believe he is doing well, his performance must ultimately be tested by him against the reality of the experience. If failures are handled in an atmosphere of warmth and acceptance, the underachiever may come to learn more about himself. Handled constructively, failures will show the student his present abilities, knowledge, and skills. An important change in self-concept comes as the individual begins to accept himself and develop an understanding of his abilities.

For years, educators have realized that a discrepancy exists between intelligence predictors and actual academic achievement. Those students who have performed below their predicted ability have been termed, "underachievers." Since available research tends to support a positive relationship between self-concept and achievement, an important concern in education should be the social-emotional growth of the student, as well as his intellectual progress.

In order for the underachiever to develop a positive self-concept and to fully realize his academic potential, the teacher must employ methods which will give the student a feeling of acceptance as well as success in the learning experience. Although the enhancement of the self-concept is in itself a worthwhile goal, more research should be conducted in determining methods which have shown an actual gain in scholastic performance.

REFERENCES

1. Wallace D. LaBenne and Bert I. Greene, *Educational Implications of Self-Concept Theory* (Pacific Palisades, California: Goodyear Publishing Co., Inc., 1969), p. 18.
2. LaBenne, p. 10.
3. LaBenne, p. 13.
4. William Watson Purkey, *The Self and Academic Achievement* (Gainsville, Florida: W. Florida Educational Research and Development Council, 1967), p. 47.
5. Purkey, p. 30.

BIBLIOGRAPHY

Cambell, Paul R. "School and Self-Concept," *Educational Leadership*, March, 1967, pp. 510-513.

Deo, Pratibha and Sagar Sharma. "Self-Ideal Discrepancy and School Achievement," *Adolescence*, Vol. 5, 1970, pp. 353-360.

Ebel, Robert L. (ed.) *Encyclopedia of Educational Research*, fourth edition. London: Collier-Macmillan Limited, 1969.

Fink, M. B. "Self-Concept As It Relates to Academic Achievement," *California Journal of Educational Research*, March, 1962, pp. 57-62.

Fisher, William. "Better Self Images," *The Instructor*, August, 1968, pp. 95-96.

Gill, Mohindra P. *Pattern of Achievement As Related to the Perceived Self.* Washington, D.C.: American Educational Research Association, February, 1969.

Horrocks, John E. *The Psychology of Adolescence: Behavior and Development,* third edition. Boston: Houghton Mifflin Company, 1969.

LaBenne, Wallace D., and Bert I. Greene. *Educational Implications of Self-Concept Theory.* Pacific Palisades, California: Goodyear Publishing Co., Inc., 1969.

Lavin, David E. *The Prediction of Academic Performance: A Theoretical Analysis and Review of Research.* New York: Russell Sage Foundation, 1965.

Mandel, Harvey P., Robert M. Roth, and Harris L. Berenbaum. "Relationship between Personality Change and Achievement Change as a Function of Psychodiagnosis," *Journal of Counseling Psychology*, November, 1968, pp. 500-505.

Purkey, William. *The Self and Acdemic Achievement.* Gainsville, Florida: W. Florida Educational Research and Development Council, 1967.

————. *Self-Concept and School Achievement.* Englewood Cliffs, New Jersey: Prentice-Hall, Inc., 1970.

Ringness, Thomas A. *Mental Health in the Schools.* New York: Random House, 1968.

Shaw, M. C., and G. J. Alves. "The Self-Concept of Bright Academic Underachievers: Continued," *Personnel and Guidance Journal,* December, 1963, pp. 401-403.

————. and K. Edson, and H. Bell. "The Self-Concept of Bright Underachieving High School Students as Revealed by an Adjective Checklist," *Personnel and Guidance Journal,* November, 1960, pp. 193-196.

Smith, Barry D., and Richard C. Teevan. "Relationship Among Self-Ideal Congruence, Adjustment, and Fear of Failure Motivation," *Journal of Personality,* March, 1971, pp. 44-56.

VanKoughnett, B. C., and Merle E. Smith. "Enhancing the Self-Concept in School," *Educational Leadership,* December, 1969, pp. 253-255.

Wylie, Ruth C. *The Self-Concept: A Critical Survey of Pertinent Research Literature.* Lincoln: University of Nebraska Press, 1961.

A Study of Self-Concepts of Negro and White Youth in Segregated Environments*

BENJAMIN J. HODGKINS AND ROBERT G. STAKENAS

Recently Thomas Pettigrew, a noted authority on Negro-white relations, lamented the lack of knowledge about the Negro personality in spite of innumerable studies conducted in this area. Noting the methodological inadequacies and limitations, as well as the narrow atheoretical approach of many studies, he advocated the development of a social psychological theory which takes into account both personality dynamics and their social origins.[1]

This need for a systematic approach is evident in the study of the effects of segregation upon the Negro's self-concept as an important element of personality. Many studies on the self-concept of the Negro suggest the presence of a negative self-image if not a self-hatred.[2] On the other hand, in a study on educational equality Coleman et al. found no difference in the self-concept of Negro and white youth in the educational setting.[3] Such inconsistencies

support Pettigrew's evaluation of the situation and reaffirm the stated need for a more systematic approach.

Although there are many aspects to be considered when selecting an approach to the study of Negro personality generally and Negro self-concept specifically one of the most basic considerations would be the avoidance of a conceptual framework that relies heavily upon phenotypic traits which could arise from social stereotypes or be spuriously related to the Negro's social and cultural status in American society. This is particularly the case when criteria for psychological adjustment are sought. For example, what is thought to be "normal" from a middle-class point of view could be perceived as "abnormal" from a lower-class perspective and vice versa. Cultural differences in suppression of physical aggression would be one case in point.

To avoid some of the pitfalls suggested above, the position taken here is that personality dynamics are best understood in terms of the social context and social forces which impinge directly upon the individual. In support of this view, we turn to theory developed by Theodore Newcomb.[4] Integrating both psychological and social determinants in his discussion of self-concept, Newcomb places great emphasis upon the importance

* A revision of a paper presented at the annual meeting of the Southern Sociological Society, Atlanta, Georgia, April 11, 1968.

1 Thomas F. Pettigrew, "Negro American Personality: Why Isn't More Known," *Journal of Social Issues*, XX (1964), 23.

2 See, for example: R. M. Dreger and K. S. Miller, "Comparative Psychological Studies of Negroes and Whites in the United States," *Psychological Bulletin*, LV (1960), 360-402; F. G. Edwards, "Community and Class Realities: the Order of Change," *Daedalus*, XCV (1966), 1-23; Thomas F. Pettigrew, *A Profile of the American Negro* (Princeton, N. J.: D. Van Nostrand, 1964).

3 James S. Coleman et al., *Equality of Educational Opportunity* (Washington, D. C.: U. S. Government Printing Office, 1966), pp. 319-321.

4 Theodore M. Newcomb, *Social Psychology* (N. Y.: Holt, Rinehart and Winston, 1950).

of the social context in which an individual finds himself. In effect, according to Newcomb, self-concepts develop consistent with the meaning of experiences interpreted in the context of values and beliefs learned from primary reference groups. They provide the frame of reference within which one's "self" is perceived.[5]

Relating this to the effects of segregation on the development of the Negro's self-concept, we would expect that in a segregated community the incidence of a negative self-image should be no greater among Negro subjects than among white subjects since in both cases primary reference groups are for the most part family and friends of the same race. But, as previously noted, some findings and interpretations do not support this expectation. One possible explanation frequently advanced is that Negroes, as members of a prejudiced white society, internalize this prejudiced frame of reference against themselves and transmit it to their children. If such is the case, however, Coleman's findings seem suspect. Indeed, Coleman himself suggests that such a finding may be an artifact of situational factors.[6] On the other hand, one might reasonably argue that interpretations based on the assumption that Negroes subscribe to a rejection of themselves, both individually and collectively, suggest a group passivity inconsistent with our knowledge of the social psychology of self-concept development.[7]

An alternative explanation which could synthesize the seemingly contradictory results of previous research, suggested by Newcomb's theory and not usually considered, is that there are at least two aspects of one's self-concept associated with a given situation; that derived from the behavioral role played by the individual and that derived from evaluations of his experience based upon a learned frame of reference.[8] Since the two need not be congruent, disparate findings could be a function of which of these individual frames of reference relative to a specific situation were tapped by the various investigators. It seems necessary to consider this alternative explanation further.

Intrinsic to part of the meaning a person associates with his own performance in any situation is his perception of himself in a role which is situation bound. In Thomas' terms, the person would include himself in any "definition of the situation."[9] Such a self-perception in normal circumstances would take on meaning by virtue of learned role expectations associated with the position assumed by the person. Thus, for the Negro, as for any individual, his self-concept in part is a reflection of the meaning of his performance in specified relatively enduring roles in addition to previously learned attitudes and values. For example, by virtue of a person's knowledge of the requirements associated with an occupational role, and his experience in that role, an occupational self-concept will develop which is situationally relevant. The individual is, in Newcomb's theory, perceiving himself as a "resource." Although a measure of consistency in how one perceives oneself across situations undoubt-

---

[5] *Ibid*, pp. 323-327.
[6] Coleman, *op. cit.*, p. 288.
[7] Newcomb, *op. cit.*, pp. 319-321.

[8] *Ibid*, p. 330.
[9] W. I. Thomas, "The Four Wishes and the Definition of the Situation," in T. Parsons (ed.), *Theories of Society, Vol. II*, (N. Y.: The Free Press of Glencoe, 1961), pp. 741-744.

edly occurs, different expectations in various situations, associated with the social role an individual plays, would result in a differentiated definition of one's self dependent upon how successfully he meets the role requirements.[10]

Behavioral role expectations, as stated previously, are not the only foundation upon which the self-concept is based. Equally important is the individual's evaluation of himself in the situation dependent upon previous general experience interpreted within his established frames of reference. In this latter instance, according to Newcomb, the individual perceives himself as an object of "value."

As Newcomb has noted, no individual (except perhaps a very young child) enters a situation without a latent self-concept of his performance in that situation based upon his prior general experience. Subsequently, within the situation, the individual appraises his performance in terms of the role expectations associated with a specific position as he understands them, and in terms of past experience based upon shared frames of reference. Ultimately, these two factors contribute substantially to a determination of the nature of his situational self-concept.

Considered in this light, the social condition of the American Negro is important for self-concept development to the extent that it determines the nature of past experiences and who will be significant others in various situations. Within the segregated community, where most if not all significant others are Negro and the majority of prior experience is with other Negroes, no difference would be expected in the incidence of positive or negative self-concepts in a specific situation in the Negro or white segments of that community. Because the Negro is segregated, race as a basis of self-evaluation is eliminated within situation boundaries. Accordingly, the probability of a Negro developing a negative or positive self-concept within most segregated situations would seem to be no greater than among the white population. The social structural fact of segregation that determines the incidence of interaction and the selection of significant others militates against it.[11]

Disparate findings previously noted could be reconciled as follows. Cases where Negroes have been found to hold predominantly negative self-concepts would be those circumstances where white individuals and groups are most likely to be relevant sources for frames of reference. Conversely, where other Negroes are the likely reference points, race is not a significant criterion for self-concept appraisal. Furthermore, unless racial characteristics are an intrinsic part of the situation, role behavior is consistently evaluated by the subject in terms of nonracial role expectations. Accordingly, findings of Coleman et al. of no overall difference in self-evaluation in school could reflect the segregated circumstances under which the Negro subjects were asked to appraise themselves. Other studies where negative self-concepts for Negroes were reported could have been tapping an area where either the role of "Negro" was of concern, or situations where white frames of reference were employed.

10 Wilbur Brookover et al., Self Concept of Achievement and School Ability (East Lansing, Michigan: Bureau of Educational Services, 1965).

11 Tomatsu Shibutani and K. M. Kwan, Ethnic Stratification: a Comparative Approach (New York: Macmillan, 1965).

To partially test out this alternative explanation an analysis of self-concept measures on segregated Negro and white subjects was performed. Consistent with the preceding discussion, it was hypothesized that no significant difference in the incidence of favorable or unfavorable self-concepts would be found between Negro and white subjects.

METHOD

Sample

The subjects were chosen primarily on the basis of their accessibility within the schools which they attended. Cluster sampling procedures resulted in a sample of 142 Negro and 100 white subjects of high school and college age. Three subjects had incomplete questionnaires leaving 239 for purposes of analysis. Fifty of the white subjects were college freshmen and sophomores attending a state university while the remaining 45 were high school students selected from a class in a rural community some 50 miles from the two universities. One hundred and two of the Negro subjects were college freshmen, sophomores and juniors attending a segregated university, while 37 were of high school age selected from a segregated high school in the rural community mentioned above. While these samples were not randomly chosen, they are fairly representative of Negro and white college and high school students in that region of the Deep South.

The universities from which the college subjects were chosen both have student bodies drawn mainly from the Southeastern United States. Both schools may be characterized as primarily vocational in nature, with emphasis upon teacher preparation, business administration, and

the like. The community from which the high school subjects were selected has a population of around 3,300. A county seat, it is the focus of most social and political activity in the county.

It should be noted that in both instances, the universities and high schools are moving toward desegregation in compliance with Federal Government directives. For most Negroes, however, the effects must be considered nil. Only a few Negro or white college students are found on the racially opposite campus; nor are any white students attending the Negro high school. Beyond this, except for personal friendships of a few faculty members and special open events such as county or regional fairs, social life is segregated. In the university town itself, no public swimming pools were open, nor were other public recreational facilities integrated at the time the data gathered.

Measures

A short questionnaire was used to gather data on the subjects' social origin.

To measure self-concept of our subjects, use was made of the semantic differential as developed by Osgood et al.[12] This method assumes that the connotative meaning of a concept can be secured by ratings on a series of bipolar adjective scales. The resultant measures are considered connotative meanings associated with the concept.

Drawing from Osgood's work and the investigators' vocabulary, 27 bipolar items were developed and arranged in random fashion under self-situation concepts. The instructions, basically similar to those used

---

[12] Charles E. Osgood, G. J. Suci and P. Tannenbaum, *The Measurement of Meaning* (Urbana, Ill.; University of Ill. Press, 1957).

by Osgood, directed the subjects to rate themselves on each of the scales relative to how they perceived themselves in the situation. The self-situation concept used and discussed herein is "Me in School." The instrument was administered by the authors in the classroom content. Anonymity was assured by the experimenter in preliminary remarks and the subjects were not required to identify themselves on the instrument in any way.

An item analysis procedure suggested by Stouffer[13] was applied to a 50 per cent random sample of the data cases to select those items and those cutting points which best represented two unidimensional attributes of self perception. Each set of items was then scaled for each half of the sample according to the Guttman criterion.[14] The results indicate adequate coefficients of reproducibility with adequate stability under this form of internal replication.

Inspection of the nature of the items led us to identify the dimensions derived as "self-adjustment" and "self-assurance." While relation to Osgood's evaluation and potency dimensions are apparent, differences in method of analysis and theoretical interpretation led us to adopt the terms indicated above. In this instance, adjustment refers to the subject's perceived self-emotional adjustment to the situation. Assurance, on the other hand, refers to the subject's perceived self-confidence in the situation.

13 Samuel A. Stouffer, *Social Research to Test Ideas* (New York: The Free Press of Glencoe, 1962), Chapter 14.
14 See, L. A. Guttman, "The Cornell Technique for Scale and Intensity Analysis," *Educational and Psychological Measurement,* VII (1947), 247-279; R. N. Ford, "A Rapid Scoring Procedure for Scaling Attitude Questions," *Public Opinion Quarterly,* XIV (1950), 507-532.

It should be noted that these scales are relative measures of the dimensions considered, not absolute. Using item and scalogram analyses requires cutting the seven point scales by rank order of proportion of bipolar item endorsement and utilizing scale geometric pattern scores. This means that it is possible to respond favorably in terms of the bipolar item and still score low on the measure relative to others in the sample.

RESULTS

Median scores were computed for the total sample on each scale in each situation. These medians were subsequently used to denote those high or low on self-assurance or self-adjustment in the school situation. Median tests were subsequently made to establish the significance of possible variation in the frequency of high or low scores between Negroes and whites.

Consistent with our theory we would expect no significant differences between Negro and white subjects in the proportion who score high or low on the two measures of self in school. Significance in this instance was set at equal to or less than the .05 level of probability as estimated by the X^2 test.

Self-Adjustment

Our data allow us to appraise Negro-white differences on the Self Adjustment Scale in the school context. Contrary to our expectations, significant differences do exist. Of particular interest, however, is that a greater proportion of Negro subjects than white subjects score above the median. Such a finding is in contrast to the traditional view of the "negative" self-concept of Negroes, but may be an artifact of sex or socioeconomic status differences in the Negro and white samples.[15] To appraise the effects of these variables on the distribution, sex and social status were controlled within race. Socio-economic status was determined using the Duncan Occupational Index.[16]

Differences are significant between races for females, but not for males although the tendency is obviously there. This suggests that differences noted cannot be accounted for purely on the basis of sex differences in the Negro and white samples. No significant differences obtain between races when socio-economic status of parents is controlled although it is apparent by inspection that the same tendencies exist for both social groups.

Self-Assurance

When self-assurance is the dependent variable, a significantly greater proportion of Negroes again scored above the median.

When sex is controlled, however, the data indicate that such differences are due primarily to the high proportion of white females falling below the median, while Negro females are proportionately overrepresented above the median. No such discrepancy is found for the white and Negro males who tend to distribute themselves rather evenly on both sides of the median.

When social status is controlled for within race, our Negro subjects do not differ significantly from our white subjects in self-assurance in the school situation.[17] These results are consistent with our expectations generally, and lend a measure of qualified support to our reasoning.

SUMMARY AND DISCUSSION

Summarizing the results of our analysis, it was found (a) that significant differences between Negro and white subjects existed in self-adjustment and self-assurance in the school situation with Negroes tending to score higher than whites; (b) but, when social status level was controlled within race, these differences were not maintained, although the tendency still existed. Although these results offer only partial support to the explanatory schema presented earlier, they are consistent with that explanation insofar as they suggest that Negro subjects who are segregated within a relatively hostile racial environment have the same likelihood of developing a favorable or unfavorable self-concept relative to a situation as do white subjects. If this interpretation is correct, it suggests that successful social integration without a significant modification of prejudiced white attitudes could lead to negative consequences for the development of Negro self-concepts. We would speculate that previously segregated Negroes who enter integrated situations where prejudiced whites become significant others, would collectively reveal an increase in the incidence of "negative" self-concepts.

The generality of the results reported herein is, of course, limited by the restricted nature of the sampling procedures.

---

15 William F. Brazziel, "Correlates of Southern Negro Personality," *Journal of Social Issues*, XX (1964), 46-53; E. F. Frazier, *The Negro in the United States* (N. Y.: MacMillan, 1957).

16 Otis D. Duncan, "A Socioeconomic Index for all Occupations," in A. J. Reiss, ed., *Occupations and Social Status* (N. Y.: The Free Press of Glencoe, 1961), Chapter VI.

---

17 Although not reported here, statistical analyses were carried out while controlling for grade level in school. The results failed to reveal any significant differences as a function of grade level.

Still, the finding that Negroes in a highly segregated community do not differ significantly in the incidence of favorable self-concept when social status origins are controlled, has suggestive implications. For example, the reduction of apparent racial differences, as a function of socioeconomic level, suggests the strong influence of economic determinants cutting across racial lines and lends credence to Frazier's argument on the Negro middle and upper classes.[18] The influence of the Southern socio-cultural milieu is suggested by the low proportion of white female subjects scoring above the median. While it must be remembered that the measures used are relative and do not reflect a "low" self-concept in any absolute sense, the low proportion above the median in every instance is in marked contrast to the consistently high proportion of Negro females above the median. It is possible that the traditional Southern pattern of idolizing white femininity and rewarding dependent female behavior is not conducive to high self-assurance and adjustment in the school. On the other hand, the matriarchial nature of Negro family life, particularly among lower status Negroes, has been well documented.[19] Negro females, raised in such an environment, possibly benefit from such an experience in that it encourages the development of a favorable self-concept of adjustment and assurance in various contexts including the school.

The findings in no way suggest that these Negro subjects like segregation and the suppressed status associated with it.

Quite the contrary it is possible to suggest that generally the greater the segregation in a community, the more resentment Negroes may have toward whites, particularly when they hold favorable self-images and quite correctly perceive that white group sanctions are preventing them from personally achieving goals consistent with their values. Thus, the results reported herein may explain why militant appeals within the Negro community are frequently voiced by the young well-educated Negro, who shares a common intellectual framework with his white counterpart and, having previously developed a positive self-image, adopts aspirations consistent with the achievement norms of white America. Furthermore, such an interpretation is indirectly supported by the findings of Johnson who reported that hatred of whites by Negroes tended to be associated with Southern birth, youth, and Negroes who had minimal interracial contact.[20]

It should be noted that the approach used in this study has not been consistent with the clinical view of self-concept. The approach has been, rather, to appraise the subject's perceived self-conception as an object in a social situation. Such a self-perception is not dependent upon the values of the total society, but upon an individual's evaluation of his performance in terms of role expectations and in terms of who his significant others are, whom he interacts with, and who has the greatest direct social control over him. Such an argument is not inconsistent with traditional reference

[18] Frazier, *op. cit.*
[19] Ruth S. Cavan, "Negro Family Disorganization and Juvenile Delinquency" *The Journal of Negro Education* XXVIII (1959), 230-238.

[20] R. A. Johnson, "Negro Reaction to Minority Group Status," in B. E. Segel (ed.), *Racial and Ethnic Relations: Selected Readings* (N. Y.: Thomas Crowell, 1966), pp. 251-270.

group theory, nor is it inconsistent with much psychological theory which recognizes the dependence of the individual's self attitudes upon the reference group's definition of social reality. In the final analysis, however, while the results are explicable in terms of contemporary social and psychological theory and knowledge, a systematic program designed to test out the above relations on random samples of Negroes and whites in both segregated and integrated environments is needed.

The Beginnings of the Self: The Problem of the Nurturing Environment

By IRA J. GORDON

The concept of the self is an old one in religion and philosophy and has been discussed endlessly as a part of man's search for identity, as he sought to answer the question, "Who am I?" For Descartes the answer was, "*Cogito ergo sum*"—I think, therefore I am. This statement marked a sharp break with medieval thought, and contributed to the age of reason. For Descartes, cognition or reason was superior to emotion. Knowing was the self's primary function. The self was active, aware, free; the senses and emotions were passive, or confused influences upon the mind. From the early seventeenth until the late nineteenth century, this view reigned.

Freud broke with this tradition by centering upon the emotions, by denying free will, and by focusing upon the influence of the child's experiences in the earliest years. Since Freud, the Descartian answer is insufficient. We now seek to define ourselves in ways which include our feelings as well as our thoughts, and look for the origins of our personality in the first dim moments of life long before cognition seemed possible. Because of Freud, our notion of self-definition has required that its origins be in early childhood and that it be developed from the experiences we have had in that most intimate of circles—our family. For modern man, this is a truism; but it also leaves unanswered a myriad of questions concerning how we got that way.

The first step in self-awareness is both affective and cognitive: the discovery of one's own body as distinct and pleasurable. When the infant puts thumb in mouth, he experiences sensation in both his thumb and his mouth and learns that the thumb is part of him. When the numerous other objects that the infant places in his mouth do not yield the double sensation, he separates self from other. This process, labeled "self-sentience" by Sullivan,[1] provides the infant with his first anchorage point, his first awareness of separateness. To paraphrase Descartes, if the infant could speak, he might say, "I experience me,

PHI DELTA KAPPAN, 1969, Vol. 50, pp. 375-378.

therefore I am."

The second marking point is the awareness of "other." The separation of "I" or "me" from "not me" requires the introduction of people and objects from outside the child. **The child needs enough of them, with enough frequency and consistency, that they can be differentiated.** The infant at three months engages in social smiles,[2] but much has gone on before this time to enable the child to reach this major social event. It is not purely the "maturation" of an inadequate organism toward social behavior. William James, at the turn of the century, defined the world of the infant as a blooming, buzzing confusion, but current research in learning indicates that infants are able to make much more elaborate differentiations of their physical environment in terms of sight and sound and sense than James would have thought possible.

For example, Lipsitt's research at Brown[3] indicates the ways in which both operant and classical conditioning can occur in infancy. Although its approach is not psychoanalytic, current research in infant learning substantiates the psychoanalyst's view of the infant's ability to learn and thus supports the notion of the importance of this early period. But what is it the child learns, in addition to such behaviors as feeding or cooing responses, smiles, and cries? The period of infancy has been seen as the time the child learns basic trust.[4] The nature of the inputs—that is, the way he is handled and fondled, dealt with and responded to, and how his body reacts to these events—teaches the child whether or not the world is a safe or terrifying place, and whether he can trust it or not.

Since the separation of self and world is incomplete, the self-concept, the "I," is part of the world. It is both cognitive and affective, active and passive. "I" is not only in the brain but also in the viscera. It is both Cartesian and Freudian.

Specifically, what are some of the inputs in the very early years which influence the initial picture of the self? Robert Sears and his colleagues,[5,6] in a series of studies which applied learning theory rigor to psychoanalytic concepts, indicated that parental attitudes and behavior (disciplinary techniques, permissiveness, severity, temperamental qualities, and aspirations) exhibited in the areas of hunger, elimination, dependency, sex, and aggression were important factors in development and in sex-role identification, a major dimension of the self-concept. But these external inputs emphasize the affective side of life. They do not adequately consider either the cognitive dimension or the role of the child himself.

Current thought emphasizes the competence of the infant and brings together both the cognitive and affective elements of the child into one system. It emphasizes the importance of not only the characteristic child-rearing patterns described by Sears, and the family drama so dear to the psychoanalyst, but also the role of the infant himself as an active, striving, curious, learning organism who makes his impact on his family. This is no *tabula rasa* child. And the child's view of himself is not simply a mirror image of the external events which surround him early in life. From the very beginning it includes his own organism as it senses, feels, learns, and assigns meaning to these external stimuli. The child learns who he is from what happens to him, from the language that surrounds him, from the people who are dear to him, from the opportunities to deal with the objects and events in his immediate world, and from his own responses to the welter of stimuli. His self-esteem represents his unique organization of his own biological makeup, the evaluations made of him by significant adults, and his own learning from trial and manipulation and feedback from his world. Cognitive development is inseparable from personality development.

The child obviously cannot define "self" as distinct from "other" before he has a permanent frame of reference. One measure of this frame is Piaget's "object permanence," manifested by the individual's recognition that an object continues to exist even though it is no longer visible to him. He arrives at this point somewhere in the second year of life. It is a growth marker because now he can relate affectively to other individuals in some consistent fashion, and cognitively he has achieved a level where he can actively engage in searching his environment. Gaining this ability is a giant step forward and gives the child a sense of competence in relating to his world.

We can make an intuitive leap from object permanence to Erikson's basic trust. Both mean that the child has now organized at least a portion of his world so that it is orderly and predictable—and therefore manageable. With this he can structure a positive self-concept. Without a sense of object permanence, he is powerless. Psychological inputs are important here, because only on the basis of broad experience can the child discover that both people and things have external reality. With the establishment of "other," the child's own behavior can now include role-taking and role-playing.[7] This process enables him to shift from Piaget's "egocentric" stage toward "decentration." That is, he develops from seeing others as just like him toward a recognition of the fact that what one sees and believes depends upon where he stands and what he already knows. Parents not only influence opportunities for such role-playing, but also provide the basic models for imitation. Through the ways in which they teach or deny opportunities for dramatic play, they influence both the cognitive and affective dimensions of the self-concept. Smilansky[8] has described the way parents affect this phase of learning.

Piaget's theoretical exposition of cognitive development returns us to the epistemological position of Descartes, but with added knowledge from Freud and the behavioral scientists. Decarie[9], for example, was able to investigate both Piagetian and psychoanalytic views about the process, timing, and meaning of arrival at object permanence. Generally, she found empirical support for both, and concluded that parents are the most effective agents in presenting both cognitive and affective experience to the young child. Piaget wrote in 1954:

> The other person is of course an emotional object to the highest degree but at the same time is the most interesting cognitive object, the most alive, the most unex-

pected. . . . The other person is an object which implies a multitude of exchanges in which cognitive as well as affective factors play a role, and if this object is of paramount importance in one of these respects, it is, I think, equally important in the other.[10]

How important are these early years? Gardner Murphy has indicated that the self-picture is fairly well integrated by the third year of life. Once it has developed, it becomes the evaluator, selector, judger, and organizer of future experience, and the child's behavior may be seen as organized to enhance and maintain his view. Such a picture sounds harsh and deterministic if we did not understand that possibilities for change are always present. Life is not over at age three, but the general view toward the world and toward one's self is already present.

The longitudinal data which support the importance of early childhood are fairly consistent. Bloom indicated on the basis of reviews of longitudinal research[11] that half of what accounts for the variance in adults in agressiveness in males and dependence in females seems to be present by age four. Not only Bloom's summary but also the classical longitudinal studies conducted in California[12] and the longitudinal studies of the Fels Institute at Yellow Springs, Ohio,[13] demonstrated the effects of parental behavior in the child's first six years on his behavior and attitudes in subsequent years.

One of Bayley's findings is that the mother's affectional behavior toward her son in the first three years of his life was related to his friendship, cooperation, and attentiveness when he became a school child and an adolescent. These behaviors may be inferred to be reflections of feelings of security, a fundamental dimension of self-concept.

One of Freud's contributions is the concept of identification, and, more specifically, sex-role identification. We noted earlier that Sears adopted this concept and applied general behavior methodology to its investigation. It is central also to Kagan and Moss. For them, the notion of sex-role identification is a core concept in influencing stability of behavior from childhood through adulthood. Events early in life lead not only to the child's sex-role identification but also determine his general social expectancy for all behavior. Boys are expected to behave more aggressively, more competently, and in more task-oriented fashions; girls are to be more nurturant, more person-oriented. Parent behavior in the first six years of life influences the child's identity and the standards he will set for typical sex-related behavior. Kagan and Moss conclude that the individual's own desire to make his behavior agree with the culture's definition of sex is a major factor determining the stability of his behavior over time.

Longitudinal studies indicate how very important it is to analyze data about children by sex as well as by age. They indicate the differential effects of parental behavior on boys and girls. This should not surprise us, but it often gets overlooked. In both the cognitive and affective aspects of the self, boys and girls view themselves differently, tend to use different learning styles, tend to evaluate different aspects of self and world as important. The origins lie both in biology and in differential treatment.

Unfortunately, most of the children studied in longitudinal research have been middle-class, from somewhat stable families, where conditions might generally foster the mix of intellectual and emotional inputs that lead to positive views of the self. They fit Lois Murphy's observation that "Each experience of mastery and triumph sets the stage for better efforts in the next experience. Confidence, hope, and a sense of self-worth are increased along with the increase in cognitive and motor skills, which can contribute to better use of the resources."[14] Their world provides them with both intellectual challenge and emotional support. Both the cognitive and affective "matches"—the connection between the child's motives and cognitive level on the one hand and the experiences being offered to him on the other[15,16]—are in phase. His positive self-image receives verification from his competence in dealing with the world.

Unfortunately, not all children have the sense of triumph described by Lois Murphy, nor do their selves match the world's demands. Yarrow's studies[17] of maternal deprivation indicate the difficulties encountered by children who lack a mother figure to provide them with some stable anchorage points. In the social domain, Clark,[18] Deutsch,[19] Smilansky,[20] Marans,[21] and Wortis,[22] among others, point out the devastating effects of social deprivation on building positive self-esteem. Although the child's view of himself does not mirror and is not an exact replica of his world's picture of him, for many youngsters it comes quite close. If the larger society conceives of the child as not worthwhile and demonstrates consistently to him that it so judges him, it is difficult for the child to value himself. Children in the ghetto, children classified as slow learners, children who for a variety of reasons are told even in these early years that they are not quite good enough or smart enough or handsome enough tend to devalue themselves and thus to set the stage for continuously poorer levels of performance than might otherwise be their lot. These images are already set before entry into school.[23] Children growing up in psychologically disorganized homes suffer similar fates, as Pavenstedt[24] has indicated about South Boston children.

"As the twig is bent . . . " has long been part of Western folklore. Scientific data now support this view. The origins of the self lie in the early years. How the child will see himself is influenced by the way he is treated, the opportunities provided for him, how he is evaluated as he copes with these opportunities, and how he perceives these evaluations.

If these early years are crucial in determining school performance through the mechanism of the self-concept, then society cannot shrug off its responsibility. For very young children, negative self-views may be as damaging as physical illness or actual physical handicap. We are rapidly making provision for medical help. We need to create nurturing environments early in life so that children's concepts of them-

33

selves may possibly emerge as positive. Whether the school systems as now constructed are the appropriate agencies to reach down to the younger years is open to debate. The example of Head Start programs and the present Parent and Child Center movement indicate that new social agencies consisting of and requiring the participation of those for whom the service is intended may provide effective vehicles for change. What is needed is education so designed that parents can provide children not only with an *affective* climate which tells them they are loved and worthy but also with a *cognitive* climate that allows the child to be competent as well as feel loved. Adequate self-esteem requires this combination.

A characteristic of the American society is its own self-concept that it is capable of solving the problems which afflict it, once the problems are pointed out. The issue is clear. What is required now are social engineering skills. Intervention is essential. We have some ideas of what it should be and who should render it. Now we need to develop the types of programs which provide for all children the psychological inputs which lead to positive self-esteem.

[1]H. S. Sullivan, *The Interpersonal Theory of Psychiatry*. New York: W. W. Norton, 1953.

[2]René Spitz, *The First Year of Life*. New York: International Universities Press, 1965.

[3]L. Lipsitt, "Learning in the Human Infant," in H. W. Stevenson, E. H. Hess, and H. L. Rheingold (eds.), *Early Behavior: Comparative and Developmental Approaches*. New York: Wiley, 1967, pp. 225-48.

[4]E. Erikson, *Childhood and Society*. New York: Norton, 1951.

[5]R. Sears, E. Maccoby, and H. Levin, *Patterns of Child Rearing*. Evanston, Ill.: Row Peterson, 1957.

[6]R. Sears et al., *Identification and Child Rearing*. Stanford, Calif.: Stanford University Press, 1965.

[7]G. H. Mead, *Mind, Self and Society*. Chicago: University of Chicago, 1940.

[8]S. Smilansky, *The Effects of Sociodramatic Play on Disadvantaged Pre-school Children*. New York: Wiley, 1968.

[9]T. Décarie, *Intelligence and Affectivity in Early Childhood*. New York: International Universities Press, 1965. (Translated by Elisabeth and Lewis Brandt)

[10]J. Piaget, *Les Relations Entre l'Affectivité et l'Intelligence Dans la Développement Mental de l'Enfant*. Paris: Centre de Documentation Universitaire, 1954.

[11]B. Bloom, *Stability and Change in Human Characteristics*. New York: Wiley, 1964.

[12]N. Bayley, "Consistency of Maternal and Child Behaviors in the Berkeley Growth Study," *Vita Humana*, 1964, pp. 73-95.

[13]J. Kagan and H. Moss, *Birth to Maturity*. New York: Wiley, 1962.

[14]L. Murphy and associates, *The Widening World of Childhood*. New York: Basic Books, 1962.

[15]J. McV. Hunt, *Intelligence and Experience*. New York: The Ronald Press, 1961.

[16]Ira J. Gordon, *Studying the Child in School*. New York: Wiley, 1966.

[17]L. Yarrow, "Separation from Parents During Early Childhood," in Martin L. Hoffman and Lois W. Hoffman (eds.), *Review of Child Development Research*, Vol. 1. New York: Russell Sage, 1964, pp. 89-136.

[18]K. Clark, *Dark Ghetto*. New York: Harper & Row, 1965.

[19]M. Deutsch and associates, *The Disadvantaged Child*. New York: Basic Books, 1967.

[20]Smilansky, *op. cit.*

[21]A. Marans, D. Meers, and D. Huntington, "The Children's Hospital in Washington, D.C.," in Laura L. Dittmann (ed.), *Early Child Care, the New Perspective*. New York: Atherton, 1968, pp. 287-301.

[22]H. Wortis, et al., "Child-rearing Practices in a Low Socio-economic Group," *Pediatrics*, 1963, pp. 298-307.

[23]B. Long and E. Henderson, "Social Schemata of School Beginners: Some Demographic Correlates," in *Proceedings*, 75th Annual Convention, American Psychological Association, 1967, pp. 329-30.

[24]E. Pavenstedt (ed.), *The Drifters*. Boston: Little, Brown, 1967.

SOCIAL DEVELOPMENT IN HANDICAPPED CHILDREN

An Essay on Metamorphosis

HANS MÜLLER WIEDEMANN

1. Introduction

This essay is an attempt to outline some fundamentals on the social development of handicapped children. It emerged from experiences in following up the ways of adjustment and rehabilitation in the children under our care. We had always realised that the problems of social adjustment are connected to human inter-relationships and that their patterns are fundamentally no different and by no means less tangible than those of the normal child. These problems however can only be understood when to begin with we accept the necessity of close daily contact with the handicapped child. In the past, knowledge of the social development of the handicapped was neglected because the handicapped child was given a kind of social status by virtue of his handicap; the term 'handicapped child' seemingly designating a particular position in society. It is of great importance to realise this since the handicapped child tends to identify himself with his handicap, particularly in early childhood, a fact which represents the real handicap as to the development of social identity he is in search of. The mere medical diagnosis and assessment of capabilities therefore misses the point of paramount importance, namely the realisation that by unconsciously identifying himself with his handicap, the child is to begin with unable to free his resources of creativeness and adaptation to the world around him. These therefore cannot be assessed. This arrest has consequences as to the child's openness and understanding of the ever changing patterns of human inter-relationships and therefore also the process of learning. The gradual loosening of the identification with the particular handicap can be achieved only in human inter-relationship,

THE CRESSET, 1964, Vol. 11, No. 1, pp. 15-26.

35

contrary to a belief that biological disturbances which cause handicaps are reason enough to regard social development as dependent on it. As long as such a view is accepted, the almost imperceptible manner in which the handicapped child learns to adjust himself will escape our knowledge and we shall have hardly any possibility to develop our imagination and insight into this process. It is decidedly different from possible improvements of overt handicaps and different in its rhythms, patterns and stages from the development of intelligence alone. Recent investigations have shown that the increase of knowledge and skill in the educationally sub-normal child pursues a steady rate, the measurement of which reveals little of the child's social maturity.

We therefore suggest that we shall have to alter considerably our attitude towards the diagnosis of handicapped children's progress in order to be able to understand the development of their Self within the group. The diagnosis and prognosis on merely medical and anatomical grounds, for instance, might have to give way to assessments of the child's handicap related to interpersonal relationship, his self-appraisal and his possibilities of becoming a member of a group of other persons. It seems that we shall have to try to clarify our notion of social development altogether. Do we really know what we mean? Are we confident that we are entitled to aim at the adjustments of the handicapped to existing values and spiritual and material patterns of our existing society? Is our concept of the teacher-pupil relationship still up to date when we have once realised that we travel together with the handicapped child along a road upon which the children are our teachers as well as vice versa? Have we perhaps failed to discover resources of our own creativeness that we are so keen on adaptation? Do we perhaps, as society, lack the necessary resources of human and other opportunities to offer to the handicapped child?

Our observations have led us to see that the handicapped child who manifests his handicap in executive and motor disorders is not only handicapped in his motor organisation but also in his freedom to make use of powers of assimilation and metamorphosis of his sensory perceptions. Thus these children do not only show overt handicaps such as, for instance, palsies, but are limited in the activation of those resources of metamorphosis and creativeness which guide social development.

In ordinary daily life, a man constantly returns to those resources whenever a crisis of Self occurs in his social contacts in order that a new Self may emerge. The handicapped child seems constantly to suffer under this crisis by being prevented from using his resources of metamorphosis. It seems therefore necessary to investigate these resources which are stimulated by the child's sensory experience and yet are not identical with it. Their coming into action alone makes it possible that *perception* turns into *experience* and only Man seems endowed with this power of metamorphosis since he is always open to the world and not bound to a particular environment, nor to specific functions and skills.

At the beginning of this century RUDOLF STEINER clearly pointed to the spiritual endowment of Man as the Ego which alone can manifest in Man as the powers of creativeness and metamorphosis alike in which the Self experiences continuity in its ever-changing status from childhood to maturity. It must be emphasised that the Self is not identical with the Ego but that the Self is only free to ever gain, lose and regain its status if it is securely related to the identity of the Ego, which makes possible metamorphosis and creativeness. Rudolf Steiner indicated that the development of the Ego, its incarnation as a spiritual entity in a body determined by hereditary and environmental factors is a slow yet perceptible process which is only fully established around the twenty-first year. To observe the gradual birth of the Ego is of importance if we are to succeed in helping the handicapped child to overcome his specific inability to bring this power into action and to bear on his emotions, his motor activities and his sense perceptions. Futhermore, if we recognise the Ego in the child, we understand where his security rests and we realise the necessity of the child's unconscious perceiving of the Ego in order that he can develop a conscious sense of individual identity. We have now recognised in the handicapped child a profound inability to use the powers of the Ego for metamorphosis and assimilation of sense perception as well as the basic security which the Ego provides as – in the words of ERIKSON,[1] 'the silent doings of Ego-synthesis'. This gradual birth of the Ego throughout childhood marks at the same time the steps towards social maturity.

---

[1] Quoted from ANSELM L. STRAUSS: *Mirrors and Masks*. The Free Press of Gencoe, Illinois.

We must therefore concern ourselves with the significance of motor development in early childhood when the Ego makes its first essential appearance. We must follow up the stages of motor development not only from its executive aspects, but we shall also have to discover the Ego activity in motor development as directed to assimilation and metamorphosis of the perceptual world around.

2. The Ego in Motor Development and Social Development in Early Childhood

In his paper on psychotic children, Dr T. J. WEIHS[2] made the following important statements concerning handicapped children. Taking up indications given by Rudolf Steiner in his course on Curative Education in 1924, Dr Weihs draws our attention to some strange remarks Rudolf Steiner made at the outset:

He (Rudolf Steiner) said that we would have to learn to understand that the handicap of a vast majority of mentally retarded children did not lie in the sphere of thinking but in the sphere of the will. He did however say that there are some very few in whom primarily the sphere of thinking was disturbed.

In the course of the years of our work, we have learned to understand one aspect of this indication of Rudolf Steiner's. In the great variety of symptoms and conditions that children suffering from all kinds of handicap show, be the handicap primarily physical, manifesting in a disability of movement or impairment of the senses or also a mental retardation, we always meet with some form of inability. When it is realised that also the faculties of speaking and even of thinking are fundamentally motor abilities, we learn to see all forms of child handicap as motor disturbances. Thereby our understanding of the child is deepened or we can feel ourselves into the child's condition. I mean that we imagine that we ourselves would be prevented from expressing what we want to express and from understanding what we want to understand.

All the many diverse forms of child handicap once they are understood as disturbances of motor development show that they are based on a physical impairment, even if the handicap is overtly a mental one. The fundamental realisation that also in a handicapped child it is the physical instrument that is imperfect and not the mind – which Rudof Steiner clearly set forth in the beginning of the century – is now gradually being accepted in scientific circles.

Taking up Dr Weih's suggestions we realise that throughout the first year of life which culminates in the child's being able to stand and to walk, yet another development takes place apart from the

---

[2] T. J. WEIHS: Psychotic Children. *The Cresset*, Christmas 1961.

conquering of the spatial world: the child learns to experience his movements as outside himself and belonging to the visual space around him. While however this process goes on very silently, a faculty appears in the small child through which the activity underlying and impulsating movement is turned inward and metamorphosed to give rise to the activity of perception of the other person as to his language, expression and gesture. At the same time the most important and significant activity in human inter-relationship – that of imitation – becomes possible. This is obviously brought about by a shift of activity from motor executive to motor assimilation of the world around. It is specifically human and creates the first and vital social dimension of experience. The movement-organisation not only becomes ordered and transformed by the Ego so that uprightness is achieved but at the same time and increasingly so, the Ego makes its appearance in the social activity of assimilation. From then on the Ego is more and more involved in those acts through which the other person appears, not only as an object or a partner in manipulation and action, but emerges as a social partner. This is most clearly expressed. Dr KÖNIG[3] has shown in detail how in the first year of life, hereditary motor patterns are transformed into those movements which together with increasing acuity of perception lead the child to uprightness. He describes this transformation as an entirely new attainment which stands opposite the biological and hereditary motor functions of the newborn child. Dr König makes the important statement that this new impulse can only be seen in connection with what Rudolf Steiner described as the Ego: 'When the Ego appears, all other patterns of movement withdraw and disappear. It is as if the shepherd appeared amongst the herd to establish peace and order.'[4]

The handicapped child however remains in the grip of his particular handicap which often does not allow the free unfolding of the metamorphosis from executive function into social dimensions, with the consequence that the powers of assimilation of sensory perceptions are not fully available. The delay and slowness of man's development in early infancy which A. PORTMANN[5] pointed out become understandable when we realise the activity

---

[3] K. KÖNIG: *Die ersten drei Jahre des Kindes.* Verlag Freies Geistesleben, Stuttgart, 1957. [4] ibid.
[5] A. PORTMANN: *Biologische Fragmente zu einer Lehre vom Menschen.* Basel, 1944.

of the Ego as not only ordering movement for the sake of perfection of skills and mere motor functions, but also directed to the inwardness of active social perception. The Ego reveals itself not as the bearer of hereditary patterns but on the contrary, of potentials which in the education of the handicapped child have to be seen, guided and freed.

Whilst the animal from birth onwards is bound to patterns of communication expressed in specific skills and biologically determined functions, man's potentialities and social openness appear in sharp contrast. It is furthermore important to note that these potentialities are only slowly realised by the child and need for their development the help and communication of other human beings. This development as we have seen does not follow a continuous curve but its progress occurs in specific rhythms and specific situations which is of great prognostic importance. Only close, individual observation can perceive improvements and it is necessary to give time to the handicapped child as well as sufficient human opportunities. Foremost however we have learned to realise that the Ego activity described relies on and is sustained only through a constant relationship to other human beings which provides a basis of security in which gradually the world of objects can appear. In this security alone is man able to transcend the sensory-motor-bound states of his early months through the power of the Ego, and can be open and prepared for the crisis of transformations which can occur in the education of the handicapped and the normal child alike. This basic security needs to be established long before a conscious Self has emerged. The overt development of movement and the handicaps of executive functions can only be regarded as external communications and signposts to the wider and deeper aspects of Ego development which links man with his potentialities – the deep resources of his powers of creativeness and metamorphosis – and which can lead him later on to the unfolding of love and of work. Only if the child is able to bring this activity to bear upon his sense perceptions of the world, is he open to mature and to gradually expand his social circumference.

3. The Veiled Understanding of the Ego

Our present understanding of Ego development and altogether the recognition of the Ego have to struggle against deeply ingrained errors of scientific thinking. The one is connected with the notion of the function of the central nervous system, others with theories of developmental psychology and psycho-analysis. These errors although historically understandable have so far drawn a veil over the acknowledgement of the ego and have consequently deeply influenced our knowledge of the social capacities of handicapped children. Let us examine these errors.

The first is the notion that the central nervous system impulsates movement from the motor cortex. This theory has increasingly been put to doubt in the last few decades by eminent neurologists and already at the beginning of the century, Rudolf Steiner pointed out that the so-called motor-nerve organisation does not impulsate movement but acts as a perceptual organ for the activity connected with the Ego which is akin to intentionality in movement, a quality which transcends any overt movement in space. As K. König has shown,[6] uprightness and the ability to walk in man can only appear through that function of the motor nervous system that perceives the activity of the Ego. Observation of the individual's development shows an ever-increasing amount of perception of his own movement and it is exactly against this background of the inwardness of perception that the child can experience his overt movement as 'outside' and ceases to be identified with it. This fact as we have tried to show has fundamental social consequences, especially for the handicapped child since only then is the child able to gain distance from his initial identification with the movement organisation and its handicaps. In doing so he gains the dimension of inwardness in which the other human being appears as a social partner. Hence imitation, for instance, appears as an activity not directed to the spatial world of objects but to the object only in so far as it is part of the human world of social contacts. The notions of the functions of the central nervous system as identical with motor actions has not only prevented an understanding of the ever-changing patterns of movements and actions towards maturity, but has also created a barrier for the understanding of the powers of metamorphosis grounded in the ego and stimulated by the perceptual faculties of the so-called motor nervous system.

The second veil which has been drawn is even more dense as

---

[6] K. KÖNIG: ibid.

41

part of our general present-day thinking. It originates in SIGMUND FREUD'S psycho-analytical theories of drives and in particular in his theory of the phantasy and reality-principle. Freud believed that man's activity is biologically determined and he postulated that the activity of drives in early childhood is constantly curtailed by the givers of sensory perception to which it is forced to adjust itself. Freud was possessed by the concept of the Ego as rational which he thought to be in opposition to what he called the Id. He missed seeing that the Ego silently makes its appearance in the unconscious sphere of the Id already in the first year of life. More tragically Freud failed to see that the growing child is not forced to wrestle with the reality principle (the world of perception and environment), giving rise to suppressions, but that the human being is increasingly endowed with the spiritual entity of the Ego whose primary tasks and divine powers rest in the ability to activate metamorphosis of sense perception, to assess security of being and to develop the faculty of love, closely related to what we have called the powers of metamorphosis. Man's striving therefore does not go towards the elimination of sensory perception, the reality principle in early childhood for the sake of the motionless state, but towards metamorphosis of perception into experience, by bringing the Ego to bear on the given facts of his cultural and sensory surroundings. In more recent trends of developmental psychology, man's striving has been realised more truly as being directed towards self-realisation, the creation of the Self out of the metamorphosis of experiences which are permeated by the Ego (see the work of E. SCHACHTEL).[7]

Thirdly I wish to examine the investigations of developmental psychology, notably the profound contributions of JEAN PIAGET. His approach is centred around two polarities of functions which guide the development of the child and which Piaget calls Accommodation and Assimilation. He clearly regards these functions as biologically determined and the child as being endowed with them at birth. Piaget is fundamentally concerned with the emergence of the spatial world in his descriptions of early sensory motor development as its appearance is obviously a first and necessary step to the child's gaining distance from the world and consequently a step towards the establishing of

---

[7] E. SCHACHTEL: *Metamorphosis*. Basic Books Inc. Publishers, New York.

Selfhood. Piaget however avoided and also partly failed to see the spiritual reality of the Ego as the specifically human activity underlying assimilation, transforming executive activities into perceptual functions, or providing the activity for such metamorphosis. Hence whilst he realised the tantamount importance of the emergence of objects for the child, he neglected the part played by human inter-relationships in this process. This becomes most obvious in his interpretation of the development of language. True, both need a spatial and visual world as language needs objects to refer to, yet no operation of thoughts can create the powers of metamorphosis of the spatial world into a world in which language makes its appearance. Without realising the metamorphosising activity of the Ego, this step will forever remain ununderstandable. It reveals itself truly in language the disturbances of which we have increasingly learnt to realise as being of diagnostic and prognostic importance in the social development of the handicapped child. Piaget constructed the emergence of language most extensively as to its relationship to objects as means of reference which he holds comes about by the child discovering more and new aspects of objects, all called by the same name, so that finally the word appears as signifying something which eventually need not be visible. Yet long before this happens, language is endowed with specific communicative values between the child and the parents, preceeding the activity of naming and through which the child enters into social dimensions. Whilst to begin with the Ego has ordered movement, here it is born in the community and reveals itself as the divine artist in man who does not paint the picture of the visual world, but creates his own central tool of human inter-relationship – language.

4. Conclusion – Some Attitudes and Observations

The limitations and the arrest of the unfolding powers of metamorphosis of the Ego in the handicapped child severs these children from being related to the ground upon which the security of man rests as a being endowed with ego-hood. Through the handicap this divine ground is prevented from unfolding its potentialities with the consequence that the social circumference of these children is limited to different degrees. The power of metamorphosis in early years is not free and the child is forced to identify itself with this limitation. Thus also the possibilities for adaptation are more confined. The handicap reveals itself foremost not as an intellectual incapacity *per se* but as a limitation of the transformation of sensory perception into what we have called experience. Experience in man comes about when what happens in the world around can be freely related to the Ego. In the first three years of childhood development, the increasing assimilation of the world arises to begin with out of this process until in the third year, the child experiences Selfhood when he begins to take his stand more and more consciously in his social surroundings. It is therefore always the first task of teachers and parents of handicapped children to give the child security in order to allow the Ego to widen into experience. The handicapped child who is denied this help will have difficulty in establishing his conscious Self which rests on this inter-relationship of security with the other person. It is then of great importance to follow up the very subtle patterns through which out of this basic security the flower of Selfhood blossoms. This process cannot easily be objectified by tests which call for executive or intellectual abilities, but essentially miss the evaluation of the realm where the child only spontaneously reveals his growing experience. We have learned to see that each child strives for his specific equilibrium of experience. This equilibrium emerges between sense perception and motor assimilation, and just as in exhaling and inhaling, the social self emerges in its dynamic functions. The growing up and educated handicapped child gradually learns to establish this equilibrium largely irrespective of the more overt capacities of motor skill and development of intellectual achievements. Intellectual and motor abilities can only provide readings but their meaning can be revealed only if they are understood against the background of social behaviour. It then becomes obvious that the handicapped child is not born into this world to conform but to be given the opportunity of unfolding his individual specific social Self, and this notion exactly marks the line between education and training. It is necessary to realise that the teacher has at times to give up his status of particular modes of self-assertion through increased self-knowledge to be free for metamorphosis. He must needs pass through many crises with his pupil, relying on the firm ground of his own egohood, on the divine powers in himself which he must reveal to the child. The handicap of a child is always a result of the past; the attitude of teacher and the community in general in their social value to the child depends on their considered judgement of where his future lies. Without recognition of the Ego in man, this future can only be adapted to existing cultural patterns. Yet if the Ego is recognised and acknowledged in its divine origin the future of the handicapped child might well lead him beyond those patterns and in the process, the handicapped child might well become able to create new values. Being bound to the past by his sensory perception, the handicapped child frequently suffers additional and perhaps his most severe disappointment by encountering a community which is similarly bound in its particular level of perception and concepts. The child longs to regain the powers of creativeness which display their wealth particularly in the first fourteen years of life. If the child is helped to do so, the age of puberty as also for the normal child marks not only a new crisis but gives new opportunities. We have observed that many handicapped children are just then actively able to adjust themselves to their handicap, an important step towards self-realisation which frees the growing child from his identification with his particular limits the handicap has imposed upon the unfolding personality. A new social status can thus be reached with the expectancy that the handicap becomes gradually accepted by the Other Self and new possibilities of metamorphosis can come about once adjustment makes its appearance.

The teacher has to learn more and more to be a brother to the handicapped child and *education* must become *conversation*. Thus in the growing child the divine power of the Ego begins to manifest, individualised in the acknowledgement of limitations and in the conscious expectancy of the teacher that the child is able to contribute to the community in which he lives. It is obvious that the history of the social development of the handicapped child is at the same time the history of his teachers and the community at large. Once this is realised we shall understand that the problem of the handicapped child is our problem, that we either mirror his handicap by providing for him old facets of life and thought, or accept the handicapped child as a brother in our own metamorphosis towards new concepts and new ways of life.

Attitudes and thoughts have here been put forward which might be the basis for further research into the ways the handicapped child seeks for self-realisation out of the divine ground of the Ego.

In conclusion I wish to emphasise that in this essay I have taken up suggestions made by Dr König as to the two aspects of child development which were then described by Dr Weihs in his last Superintendent's Report:[8]

Basing our assumptions on Rudolf Steiner's teaching, we regard child development as a process of integration – one might say, incarnation – in which the spiritual entity tries to manifest as a personality in a body determined by heredity and environment factors. Here Dr König has pointed out two main aspects: the one is that the integration process must lead to the child's appreciation of what surrounds it. The development of consciousness, the integration of the sense processes, the sphere of human contact – all these belong to this aspect. The other aspect is that in which the personality takes hold of its own body as well as of all the executive faculties or motor abilities not only of the body and limbs but also of speech and even thinking. Even when frequently both aspects of the incarnation process are involved, we are inclined to regard our children from the polar aspect of personality-disorder and sensory defect on the one hand, and executive and motor disorders on the other hand.

I have only dealt with the second aspect in order to show the implications of executive and motor disorders as to social development. The growing experience and social maturity of the handicapped child with executive disorders can be seen as related to the attempts to give birth to the freedom of the spiritual powers of creativeness and metamorphosis manifest in the Ego of man.

IMITATION AND THE BODY-SCHEME

Dr. med. GEORG VON ARNIM

"Imitation is the central element of behaviour in pre-school development," writes Lutz in his text-book on Child-Psychiatry.[1] He emphasizes that "the child does not only imitate what it consciously perceives, but also makes use of every example of behaviour in its environment, be it physical or psychological, conscious or unconscious." Finally Lutz suggests that "the pre-school child does not yet understand intellectual arguments or casual explanations." As early as 1907, Rudolf Steiner, in his essays on the "Education of the Child", had already expounded this idea in detail: "Two magic words," he wrote, "describe the manner in which the child relates itself to the environment: Imitation and Example. The Greek Philosopher Aristotle described man as the most imitative of all animals. There is no age to which this view is more applicable than to the age between birth and the second dentition, the time when the first set of teeth is replaced." [2]

According to Rudolf Steiner the effects of imitation penetrate deeply into the formation of the physical organs of the pre-school child. He writes: "Everything in the child's physical environment is imitated and, by imitating, the child moulds its organs into permanent forms. However, the physical environment must be taken in its broadest possible sense. To this environment does not only belong the material world but everything that the child can perceive, everything that by happening in a physical space, can influence the child's spiritual forces. To these influential factors belong all moral and immoral deeds, all forms of reasonable and unreasonable behaviour visible to the child. Moral statements or rational teaching are of no effect. The deeds of the adult performed in the child's sight are effective."

Everyone who meets these problems for the first time will be surprised how widely Rudolf Steiner interprets the meaning of imitation. One must, however, be aware of the fact, that this situation is encountered only by the

THE CRESSET, 1967, Vol. 13, No. 4, pp. 15-31.

small child. At a later stage, notably at the beginning of the second dentition, the ability to imitate decreases and loses its intimate character.

Indeed, closer observation reveals imitation as the only means by which the child relates itself to its environment. Furthermore we can grow aware of the fact, that for the small child imitation is a strong inner necessity. We encounter therefore the important double aspect of imitation: On the one hand imitation is an ability, on the other hand it is an inborn *necessity*, and the child is compelled to imitate whatever may happen in its environment. "At this stage of development there is an intrinsic connection between the child and its acting environment which disappears later." (R. Steiner [3]).

But how does imitation really come about and what are its elements?

The German word "Nachahmen" already points to the fact, that imitation is not passive but an act. Language itself then provides the first indication. What is the nature of this act which allows the child to absorb the moral or immoral character of a deed? We realize that generally the action of the other person is not explicitly imitated. Is it perhaps observation, i.e. perception which leads to the effect we call imitation? However, mere observation could hardly suffice to create the penetrating influence on the child which we referred to earlier on.

Rudolf Steiner, in a lecture to teachers,[4] has elucidated the process which leads to imitation: "The pre-school child," he says, "is interested only in what one can call gestures, relationships of movement and expressions." The importance of this statement is that this interest is not directed towards the logical or casual meaning of an expression or movements nor towards its outer effect. On the contrary, it is only the expressional value, connected with the personality through which it occurs, which the child is able to imitate. The fact, for instance, that I move the coffee pot in order to pour some coffee for a visitor is not of interest, but the child perceives in my movements and expressions whether I act in a friendly and warm-hearted way or in an empty, conventional way. This the child imitates. "Between birth and the second dentition the child relates his

perception to all that is gesture, expression and movement. Whenever the child perceives movement it
experiences the inner drive to imitate it." (R. Steiner [5]).

The child cannot subdue this drive. Following the
descriptions of Rudolf Steiner, we can conclude that
only in this way does the child relate itself meaningfully
to its environment and understand it. This form of
communication exceeds verbal and explicit understanding
to a degree which is usually not sufficiently understood.
Generally speaking, the child understands verbal communication from its expression rather than from its
logical meaning. "It is therefore necessary to abstain
from everything in the presence of the small child that
the child should not imitate. By doing so the child is
educated. To admonish 'Do this! Don't do that!' has no
lasting influence on the child in the first seven years.
Such demands not only become effective by being
clothed in a different way; for instance by saying: 'Look,
you have done this, I would never have done it'. Such
a subtle admonishing becomes effective by being as it
were camouflaged as a verbal gesture." (R. Steiner [6]).
One might say that the small child swims in a sea of
what appears to be expression, gesture and movement.
As we co-ordinate ourselves by swimming with the
movements of the waves of the water the small child's
imitations coincide with the waves of expressive movement and gesture into which it is immersed.

The influence of this process goes extremely deep
especially since, for the most part, it is not consciously
perceived. The separation of the Self from the environment cannot yet be achieved. Only later does the Self
emerge when the child begins to establish its own
individuality through the peculiarities of its own individual movement. In the early stages, however, the
movement of the child takes on forms and meaning from
the environment. To begin with, the child's movement
remains orientated to those expressions which the
environment has to offer. There exists a large literature
of observations which show to what great extent the
child imitates, for example the movement-patterns of its
parents.

For the following investigations I suggest to consider

the unity of movement and the sum of single movements of a group of people as an organic unity. That is to say, that there exists a common space in which all our movements flow together, are singled out, meet, are related to each other or become separated. In exactly the same way as the space in which we live together can be perceived as a unity can we consider all movements happening in such a space as a wholeness. Of course, this cannot be said to be true of a physically conceived space but more of the space of human communication. Since it constitutes the space of our movement and expression it can also be called our space of experience or of communication. O. F. Bollnow, the German philosopher, has given a description of the space we mean: "Man is not placed in space like an object in a box. He does not behave as if he existed as a non-spatial subject that afterwards relates itself to a given space; human life has *initially* a given relationship to space and cannot be divorced from it even in thought." [7] Life, therefore, seems to include space from the beginning and even the operations of thought cannot fully overcome this unity. Therefore O. F. Bollnow later writes: "Space becomes a general formation of human communication." To illustrate the point one may visualize a gathering of people whose discussion or conversation is accompanied by animated gestures. In such a situation the bond of communication can be experienced as "gelebter Raum" (a lived-in-space). It could also be called "the space of loving togetherness" (Binswanger). This space is not the space of the physicist but the space of living together. It may be suggested that the whole dimension of movement has a similar meaning as the lived-in-space has, if one considers its communicative unity. The wholeness of "life-space" and the movements which we perform in it seem to form an inseparable unity. Space is built up from the sum of our movements and is filled with the expression that accompanies those movements. The small child is immersed in this space and lives in it without restriction. In shaking hands we experience the meeting of movements as a form of communication. The small child does not yet employ this gesture of communication but it may reach for its mother's hand when it feels insecure. It still lives in the immediate perception of the movement in its environment. The small child is not yet confronted with its environment as is the case when we reach out to shake hands in greeting each other or in saying good-bye. The child is still part and parcel of the environmental movement and imitates it.

We can now imagine that the child imitates its surroundings with an inner movement not with a physical one. In tuning in to its surroundings it absorbs meaning and expression of imitated movement. Here we must add another important phenomenon. The more we understand that it is not only words and concepts but also the inner imitation of expressional movements that bring about the communication of one man to another, the easier we can grasp the following: Words might be wrong, affection might be deceiving but the expression which goes with a movement has a particular power of truthfulness and conviction. The inner value of a gesture corresponds to its outer appearance. It cannot be deceiving. In practical experience nobody would think that in his movements could be seen anything other than his soul. What the child perceives in imitating the movement of its environment reveals to it all that lives in the soul of the adult and this both unconsciously and in the most immediate way. Because of this the effect of imitation is all the more lasting. It seems to be a profound truth that the small child lives in a world in which no deception is possible. Absorbing its environment by imitating movement, the child meets unadulterated reality. The child gives itself up to this reality, unconsciously by trusting that it is only the good that it meets. If it were otherwise, the overwhelming openness of the infant would not be understandable. This relationship to the world, the manner and quality of which is characterized by a complete lack of pre-conception and by the fullest possible submission may only be compared to the adult's later religious experiences. All this points to further understanding of "the particular intrinsic connection between the child and the actions in its environment", so important in the early ages and lost in the course of development. This form of early communication decreases at the age when the child hitherto went to school. This environmental relationship is no longer possible when the child has to learn to read and write and to manipulate the symbolic character of letters and numbers.

When even only gropingly the child begins to *think* about the world, it severs itself from its relationship with it. A new stage of consciousness dawns. The Self, the individual begins to separate itself from the general in the same way as earlier the body of the child became independent at the moment of birth.

Recent observations have shed new light on this process. They are related to the development of what is called the body-scheme. This development can be seen as closely related to the dawn of the new consciousness described earlier on. It has been found that the development of the body-scheme is paralleled by the experience the child gains of his own body as compared to the experience of the bodies of others. The child's consciousness of the relationships of the parts of his own body as well as of the bodies of others does not exist at birth. This fact has been again verified through more recent observations on children with malformed, under-developed or missing limbs. In a report on children with "Dysmelia" (underdeveloped limbs), the authors investi-gated the psychological situation of these children and wrote: "We noticed that the playmates [of these children] at the age of under three years did not notice their handicap. They play with such a handicapped child as if it were entirely normal.[8] "

Lack of a developed body-scheme of the child's own body seems to make the perception of parts of the body of others difficult. Therefore the malformations of the children with Dysmelia had not been noticed by their playmates. Only in the course of Kindergarten and school age the child, by developing its own body-scheme, becomes able to perceive its own body or the bodies of others.

What is meant with the child's experience of his own body Karl König has formulated: "We experience our feet and hands, our own limbs, our head, our trunk. We also have a dim experience of our organs, we perceive unconsciously our breathing and know exactly at every moment how the single parts of our body are inter-related. We notice when we bend or stretch our fingers, whether we move them upwards or downwards. We know which way we turn our head; our whole movement-organization is perceived in its entirety.[9] "

The presence of this body-scheme in childhood development has been extensively studied in recent years.[10] It has been visualized as a function of the central nervous system although its true nature is difficult to understand. It has been suggested however that in the course of childhood the function of the body-scheme impresses itself in some way on the central nervous system. This process was thought to lead finally to a kind of scheme, imprinted on the central nervous system, to which the real conditions of the body at any one time can be related as it were by a kind of comparison. However, a full understanding of this process has remained vague up to the present day.

Poeck and Orgass have collected together the older theories and, although opinions differ, a general trend of thought can be observed: "The function of the body-scheme is conceived as the inner experience of one's own limbs together with their optical perception and the optical perception of other bodies." Obviously this is not an easy concept to grasp. We must imagine that the central nervous system is able to abstract such a scheme from the great number and variety of all possible movements and postures, which are in a continual flux, changing every moment. For the central nervous system being as it is a perceiving organ such a task would surely be a very creative achievement. The investigations of Poeck and Orgass have shed a different light on the problem.

Detailed investigations on the development of the body-scheme in normal children have been carried out from different aspects: Differentiation of right and left under different conditions, the child's ability to point out different parts of its body as well as parts on models, differentiation of the body-scheme especially in relation to hand-perception and the identification of single fingers. In all aspects the child's ability to discriminate and perceive takes a leap when it reaches the age of 6 or 7

By the age of 8 to 10 the development of a stable body-scheme has been more or less completed.

The investigation of blind children has shown striking and far-reaching results: Compared with normal children no differences were found in the development of the body-scheme with respect to hand-perception. "This lack of difference between the normal and the blind child has been found in all aspects of body-scheme development. All our investigations have shown that the blind child is neither worse nor better off than the normal child.[11]" It can therefore be concluded that the child's visual perceptions of its own body and of the body of others has no influence on the development of the body-scheme. Finally children, born with missing limbs, were investigated. The result was even more startling: These children showed body-scheme perception for all limbs which had been missing from birth onwards. Previously such a possibility had never been accepted. The body-scheme of the missing limbs appeared in the form of so-called "phantom-limbs". It had been known, that after amputation a real sensation of the lost limb persists—the phantom-limb. Now it became clear, that phantom-limbs appear not only after amputation at an early age but develop gradually in children where no "physical limb" (hand, arm or leg) was present at birth. One might say that the phantom-limbs "grow".

Recent observations by S. Weinstein and others [12] have shown, that among 101 children born with limbs missing, 18 had clear perception of phantom-limbs. Taking into account the difficulty with which a crippled child can describe such subtle sensations, the percentage must be regarded as high. The intensity of the phantom-experience seems to vary in these children. Weinstein and his colleagues state that physical activity, emotional state and bodily position seem to intensify the experience, whereas wearing of the prosthesis, fatigue and rest have the contrary effect. Suggestion by the examiner could be excluded. The authors write: "A strong argument against the role of suggestion by the examiner is illustrated by the report of case eight: After the child (a girl) reported the existence of phantom-fingers to the examiner, the mother confirmed that she too had, on a number of occasions, heard her report such feelings spontaneously. These statements, however, had been discounted by the parents." [13]

Poeck and Orgass give another impressive description: A girl with both lower arms and hands missing (Peromelia) experienced phantoms of both hands at the age of six. She experienced these limbs as clearly differentiated and freely moveable. During her first school year she had used her phantom-fingers to help her solve simple tasks of arithmetic. At the age of 11 the phantom had become so intensive that the child could experience the touch of objects as well as the hand of the examiner including the differences of consistence and temperature. The hand-scheme had been developed without the corresponding somato-perceptive "experience".[14] The reality of such experiences cannot be doubted.

Now, the question arises of the relationship of the body-scheme to the appearance of the phantom-limbs.

Poeck and Orgass argue in the following way: They conceive of the body-scheme as an autonomous function of the central nervous system which develops from inner causes and necessities. They believe, however, that this process does not happen entirely autonomously. The authors suggest that, according to their investigations of blind children with intact limbs as well as of seeing children without limbs, a kind of perception is necessary in order to give an impulse to this autonomous development. Either the inner (proprioceptive) perception or the outer (visual) perception of the child's own limbs or (as in children without limbs) of the limbs of others must be thought as necessary. The authors therefore presume, that blind children without limbs could not develop a body-scheme.

A body-scheme, developed in the above-mentioned fashion is conceived as a condition for the appearance of phantom-limbs. The authors write: "From our investigations the question can be answered whether the rare appearance of phantoms in children is related to the fact that the body-scheme is not yet fully developed enough to allow the perception of these phantom-limbs: by the age of 5-6 years at the latest, the child can

utilise a sufficiently differentiated body-scheme to create the physiological conditions for phantom-perception.[15] "
According to this statement we would have to visualize the phantom-limb only as a part of the body-scheme which becomes conscious, as it were, as an isolated part of this scheme. Seen in this light, both body-scheme and phantom-limb would indeed appear only as functions of the central nervous system. The investigations of Weinstein, however, give rise to serious doubts concerning these conclusions. He and his colleagues could show that the child can in some cases experience phantom-limbs already at the early age of four. It is therefore unlikely that the body-scheme is sufficiently mature at that stage to provide conditions for the experience of phantom-limbs (if one follows the arguments of Poeck and Orgass).

No doubt, the general concept of an autonomously developing process of maturing of a body-scheme shows definite progress as compared with previously held views, which presupposed the necessity of visual *and* proprioceptive perception for the development of the scheme. We must ask ourselves, however, whether the perception of phantom-limbs is not in fact more fully autonomous, whether perhaps the body-scheme as a function of the central nervous system is *not* the condition by which phantom-limbs "grow". Perhaps the body-scheme cannot be at all conceived as such a function inscribed into the central nervous system as if it were a certain reflex.

The results of the above-mentioned investigations must give rise to a new interpretation that the children's experience of a growing phantom-limb is an expression of a real, new "Gestalt". In 1907 appeared Rudolf Steiner's notes on general child development;[16] they allow a new and more realistic appreciation of the phenomena described as compared to purely neurological interpretations. At the age of seven a new "Gestalt" is formed besides the bodily external forms of the child. It can be called a "functional Gestalt". This new inner supersensual formation can also be seen as the foundation of those functions which are related to the body-scheme. Rudolf Steiner has called this "functional Gestalt" the ether-body, or the body of formative, creative forces and he has described it in detail on many occasions. "We must assume, that the development of a body-scheme in childhood is related to the birth or the freeing of the child's formative body or life-body. On account of this "birth" the first "Gestaltwandel" occurs around the 7th year and the child experiences its body in a new way. This experience increases and is fully completed at the age of 9." (K. König [17]). In using the term "Gestaltwandel", K. König refers to the metamorphosis of the child's Gestalt at the age of six to eight which has been described by W. Zeller [18]: The child relinquishes the physical proportions of the infant, the relatively big head, the hardly developed neck, the relatively big trunk as compared with the small and still helpless limbs. Now, at this age the limbs grow considerably, chest and abdomen flatten out, the lower part of the face increases in size and becomes well proportioned, instead of being dominated as previously by the forehead. The child's body becomes well proportioned and loses its infantile roundness. Indeed, one is now able to see that the phantom-limbs are part of this inner "Gestalt" and can be perceived by the child because its material counterpart is missing. It seems to be justified to concede to the development of this "inner Gestalt" the same autonomy by which the "Gestaltwandel", described by Zeller, takes place. The qualitative similarity of the process that we have experienced by the little girl with her hand-phantom develops at the age of six to eight for the *whole* "Gestalt" of the child. "The phantom-limb is a perceived reality". It must be seen as the same supersensual limb which normally also moves the material limbs, arms, hands and fingers. With amputation only the material limb is eliminated. The supersensual limb however remains intact provided it has already developed. If this has not happened, as in the case of the small infant, the experience of the phantom-limb will be delayed until school-age. Only then does the "birth" of phantom-arms and hands take place.[19]

Seen from the viewpoint taken by Rudolf Steiner of the birth of the ether-body in the child, the outer aspect of "Gestaltwandel" (Zeller), the development of a body-scheme and the experience of phantom-limbs are different expressions of the same underlying process. The body-scheme is therefore not the condition for the appearance of phantom-experiences in limbless children. Both developmental phenomena are expressions of the process described by Rudolf Steiner as the etheric-body of man. It is therefore conceivable that a blind child born with missing limbs can also develop phantoms. Following Rudolf Steiner's notes further we can see that the forces of growth undergo a certain metamorphosis at the age of seven. They cease to be connected with the organic growth of the child, and by becoming free and more independent, create new functions. The creation of a stable body-scheme is one of them.

Time and again Rudolf Steiner has emphasised the importance of this archetypal process of childhood development round about the seventh year: The metamorphosis of those forces which underlie the organic growth of the child during the first seven years. Whilst new functions develop, intensity and speed of growth decrease. Through these new functions not only the body-scheme and the phantom-limbs appear but the child gains new possibilities of thought at this age, the age which until recently has rightly been the first school year. The new abilities of thought do not arise out of nothingness. They are transformed forces of growth.

Going back to our reflections on imitation in early childhood, I referred to the particular form of openness the child has to the world and its intimate relationships to the environment. At the end of this period of imitation the Self sees the perceived unity of the environment from a distance. We can now recognize the physiological conditions which lead to this new step. The appearance of inner formative forces means the end of outer imitation.

Beginning round about the age of six this development is completed between the ninth and tenth years of age. The new achievement, the creation of the inner "Gestalt" allows the child to enter anew the space of communication. At puberty a new step will be taken by the child, the importance of which cannot be discussed in this article.

The idea that the small child should not be treated like an adult gains deeper meaning if seen in the light of the processes described. It is necessary to realize that any manipulation of the space of time of these developments has its effect, as we are dealing with the most intimate foundations of human existence. One is forced to assume that the child who begins to read and write at the age of three or four has to advance the development of body-scheme, the "inner Gestalt". In order to learn to read and write the child has to consolidate the relationship of the right and left side and so on. According to our knowledge now one has also to assume that this relationship can only be established with the help of a stable body-scheme. This means, however, that the development of the body-scheme has to be advanced and the phase of imitation is shortened.

Both processes, happening concurrently—imitation and a functioning and fully established body-scheme—represent an impossibility in the development of the child, although every stage of development can persist after a new stage, not, however, in the same way as before. This law is contained in the phenomena of metamorphosis as expounded in the educational teachings of Rudolf Steiner. The possibility of imitating can be utilised to a certain extent in adult life, but not in the way the infant uses it. The essence of the infants imitation is characterized by the fullest, most immediate and intimate devotion to the expression of movement which is connected with people. The child imbues the deepest layers of its existence with the experience which comes from imitation, an experience which it could neither imagine nor conceptualize. From the mother's smile to every

59

single everyday action stretches the range of expressions which are imitated. This form of relationship to the world ceases when the child can distance itself from the world in the established body-scheme and its consequent abilities. It changes into an imitation further from the centre of the child's existence, more abstract. The child has now to grasp that a letter or a written word has meaning, pointing to something different and becoming a symbol. Imitation at the early age does not take place in the dimension of symbols, it reaches deeper into the realm of immediate being. Being is not perceived as relating to an image or a concept; it is a given, immediate experience. The child partakes as it were in an unbroken heavenly existence. Good and evil are not yet differentiated and the child perceives human existence in the most general sense. The child lives in what E. H. Erikson has called "Urvertrauen" (primary confidence [20]). It must however be emphasised that the child does not gain this confidence through the way in which people, for instance the parents, turn to it. This confidence is primal since the child brings it into the world. Imitation appears as the phenomenalistic expression of confidence. The later development of the child, however, is largely determined by the good and the evil, the moral and the immoral which the child perceives in others through its imitation as well as whether opportunities for imitation exist.

The archetypal confidence that all human expression is worthy to be imitated represents the most child-like and perhaps also the most human of all possible forms of behaviour. This gift represents the foundation of the world-openness of man in comparison with the inborn and limited behaviour-patterns of the animal.

The child cannot stand with one foot in paradise and the other outside. Once the child has made the step to understand signs and symbols, the immediacy with which it perceives the being of others can no longer persist. To repeat, the metamorphosis which the "physiological" functions of the child undergo at the end of the imitative phase and at the beginning of school age does not simply mean an extension of already existing abilities. Metamorphosis means the appearance of a new phase of life. The child seems to need 5-7 years time to complete the process of imitation to an extent enabling it to be inwardly ready to enter a new phase. This need cannot be questioned as it emerges from inner necessities of human existence. The manipulations by which the child is forced to advance the development of the body-scheme and thereby to shorten the phase of imitation are bound to lead to severe disturbances in many of these children in later life. Such disturbances will first occur in those dimensions which are related to interpersonal relationships, the ability to contact others. A new form of acceleration would be created. Normally speaking, the term acceleration means increased growth of children and the advancement of the age when puberty begins. According to A. Portmann, the renowned Swiss biologist and philosopher, the first signs of this process became visible over a century ago.

During the last decades these signs became more intensive and alarming. At the same time opinion changed, being rather optimistic to begin with, then changing to a more cautious negative viewpoint. Portmann writes: "Wherever acceleration has occurred. there has been a noticeably increased susceptibility to certain diseases, especially those of psychological origin." [21]

The speeding up of the stages of development is always connected to a loss in quality of development. Shortened processes of maturing cause later immaturity. If this is true already for the form of acceleration described by Portmann, even more obvious and striking disturbances can be expected to result from the form of acceleration discussed in this paper. The possibility to imitate means a great deal for the growing child. We must ask ourselves whether the fact can be neglected, that the adult's deepest expressions in gesture and movement are absorbed by the imitating child ? The answer is obvious. If we neglected this process, the world would become dangerously empty. Our social structure and the fullness of interpersonal relationships would receive a painful and destructive blow if the child's ability to imitate decreased generally. The adult would become deeply frustrated if the forces destined to be perceived by the imitating child were no longer utilized. In handicapped children this ability is often deeply disturbed. By living together with these children, we learn to understand imitation in a particularly striking way, because they can teach us the origins of human existence from which these forces spring.

REFERENCES:

1 J. Lutz: Kinderpsychiatrie, 2 Aufl. Zürich und Stuttgart, 1962.
2 R. Steiner: Die Erziehung des Kindes, Verlag Freies Geistesleben, Stuttgart, 1948.
3 R. Steiner: Der pädagogische Wert der Menschenkenntnis und der Kulturwert der Pädagogik, Dornach, 1965.
4 R. Steiner: Der pädagogische Wert der Menschenkenntnis und der Kulturwert der Pädagogik, Dornach, 1965.
5 R. Steiner: Der pädagogische Wert der Menschenkenntnis und der Kulturwert der Pädagogik, Dornach, 1965.
6 R. Steiner: Der pädagogische Wert der Menschenkenntnis und der Kulturwert der Pädagogik, Dornach, 1965.
7 D. F. Bollnow: Mensch und Raum, Stuttgart, 1963.
8 W. Bläsig, E. Schomburg: Das Dysmelie-Kind, Stuttgart, 1966.
9 K. König: Die Wissenschaft an der Schwelle, "Die Drei", 1965. Heft 6, pp. 385-392.
10 K. Poeck, B. Orgass: Über die Entwicklung des Körperschemas. Fortschritte der Neurologie und Psychiatrie. 32 (1964). pp. 38-555.
11 K. Poeck, B. Orgass: Über die Entwicklung des Körperschemas, Fortschritte der Neurologie und Psychiatrie, 32 (1964),
12 S. Weinstein, E. Sersen, R. Vetter: Phantoms and somatic Sensation in Cases of Congenital Aplasia. Cortex, Vol. 1 (1964), pp. 216-290.
13 S. Weinstein, E. Sersen, R. Vetter: Phantoms and somatic Sensation in Cases of Congenital Aplasia. Cortex. Vol. 1 (1964), pp. 216-290.
14 K. Poeck, B. Orgass: Über die Entwicklung des Körperschemas, Fortschritte der Neurologie und Psychiatrie. 32 (1964). pp. 38-555.
15 K. Poeck, B. Orgass: Über die Entwicklung des Körperschemas, Fortschritte der Neurologie und Psychiatrie. 32 (1964). pp. 38-555.
16 R. Steiner: Die Erziehung des Kindes, Stuttgart, 1948.
17 K. König: Die Wissenschaft an der Schwelle, "Die Drei", 1965. Heft 6, pp. 385-392.
18 W. Zeller: Konstitution und Entwicklung 2. Auflage, Göttingen, 1964.
19 K. König: Die Wissenschaft an der Schwelle, "Die Drei", 1965. Heft 6, pp. 385-392.
20 E. H. Erikson: Identität und Lebenszyklus, Frankfurt/M., 1966.
21 A. Portmann: "Umzüchtung des Menschen? Aspekte heutiger Biotechnik", Universitas 21, 1966, pp. 785-803.

SKIN COLOR PREFERENCE OF THE NEGRO CHILD

EARL OGLETREE

Kenneth Clark has remarked, "As children develop an awareness of racial differences of their racial identities, they also develop an awareness and acceptance of the prevailing social attitudes and values toward race and skin color."[1] To test this statement, Clark and Clark[2] conducted a "doll-test" study which demonstrated that younger Negro children reject their race more often than older Negro children. The majority of six- and seven-year-olds preferred dolls symbolizing the white race to dolls representing the Negro race. They also employed a coloring test to evaluate skin color preferences. There they found that 52 percent of the Negro children refused to color their figures either brown or black. This supported their "doll test" findings in which 60 percent of the children rejected the brown dolls.

To test the findings of Clark and Clark that Negro children reject brown as a color, the writer conducted a similar investigation on the skin color preferences of Negro children. The sample was taken from a nonsegregated Detroit elementary school, grades three, four, and five. It included 119 pupils of which 74 (67 percent) were Negro and 45 (33 percent) were white. The pupils were given a skin color preference test in which they were asked to color the two human figures as part of their regular science lesson. They were unaware that the administered paper was a skin color preference test. The analysis of the completed colored pictures revealed: (a) 72 percent of the Negro pupils colored both figures brown; and (b) 75 percent of the white children colored both figures white. The disparity in the findings of the present study and those previously cited is, perhaps, the result of differences in time and the changed sociocultural milieu of 20 to 30 years ago as compared to today.

---

[1] Clark, K. Prejudice and Your Child. Boston, Mass.: Beacon Press, 1963. Pp. 46-47.
[2] Clark, K., & Clark, M. Skin color as a factor in racial identification of Negro preschool children. *J. Soc. Psychol.*, 1940, 11, 159-169.

THE JOURNAL OF SOCIAL PSYCHOLOGY, 1969, Vol. 79, pp. 143-144.

THE OVERLOOKED POSITIVES OF DISADVANTAGED GROUPS*

Frank Riessman

I have been interested in the problems of lower socio-economic groups for about 15 years, during most of which time there has been a lack of concern for the educational problems of children from low-income families. In the last five years, however, this attitude has changed markedly. There is now an enormous interest on the part of practitioners and academic people in this problem. I think we are on the point of a major breakthrough in terms of dealing with this question.

After appraising a good deal of the recent work that has been done on the education of disadvantaged children, I feel that there is a considerable agreement regarding many of the recommendations for dealing with the problem, although there are some very different emphases. What is missing, however, is a theoretic rationale to give meaning and direction to the action suggestions. I should like to attempt to provide the beginnings of such a rationale.

I think that a basic theoretic approach here has to be based on the culture of lower socio-economic groups and more particularly the elements of strength, the positives in this culture. The terms "deprived," "handicapped," "underprivileged," "disadvantaged," unfortunately emphasize environmental limitations and

ignore the positive efforts of low-income individuals to cope with their environment. Most approaches concerned with educating the disadvantaged child either overlook the positives entirely, or merely mention in passing that there are positive features in the culture of low socio-economic groups, that middle-class groups might learn from, but they do not spell out what these strengths are, and they build educational programs almost exclusively around the weaknesses or deficits.

I want to call attention to the positive features in the culture and the psychology of low income individuals. In particular, I should like to look at the cognitive style, the mental style or way of thinking characteristics of these people. One major dimension of this style is slowness.

Slow vs. Dull

Most disadvantaged children are relatively slow in performing intellectual tasks. This slowness is an important feature of their mental style and it needs to be carefully evaluated. In considering the question of the slowness of the deprived child, we would do well to recognize that in our culture there has probably been far too much emphasis on speed. We reward speed. We think of the fast child as the smart child and the slow child as the dull child. I think this is a basically false idea. I think there are many weaknesses in speed and many strengths in slowness.

*This is a revision of an opening address at the Conference on Education of Disadvantaged Children, held by the Office of Education, May 21-23, 1962, Washington, D. C.

JOURNAL OF NEGRO EDUCATION, 1964, Vol. 33, pp. 225-231.

The teacher can be motivated to develop techniques for rewarding slow pupils if she has an appreciation of some of the positive attributes of a slow style of learning. The teacher should know that pupils may be slow for other reasons than because they are stupid.

A pupil may be slow because he is extremely careful, meticulous or cautious. He may be slow because he refuses to generalize easily. He may be slow because he can't understand a concept unless he does something physically, e.g., with his hands, in connection with the idea he is trying to grasp.

The disadvantaged child is typically a physical learner and the physical learner is generally a slower learner. Incidentally, the physical style of learning is another important characteristic of the deprived individual and it, too, has many positive features hitherto overlooked.

A child may be slow because he learns in what I have called a one-track way. That is, he persists in one line of thought and is not flexible or broad. He does not easily adopt other frames of reference, such as the teachers, and consequently he may appear slow and dull.

Very often this single-minded individual has considerable creative potential, much of which goes unrealized because of lack of reinforcement in the educational system.

Analysis of the many reasons for slowness leads to the conclusion that slowness should not be equated with stupidity. In fact, there is no reason to assume that there are not a great many slow, gifted children.

The school in general does not pay too much attention to the slow gifted child but rather is alert to discover fast gifted children. Excellence comes in many packages and we must begin to search for it among the slow learners as well as among the faster individuals.

My own understanding of some of the merits of the slow style came through teaching at Bard College, where there is an enrollment of about 350 students. There I had the opportunity of getting to know quite well about 40 students over a period of four years. I could really see what happened to them during this time. Very often the students I thought were slow and dull in their freshman year achieved a great deal by the time they became seniors. These are not the overall bright people who are typically selected by colleges, but in some area, in a one-tract way, these students did some marvelous creative work. It was too outstanding to be ignored. I discovered in talking with students that most of them had spent five or six years in order to complete college. They had failed courses and made them up in summer school. Some had dropped out of college for a period of time and taken courses in night school. These students are slow learners, often one-tract learners, but very persistent about something when they develop an interest in it. They have a fear of being overpowered by teachers in situations where they don't accept the teacher's point of view, but they stick to their own particular way of seeing the problem. They don't have a fast pace, they don't catch on quickly and they very often fail subjects.

At the present time, when there is a measure of public excitement for reducing the four-year college to three years, I would submit that many potentially excellent students need a five or six year span to complete a college education.

The assumption that the slow pupil is not bright functions, I think, as a self-fulfilling prophecy. If the teachers act toward these pupils as if they were dull, the pupils will frequently come to function in this way. Of course, there are pupils who are very well developed at an early age and no teacher can stop them. But in the average development of the young person, even at the college level, there is need for reinforcement. The teacher must pick up what he says, appeal to him, and pitch examples to him. Typically this does not occur with the slow child. I find in examining my own classroom teaching that I easily fall into the habit of rewarding pupils whose faces light up when I talk, who are quick to respond to me and I respond back to them. The things they say in class become absorbed in the repertoire of what I say. I remember what they say and I use it in providing examples, etc. I don't pick up and select the slower pupil and I don't respond to him. He has to make it on his own.

In the teacher training program future teachers should be taught to guard against the almost unconscious and automatic tendency of the teacher to respond to the pupil who responds to him.

HIDDEN VERBAL ABILITY

A great deal has been said about the language or verbal deficit supposedly characteristic of disadvantaged children. Everybody in the school system, at one time or another, has heard that these children are inarticulate, non-verbal, etc. But is not this too simple a generalization? Aren't these children quite verbal in out-of-school situations? For example, that the educationally deprived child can be quite articulate in conversation with his peers is well illustrated by the whole language developed by urban Negro groups, some of which is absorbed into the main culture via the Beatnick and the musician, if you dig what I mean.

Many questions about the verbal potential of disadvantaged children must be answered by research. Under what conditions are they verbal? What kind of stimuli do they respond to verbally? With whom are they verbal? What do they talk about? What parts of speech do they use? Martin Deutsch of New York Medical College is doing some very significant research trying to specify these factors and I surveyed some of his findings in my book, *The Culturally Deprived Child*. I think Deutsch is getting at some very interesting things. One technique he uses is a clown that lights up when the children say something. "Inarticulate" children can be very verbal and expressive in this situation.

Disadvantaged children are often surprisingly articulate in role-playing situations. One day when I was with a group of these youngsters, sometimes mistaken for a "gang," I asked them, "Why are you sore at the teachers?" Even though I was on good terms with them, I could not get much of a response. Most of them answered in highly abbreviated sentences. However, after I held a role-playing session in which some of the youngsters acted out the part of the teachers while others acted out the parts of the pupils, these "inarticulate" youngsters changed sharply. Within a half-hour they were bubbling over with very verbal and very sensitive answers to the questions I had asked earlier. They were telling me about the expressions on the teachers' faces that they did not like. They reported that they knew the minute they entered the room that the teacher did not like them and that she did not think they were going to do well in school. Their analyses were specific and remarkably verbal.

However, the quality of language employed has its limitations and I think herein lies the deficit. As Basil Bernstein indicates, the difference is between formal language and public language, between a language in a written book and the informal, everyday language. There is no question in my mind that there is a deficit in formal language. Since this deficit is fairly clear, the question might be asked, why make such an issue of the positive verbal ability to these children.

The reason is that it is easy to believe, that too many people have come to believe, that this formal deficit in language means that deprived people are characteristically non-verbal.

On the other hand, if the schools have the idea that these pupils are basically very good verbally, teachers might approach them in a different manner. Teachers might look for additional techniques to bring out the verbal facility. They might abandon the prediction that deprived children will not go very far in the education system and predict instead that they can go very far indeed because they have very good ability at the verbal level. In other words, an awareness of the positive verbal ability — not merely potential — will lead to demanding more of the disadvantaged child and expecting more of him.

EDUCATION vs. THE SCHOOL

There is a good deal of evidence that deprived children and their parents have a much more positive attitude towards education than is generally believed. One factor that obscures the recognition of this attitude is that while deprived individuals value education, they dislike the school. They are alienated from the school and they resent the teachers. For the sake of clarity, their attitude towards education and toward the school must be considered separately.

In a survey conducted a few years ago, people were asked, "What did you miss most in life that you would like your children to have?" Over 70 per cent of the lower, socio-economic groups answered, "Education." The answer was supplied by the respondents, not checked on a list. They could have answered "money," happiness," "health," or a number of things. And I think this is quite significant. Middle-class people answer "education" less frequently because they had an education and do not miss it as much.

A nation-wide poll conducted by Roper after World War II asked, "If you had a son or daughter graduating from high school, would you prefer to have him or her go on to college, do something else, wouldn't care?" The affirmative response to the college choice was given by 68 per cent of the "poor," and 91 per cent for the more prosperous. The difference is significant, but 68 per cent of the poorer people is a large, absolute figure and indicates that a large number of these people are interested in a college education for their children.

Why then do these people who have a positive attitude towards education, hold a negative attitude towards the school? These youngsters and their parents rec-

68

ognize that they are second-class citizens in the school and they are angry about it. From the classroom to the PTA they discover that the school does not like them, does not respond to them, does not appreciate their culture, and does not think they can learn.

Also, these children and their parents want education for different reasons than those presented by the school. They do not easily accept the ideas of expressing yourself, developing yourself, or knowledge for its own sake. They want education much more for vocational ends. But underneath there is a very positive attitude towards education and I think this is predominant in the lower socio-economic Negro groups. In the Higher Horizons program in New York City the parents have participated eagerly once they have seen that the school system is concerned about their children. One of the tremendously positive features about this program and the Great Cities programs is the concern for disadvantaged children and the interest in them. This the deprived have not experienced before and even if the programs did nothing else, I believe that the parents and the children would be responsive and would become involved in the school, because of the demonstrated concern for them.

SOME WEAKNESSES

A basic weakness of deprived youngsters which the school can deal with is the problem of "know-how." Included here is the academic "know-how" of the school culture as well as the "know-how" of the middle class generally. Knowing how to get a job, how to appear for an interview, how to fill out a form, how to take tests, how to answer questions and how to listen.

The last is of particular importance. The whole style of learning of the deprived is not set to respond to oral or written stimuli. These children respond much more readily to visual kinesthetic signals. We should remodel the schools to suit the styles and meet the needs of these children. But no matter how much we change the school to suit their needs, we nevertheless have to change these children in certain ways; namely, reading, formal language, test taking and general "know-how."

These weaknesses represent deficienies in skills and techniques. However, there is one basic limitation at the value level, namely the anti-intellectual attitudes of deprived groups. It is the only value of lower socio-economic groups which I would fight in the school. I want to make it very clear that I am very much opposed to the school spending a lot of time teaching values to these kids. I am much more concerned — and in this I am traditional — that the schools impart skills, techniques and knowledge rather than training the disadvantaged to become good middle-class children.

However, I think there is one area indigenous to the school which has to be fought out at some point with these youngsters; that is their attitude toward intellectuals, towards knowledge for its own sake, and similar issues.

These children and their parents are pretty much anti-intellectual at all levels. They do not like "eggheads." They think talk is a lot of bull. I would consciously oppose this attitude in the school. I would make the issue explicit. There would be nothing subtle or covert about it. I would at some point state clearly that on this question the school does not

69

agree with them and is prepared to argue about the views they hold.

In my book, *The Culturally Deprived Child,* and in various speeches, I have elaborated more fully on these and other positive dimensions of the culture and style of educationally deprived people. A brief list would include the following: cooperativeness and mutual aid that mark the extended family; the avoidance of the strain accompanying competitiveness and individualism; the equalitarianism, in informality and humor; the freedom from self-blame and parental over-protection; the children's enjoyment of each other's company and lessened sibling rivalry, the security found in the extended family and a traditional outlook; the enjoyment of music, games, sports and cards; the ability to express anger; the freedom from being word-bound; an externally oriented rather than an introspective outlook; a spatial rather than temporal perspective; an expressive orientation in contrast to an instrumental one; content-centered not a form-centered mental style; a problem-centered rather than an abstract-centered approach; and finally, the use of physical and visual style in learning.

SUMMARY AND IMPLICATIONS

I have attempted to reinterpret some of the supposedly negative aspects — e.g., slowness — that characterize the cognitive style of disadvantaged individuals. I have given particular attention to the untapped verbal ability of these individuals and have indicated the basic weaknesses of the disadvantaged child which the school must overcome, such as the lack of school know-how, anti-intellectualism, and limited experience with formal language. Others which should be noted here are poor auditory attention, poor time perspective, inefficient test-taking skills, and limited reading ability.

The school must recognize these deficiencies and work assiduously to combat them. They are by no means irreversible, but even more important, because neglected, the positive elements in the culture and style of lower socio-economic groups should become the guide lines for new school programs and new educational techniques for teaching these children.

There are a number of reasons why it is important to emphasize the positive:

1. It will encourage the school to develop approaches and techniques, including possibly special teaching machines. appropriate for the cognitive style of deprived children.

2. It will enable children of low income backgrounds to be educated without middle-classifying them.

3. It will stimulate teachers to aim high, to expect more and work for more from these youngsters. Thus, it will constrain against patronization and condescension, and determinate, double-track systems where the deprived child never arrives on the main track.

4. It will function against the current tendency of over-emphasizing both vocational, non-academic education for children of low-income background.

5. It will provide an exciting challenge for teachers if they realize that they need not simply aim to "bring these children up to grade level," but rather can actually develop new kinds of creativity.

6. It will make the school far more

pluralistic and democratic because different cultures and styles will exist and interact side by side. Thus, each can learn from the other and the empty phrase that the teacher has much to learn from deprived children will take on real meaning. General cultural interaction between equal cultures can become the hallmark of the school.

7. It will enable the teacher to see that when techniques, such as role-playing and visual aids are used with deprived children, it is because these techniques are useful for eliciting the special cognitive style and creative potential of these children. All too often these techniques have been employed with the implicit assumption that they are useful with children who have inadequate learning ability.

8. It will lead to real appreciation of slowness, one-track learning and physical learning as potential strengths which require careful nurturing. The teacher will have to receive special training in how to respond to these styles, how to listen carefully to the one-track person, how to reward the slow learner, etc. Special classes for slow learners will not culminate in the removal of these youngsters from the mainstream of the educational process on a permanent second track, and longer periods of time in school and college can be planned for these students without invidious connotations.

Dr. Irving Taylor, who has been concerned with various types of creativity in our American society, has observed that the mental style of the socially and economically disadvantaged learners resembles the mental style of one type of ·highly creative persons. Our schools should provide for the development of these unique, untapped national sources of creativity.

PSYCHOLOGICAL IMPLICATIONS FOR SCHOOLING

Understanding Readiness: An Occasional Paper

Arthur R. Jensen

Recent research papers in child development and educational psychology reflect a renewal of interest in readiness among educational researchers. There is a new awareness of the importance of the really old notion of readiness and of the need to reexamine the diverse phenomena associated with this concept in light of recent theory and research in child development, individual differences, and the psychology of learning and instruction. The fact that empirical researchers in psychology and education are again seriously approaching the problems of readiness, now with more sophisticated theories and research methodologies than were available in the former heyday of the concept, is an important trend in the right direction.

A generation ago, readiness in a biological-maturational sense was of greater interest to educational psychologists and was regarded more seriously than it has been in the past decade, which has been dominated largely by conceptions derived from theoretical positions of extreme environmentalism and behavioristic learning theory. In its most extreme form, this view holds that the degree of readiness for learning at any given age is merely the product of the amount and nature of the learner's previous experience. Readiness is viewed as the amount of previous learning that can transfer to new learning.

There can be no doubt about the *fact* of readiness; that is, the common observation that certain kinds of learning take place much more readily at one age than at another. No one disputes this. Disagreements arise only when we try to *explain* readiness. The theoretical explanation of readiness is important, of course, because much of what we do about readiness in educational practice will depend upon our conception of its nature.

ERIC Clearinghouse on Early Childhood Education, 1969, pp. 1-16.

For the sake of conceptual clarity, one can state two distinct theories of readiness. One theory can be called the *growth-readiness* view of mental development. It is associated with such eminent psychologists as G. Stanley Hall and Arnold Gesell, and it holds that certain organized patterns of growth of neural structures must occur before certain experiential factors can effectively contribute to development. The rate of intellectual development is seen as due primarily to internal physiological mechanisms and their orderly, sequential growth, rather than to inputs from the environment.

The contrasting viewpoint emphasizes learning as the major causal factor in development. The simplest, most extreme statement of this position is simply that humans, like all mammals, possess the neural structures for the formation of associations between the sensory inputs from receptors and the output mechanism of the effectors. This is, in short, the capacity for acquiring stimulus-response connections or habits. The sets of habits which we identify as intelligent behavior are seen as being built up through the acquisition of habits and chains of habits which interact to produce complex behavior. Thus mental development is viewed as the learning of an ordered set of capabilities in some hierarchical or progressive fashion, making for increasing skills in stimulus differentiation, recall of previously learned responses, and generalization and transfer of learning. In recent years this viewpoint has been most notably developed by Gagné (1965, 1968), who refers to it as the *cumulative learning* model of mental development.

Probably everyone who has attended to the relevant evidence in this field would agree that *both* the *growth-readiness* and the *cumulative learning* theories are necessary for comprehending all the facts of the matter. These two aspects are not at all mutually exclusive but work hand in hand to produce the phenomenon we observe as cognitive development. There is little doubt that the physical maturation of the brain, particularly the cerebral cortex, underlies the development of particular cognitive abilities. The developmental sequence of these abilities or, more exactly, of the readiness to acquire them through interaction with the environment, is especially evident between birth and seven or eight years of age. In fact, we know that not all of the brain's potential neural connections are physiologically functionable until at least seven or eight years of age in the vast majority of children.

The orderly sequence of maturation of neural structures is such that the capability for certain kinds of learning and performance falls along an age scale. Standard intelligence tests, such as the Stanford-Binet, yield scores in terms of mental age and attempt to index the child's level of mental maturity. These standard indices, especially in childhood, unquestionably measure a composite of factors associated with both neurophysiological maturation and cumulative learning; there are more specialized tests which clearly measure more of one of these factors than of the others. Acquiring the names of objects — learning common nouns, for example — is highly dependent upon experience once the child begins to talk; the child's vocabulary of common nouns at a given age may thus be conceived of as cumulative learning. The ability to copy geometric forms of increasing complexity, however, seems to depend more upon maturational than upon experiential factors. For example, many children who can easily copy a circle or a square cannot copy a diamond, but the reverse is not true. There is a sequence or hierarchy in the emergence of some abilities. The average five-year-old can easily copy a square. But he must be six before he can easily copy a square containing a single diagonal, and he must be seven before he can copy a diamond. Intensive training in the specific act of copying a diamond is surprisingly difficult and generally ineffective in the average five-year-old. At seven, no training is necessary.

Everyone will agree, too, that these sequential stages of capability are not abrupt steps but that these are transitional stages from one to another. Some transitions are relatively rapid, so that in the preschool years an age difference of just a few months can make for quite striking differences in the child's learning capability for certain tasks.

Levels of Complexity

In learning, as in perception, often the whole equals more than the sum of the parts. It is in the child's progressing ability to *integrate* the component subskills that the phenomenon called readiness is most apparent. Prior acquisition of the subskills is usually necessary but often not sufficient for learning a particular skill requiring the integration of the subskills. It is the integrative process, the development of a higher-order "master plan," that depends most upon the maturation of brain structures. The physical and mental *subskills* for drawing a diamond are clearly possessed by the five-year-old child. The abstract concept of a diamond, however, is still beyond him, and he therefore cannot integrate his subskills into the total performance of copying the figure of a diamond. He lacks the necessary program, the master plan, so to speak. If anyone doubts this, let him first try to teach a typical five-year-old to copy a diamond, and then to teach a seven-year-old. It is a highly instructive experience to the teacher and provides a most tangible demonstration of the meaning of readiness.

A task with more clearly defined subskills lends itself even more readily to a demonstration of the interactive effects of mental maturation and cumulative learning. Learning to play chess is a good example. I was able to observe the simultaneous roles of maturation and cumulative learning quite clearly while trying to teach my daughter to play chess when she was five years of age. At the time, I was especially interested in Gagné's formulation of cumulative learning in terms of learning hierarchies — the idea that each new step in learning is dependent upon the prior acquisition of certain subskills, and that learning takes place most efficiently when we insure that all relevant subskills have been mastered prior to the next-to-be-learned skill in the learning hierarchy. The notion of a hierarchy of skills seems clearly applicable to the teaching and learning of chess, and I proceeded carefully to teach my five-year-old daughter the game of chess with this hierarchical model in mind.

First, I had her learn to group the chess pieces into their two main categories, white and black. At five this was so easy for her that it hardly needed to be taught, as shown by the fact that she would spontaneously sort out the shuffled pieces in terms of their color when putting them away in the two compartments of the chess set's wooden storage box. If she had been only four years old, it might have been necessary to spend some time teaching her to categorize the items on the basis of color, but by five she had already acquired some concept of classes of objects that look alike in terms of some attribute — in this case, color. The next step was to learn the names of the six chess pieces, an example of paired-associates learning. Mastery of this was attained within a few trials and was accomplished with evident pleasure at having learned something new.

The next day's lesson consisted of learning the proper placement of the pieces on the chess board. This was learned, also with evident pleasure, in one brief session, but there was a slight retention loss before the next day, and further practice in placing the pieces was needed to bring this performance up to mastery. Then, one by one, the rules for moving each of the pieces were learned — another instance of paired-associate learning, but this time requiring practice with each piece in a number of different positions so that the general principle of each piece's movement could be acquired. This aspect of the learning also progressed quickly and easily. It seemed like fun to my daughter, and she appeared "motivated" and eager to learn more in the next lesson. Her learning had proceeded so smoothly and easily up to this point that I almost became convinced that if each step in the learning of the sub-skills of chess were carried to mastery and if interest and motivation persisted, each subsequent step would prove as easy as the preceding one. This was conspicuously not the case.

After the subskills of chess had been learned and the object of the game was explained and demonstrated repeatedly, we tried to play the game of chess, using all that had been learned up to that point. But a game did not emerge; good moves were reinforced by praise, illegal moves were prohibited and had to be taken back, poor moves resulted in the loss of a piece, and half the time bad moves were not made to result in a loss, in order to avoid too much discouragement. Further coaching resulted in no discernible improvement, there was no coordination or plan in the movement of pieces such that an actual chess game would result, and learning seemed to come to a standstill. Moreover, at this stage interest and motivation took such a slump that even some of the earlier acquired, simple component skills deteriorated. Further lessons led to boredom, inattentiveness, restlessness, and finally complete rejection of the whole enterprise. To continue would have required extreme coercion on my part, so we quit the lessons completely. A few weeks later we tried checkers, which she learned easily. It was sufficiently less complex than chess, and she had no trouble playing a reasonably good game. Learning and improvement in performance in checkers was a smooth, continuous process, and at no point did my daughter show signs of "turning off." Checkers became her favorite game for a time, and she often coaxed me and others to play with her.

What was the difference between chess and checkers? I doubt that I was a better teacher of checkers than of chess; I doubt that my daughter was more motivated to learn checkers than chess or that checkers was in some way more "relevant" to her than chess. I believe it was a difference in the complexity of checkers and chess and of the level of complexity that my child at age five could cognitively integrate into the total act of playing a game of checkers or chess.

A most instructive part of this experience to me was the rapidity of motivational slump and psychological "turn-off" when instruction persisted beyond the level of readiness. The same phenomenon must occur in the learning of school subjects as well as in the present chess example.

I doubt also that what I observed could be explained entirely in terms of my having used inappropriate teaching methods at the final stage of the chess instruction.

Exactly one year later, when my daughter turned six, I again got out the chess set. By this time she had lost most of her negative reaction to it, and we ran through the component skills again; relearning was rapid. The only source of difficulty was some negative transfer from checkers; she now had to learn that chess pieces do not take other pieces by jumping over them but, rather, by displacing them on the same square. I believe she would have relearned faster had she never practiced checkers. But it was a trivial difficulty. What was interesting was that this time, though my instructional technique was no different from that used before, there was no hitch in the learning, and a smooth, easy transition was made from the learning of the subskills to learning to integrate them into playing a real game of chess. Simultaneously, there was a growing interest and motivation, and my daughter's skill in the game itself showed continuous improvement with practice. For many weeks thereafter, the first thing I heard from my daughter every night when I arrived home from the office was, "Daddy, let's play chess!"

This is a clear example of learning readiness in both of its aspects — the need to have already acquired the component subskills underlying the next level in the learning hierarchy and the need to have reached the level of cognitive development necessary for the integration of the subskills into a functional whole. Learning is a normal biological function. Children do not have to be cajoled, persuaded, coerced, manipulated, or tricked into learning. Given the opportunity and the appropriate conditions, including readiness, children simply learn. The most effective reinforcement for learning or the behaviors that promote learning (such as attention, effort, persistence, and self-direction) is the child's own perception of his increasing mastery of the skill he is trying to acquire. When this perception is lacking, learning bogs down, and external reinforcements or rewards are usually inadequate to maintain cognitive learning. The child's *efforts* are rewarded, but not the cognitive processes that lead to further mastery; and the end result is frustration and turning off in the particular learning situation. This reaction can become an attitude that generalizes to many similar learning situations; for example, school learning in general.

An important aspect of readiness is the child's ability to perceive discrepancies and approximations in his own behavior in relation to a good model or plan. It is becoming increasingly clear from the research on cognitive development that the child's capacity for plans increases with age and is underpinned by genetically coded neurophysiological developments. Any complex integrative activity — playing chess, reading with comprehension, doing arithmetic thought-problems — depends upon the development of these plans or cognitive structures. The child adapts his behavior to the model or plan and the self-perception of successive approximations provides the reinforcement (reward) that shapes behavior in the desired direction. This is the essence of cognitive learning. Though several years ago I believed that the child's learning of language was the chief instrument of his cognitive learning abilities and that these abilities were almost entirely dependent upon his use of language and his acquisition of habits of verbal mediation, my reading of more recent research in this field inclines me to reject this view. The evidence leads me to closer agreement with the position expressed by Sheldon White that ". . . the gathering evidence seems more and more to suggest that the child's progressive sophistication in language between five and seven is not the cause, but is rather the correlate of, his progressive sophistication in learning" (White, 1968, p. 3).

The Relativity of Readiness

The age for readiness for some particular learning is rarely confined to a single point on a developmental scale for any given child. Readiness cannot be determined independently of the method of instruction. A child can evince readiness for learning to read, for example, at age three by one method of instruction and not until age six by another method. The materials and methods that will work at three will work at six, but the reverse may not be true. For example, most three-year-olds would not learn to read in the typical first grade classroom nor with the size of type typically used to print first-grade primers, nor by a phonic method. Individual instruction, using very large, poster-sized type, and a "look-say" method will permit many three-year-olds to learn to read, although such reading at three is probably a quite different process psychologically than reading at six. In other words, what appears superficially as the same behavior may be acquired by different means and involve different psychological processes at different developmental stages. The often superficial nature of the resemblance of the two behaviors can be observed in the extent and nature of the transfer of learning. The three-year-old who learns to read "leg," for example, will be at a loss when the new word "peg" is presented, and it will take as long to learn "peg" as it would to learn "can." For the six-year-old, reading need not be so much a form of audio-visual paired-associate rote learning as it is a form of problem-solving using phonetic mediators. Therefore there will be a high degree of transfer from "leg" to "peg."

Little is known about the extent to which the readiness factor can be minimized in learning by manipulating instructional techniques. Experiments on such tasks as copying a series of geometric figures of increasing complexity suggest that, at least in this realm, performance is far more dependent upon maturational factors than upon any variations that different instructional techniques can produce. Differences in instructional techniques in most forms of school learning may well be of maximum importance at the threshold of readiness, although beyond this threshold a variety of techniques may be relatively indistinguishable in their effectiveness.

Ignoring Readiness

What happens when we ignore the readiness of children who are of approximately the same chronological age but different readiness levels and attempt to teach all the children the same thing in the same way? Obviously we will observe marked individual differences in the speed and thoroughness with which the children learn, and we may be inclined to increase our efforts and persistence in teaching the slower learners in order to help them catch up to the others, or at least to try to achieve the same degree of mastery of the subject as attained by the faster children, even if it takes somewhat longer.

Aside from the accentuation of individual differences in the classroom, are there likely to be other effects of ignoring readiness with possibly greater psychological consequences than those of merely making more visible individual differences in scholastic performance? We do not have any firmly established answers to this question. However, recent animal research on readiness factors in learning and some of my own observations of certain classes in which many children appear not to be learning much of anything at all, despite heroic efforts of the teachers, lead me to hypothesize that ignoring readiness can have adverse psychological effects beyond merely not learning what is being taught at the time it is being taught.

These adverse effects seem to take two main forms: (1) The child may learn the subject matter or skill by means of the cognitive structures he already possesses; but because these structures are less optimal than more advanced structures in the sequence of cognitive development, the learning is much less efficient and results in the acquisition of knowledge and skills with lesser capability of transfer to later learning. The increasing breadth of transfer of learning is a chief characteristic of the sequence of cognitive development. (2) The second adverse effect of ignoring readiness by persisting in instruction beyond the child's present capability is to cause the phenomenon referred to earlier in the chess example as "turning off." This amounts to an increasing inhibition of the very behaviors that promote learning, and I believe it can become so extreme that it may eventually prevent the child from learning even those things for which he is *not* lacking in readiness.

"Learning to learn," or what psychologists call the acquisition of learning sets, is of greater educational importance, and requires more complex cognitive structures, than the learning of any specific associations or facts. All animals are capable of forming new associations between stimuli and responses, but only higher mammals are capable of learning-set acquisition to any appreciable degree, and this capability is not easily demonstrated below the level of primates. Much research on learning sets has been conducted with monkeys and apes. This research clearly shows that learning to learn, more than any specific learning, is dependent upon maturational factors. Since a high degree of control can be maintained over the experiences of monkeys in the laboratory, it is possible to assess the relative importance of maturational and experiential variables for different kinds of learning and to study the consequences of forcing certain types of learning before the maturational factors are optimal for that particular learning.

Research on primates leaves no doubt that learning ability increases with age up to adulthood and that the asymptote of capability for various types of learning comes at later and later ages as the complexity of the learning task increases. The five-day-old monkey, for example, forms conditioned reflexes as rapidly as the adult monkey. The speed of learning object-discriminations, on the other hand, does not reach its maximum until about 150 days of age. When monkeys are given a *succession* of object discrimination problems, each involving different visual discriminations, the monkeys' learning speed gradually increases from one problem to the next. The first problems may require 100 to 200 trials to learn a single discrimination; but after the animal has learned to learn by being given a sequence of many different object discrimination problems, these discriminations may be learned in only one or two trials. In other words, the animal is said to have acquired a learning set for object discriminations and in this type of learning is capable of close to 100 per cent efficiency; that is, learning in the fewest possible trials.

It is known that the speed with which learning sets are acquired depends upon the monkey's age; that is to say, its maturational readiness for learning set formation or interproblem learning. Young monkeys (60 to 90 days old) show much less readiness for learning set formation than older monkeys (150 to 300 days old), as reflected in the great differences in learning rates. The most interesting finding, however, is that the monkeys trained at the earlier, preoptimal age for learning set formation apparently do *not* eventually catch up with the older monkeys, even when they finally reach the same age as that at which the older monkeys were trained with much greater ease. In other words, the early training not only was less efficient, but it resulted in these young monkeys' attaining an asymptote at a lower level of proficiency than that attained by older monkeys with much less training. The too-early training resulted in a low ceiling for the subsequent development of this particular ability.

Harlow, who conducted these experiments, concluded

these data suggest that the capacity of the two younger groups to form discrimination learning sets may have been impaired by their early, intensive learning-set training, initiated before they possessed any effective learning-set capability. Certainly, their performance from 260 days onward is inferior to that of the earlier groups with less experience but matched for age. The problem which these data illustrate has received little attention among experimental psychologists. [And, we might add, educational psychologists.] There is a tendency to think of learning or training as intrinsically good and necessarily valuable to the organism. It is entirely possible, however, that training can either be helpful or harmful, depending upon the nature of the training and the organism's stage of development (Harlow, 1959, p. 472).

For the neonatal and infant rhesus monkey each learning task is specific unto itself, and the animal's intellectual repertoire is composed of multiple, separate, and isolated learning experiences. With increasing age, problem isolation changes to problem generalization, and this fundamental reorganization of the monkey's intellectual world apparently begins in its second year of life. From here on, we can no longer specify the monkey's learning ability for any problem merely in terms of maturational age and individual differences. The variable of kind and amount of prior experience must now be given proper value. (Harlow, 1959, pp. 477-78).

The shift in cognitive style in the second year of life in the rhesus monkey, described by Harlow, seems to have its counterpart in the human child between about five and seven years of age — the age at which children universally begin their formal schooling. Sheldon H. White (1965) has adduced a diversity of data in support of his hypothesis that adult mental organization is hierarchical, consisting of two main "layers": an associative layer laid down early in development and following conventional associative principles and a cognitive layer laid down in later childhood. The formation of the cognitive layer is most marked between the ages of five and seven. Between these ages children show a transition from a type of performance in learning situations characteristic of lower animals in similar situations to a type of performance characteristic of adult humans. Thus, it is during this period of most rapid qualitative changes in cognitive processes that consideration of readiness factors of the maturational type is of most importance. The period is better thought of as extending from age five to ages eight or nine, to include more or less the full range of individual differences in making this cognitive transition. Tests such as the Stanford-Binet, the Piagetian developmental tests, and the types of tests and indices described by Ilg and Ames (1964) are the best means now available for assessing readiness for cognitive learning in this age range.

As I mentioned before, the second major type of difficulty that can result when readiness is ignored is what I previously called "turning off"; that is to say, the extinction or inhibition of those forms of behavior which are essential aspects of learning — attention, self-directed effort, rehearsal, and active involvement. Signs of discouragement, waning interest, boredom, and the like are merely surface indicators of the inhibition of learning.

The psychological mechanism by which turning off comes about is well known in laboratory research on learning and was first described in detail by Pavlov under the names "experimental extinction" and "conditioned inhibition." It is a reasonable hypothesis that these processes operate in school when certain analogous conditions prevail in the learning situation. The essential condition is responding without reinforcement or with very inconsistent reinforcement. In animal learning, reinforcement or reward must be external; it is dispensed by the experimenter, usually as bits of food, to strengthen the responses defined as correct by the experimenter. Withholding reinforcement results in decrement or extinction of the response in question, and the stimuli that are present while this extinction process is underway become conditioned inhibitors; that is, the mere presence of these stimuli can come to inhibit the class of responses with which they were associated during extinction.

In humans, reinforcement can be external or internal, so to speak. External reinforcement in the pupil-teacher relationship generally involves both approval and praise by the teacher and "informative feedback" from the teacher as to the correctness or incorrectness of the child's responses. But more important in human cognitive learning is internal reinforcement resulting from the learner's self-perception of his own behavior and its approximation to self-perceived goals. Behavior is sustained and shaped by reinforcement or feedback. If there are no internalized standards or structures as a basis for feedback concerning the approximation of one's performance to the standard, then reinforcement must be external. A simple, clear-cut example is the comparison of a beginning student on the violin and a professional musician. The former must have a teacher to provide immediate feedback on the correctness or incorrectness of performance; the standard is in the teacher's head, so to speak, and not the pupil's. When the professional practices a new piece, on the other hand, his activities are reinforced by his successive approximations to his own internalized standards, which have been acquired through years of musical training, and the subtleties of which can only be referred to as musical talent.

Human cognitive learning (as contrasted with rote learning and motor learning) depends in large part on such internalized regulation of the learning process. The source of self-informative feedback is highly dependent on readiness, the capacity for plans or models to which the child's performance can achieve successive approximations. There is a difference in readiness, for example, between the child who reads by naming symbols (words) he has rote-learned and the child who perceives reading as making an effort to extract meaning from the printed words. Much of the activity of the latter child is self-instructional. Children who do not engage in self-instructional activity do not make normal progress in school. Forced practice in the absence of internal reinforcements, I suggest, can lead to extinction of the behavior being practiced.

Readiness in the cognitive sphere is largely the ability to conceptualize the learning task, to grasp the aim of one's efforts long before achieving mastery of the task. The relative ineffectiveness of shaping one's behavior to external requirements as compared with internal requirements is perhaps seen most dramatically in the child's efforts to copy geometric figures of varying difficulty. Unless the child can internalize a conceptual representation of the figure, he cannot copy it, even though the model is directly before him. Partly for this reason, as well as for its correlations with school readiness, the Ilg and Ames figure copying test is probably one of the most convincing and valuable measures of cognitive development in the preschool years and throughout the primary grades (Ilg and Ames, 1964).

Conclusion

Many school learning problems could be circumvented if more attention were paid to readiness in the primary grades, when children's learning is most easily turned off through extinction due to inadequate readiness. The risks of delaying instruction too long seem much less than the possible disadvantages of forcing instruction on a child who is still far from his optimal readiness for the subject of instruction.

We need much more experimentation on readiness; that is, trying the same instructional procedures over a much wider age range than is ever the case in traditional schools. It may well be that some sizeable proportion of children in our schools will, for example, be better readers at age twelve if they began reading instruction at age eight than if they began at age six, and this may apply to the learning of most scholastic skills. The high rate of reading failures and other deficiencies in basic scholastic skills found among high school graduates in groups called disadvantaged can hardly be explained in terms of deficiencies in basic learning abilities. It would seem necessary to invoke turn-off mechanisms at some early stage of their schooling to account for some of their marked educational deficiencies. Experimental programs of primary education that pay special attention to readiness factors in learning and actually *delay* formal instruction (meanwhile inculcating prerequisite experiential factors) until readiness is clearly in evidence are needed to test this hypothesis for its practical effectiveness in improving the ultimate educational achievements especially of children called disadvantaged. It is among this group that turning off in school is most evident.

I suggest that more of the factors which cause turning off are found within the school than outside the school and that among the prime causal factors is an inadequate recognition of the importance of readiness, both in terms of cognitive maturation and cumulative learning. Compared with the potential benefits of such experiments as suggested here in terms of the readiness concept, the risks seem almost trivial. It appears that considerably more bold and daring educational innovations are called for if we are to improve the outcomes of schooling for the majority of children called disadvantaged. The present large-scale programs of compensatory education, which so far have failed to yield appreciable scholastic gains among the disadvantaged, are psychologically and educationally probably still much too conservative. A variety of much more radical educational experiments, with the outcomes properly assessed, would seem to be indicated. At least a few such experiments should give extreme emphasis to readiness factors and to the avoidance of turn-off in school learning.

REFERENCES

Gagné, R. M. *The Conditions of Learning.* New York: Holt, Rinehart & Winston, 1965.

Gagné, R. M. "Contributions of Learning to Human Development." *Psychological Review,* Vol. 75, No. 3 (1968), pp. 177-191.

Harlow, H. F. "The Development of Learning in the Rhesus Monkey." *American Scientist,* Vol. 47, No. 4 (1959), pp. 459-479.

Ilg, F. L., & Ames, L. B. *School Readiness.* New York: Harper & Row, 1964.

White, S. H. "Evidence for a Hierarchical Arrangement of Learning Processes." In L. R. Lipsitt and C. C. Spiker (eds.), *Advances in Child Development and Behavior* (Vol. 2). New York: Academic Press, 1965, pp. 187-220.

THE CALIFORNIA REPORT:
EARLY SCHOOLING FOR ALL?

Raymond S. Moore
Robert D. Moon
Dennis R. Moore

The United States is currently witnessing one of its most remarkable educational developments — a drive for earlier and earlier schooling for all children which appears to be either overlooking or ignoring many of the most important findings of developmental research. While such oversight is not new to American education, in this instance the evidence and implications are not only clear, but also warn of formidable costs — first, in tax moneys, and second and far more important, in possible damage to young children.

A look at the early schooling (ES) movement reveals many developments, e.g., mounting problems of child behavior, parents chafing at the "shackles" of parenthood, inadequate and unregulated care of children, and federal and state interest in early schooling. Educators are intrigued by research which points up the rapid early development of intelligence. (See Bloom's review, *Stability and Change in Human Characteristics.* [1]) But many of these well-intentioned people overlook scientific findings which point in other directions than that in which early childhood education is now generally going, e.g., studies on early *vs.* later school admission, neurophysiology, cognition, and maternal deprivation. If such findings are not carefully considered, early childhood educators may threaten the very childhood development they design to improve.

In order to develop a fair and somewhat comprehensive viewpoint, the Hewitt Research Center has involved leading educators, legislators, scholars, and researchers at local, state, and national levels from

PHI DELTA KAPPAN, 1972, Vol. 53, pp. 615-621, 677.

coast to coast in a review of early childhood research. A limited cross-section of the resulting analysis is presented here.

We acknowledge, of course, the need of special education for the seriously disadvantaged or handicapped. There is also a need to care for children who have handicapped parents or whose parents are compelled to work. No position is taken here against early intervention where indicated by research. The principal questions we shall treat here are: What is the best kind of intervention or care for young children? What is generally the best — and most financially feasible — environment for early childhood development (ECD)?

We will attempt 1) to analyze typical goals of early schooling proponents, 2) to examine their use of research in support of their conclusions, 3) to see what systematic research actually says about typical ES programs and proposals, and 4) to report some practical solutions growing out of research and experimentation. In order to maintain a sharp focus this will be done primarily with reference to one state — California.

The California Report. The report of the California Task Force on Early Childhood Education[2] is relatively middle-of-the-road as ES proposals go. For example, it proposes to take schooling at first only down to four-year-olds, rather than to children aged three or three and one-half as planned in New York State and Houston. The task force plan may soon be presented to the California legislature. Because California has long been among the pioneers in U.S. education, it will exercise a telling influence among other states. Yet the California proposal, with some variations, appears typical of current ES rationale.

Typical Early Schooling Goals

The California task force offers a philosophy and goals that would build on a substantial body of research:

> The past decade has produced a new body of educational, psychological, and medical research documenting the crucial importance of the first eight years of life. And we are convinced that these early years are critical in determining the future effectiveness of our citizens and in the long-range prevention of

crime, poverty, addiction, malnutrition, neurosis, and violence.[3]

The report assumes that "even though research is still in progress and conclusions continue to evolve, enough evidence is in" to justify certain goals, namely, "to bring about the maximum development of every child" down to age four.[4] And it is proposed that this goal will be accomplished by providing for *academic* as well as personal development and requiring "school districts to restructure and expand existing programs."[5]

Typical Use of Research

The California goal of maximum development surely is consistent with the ideals of most Americans. The report cites many examples of ECD research and experimentation which it assumes will provide substance for its implementation plan. Yet in no case does it clearly show how this research supports its plan. In fact certain research quoted in the report actually contradicts the task force's conclusions that *schooling* under carefully selected teachers is desirable for *all* four-year-olds. For example:

1. Harold Skeels's study[6] of orphanage children is quoted as demonstrating how the young child, given a favorable environment, can make marked intellectual growth. But the report does not continue its analysis to show that Skeels's "environment" was an institution in which *retarded teenagers* provided the orphans a *warm, free, one-to-one, continuing* mother or mother-surrogate relationship. Skeels's study had little to do with academic instruction or credentialed teaching.

2. The report quotes findings of the White House Conference of 1970: "We must free ourselves from our antiquated and erroneous beliefs that school is the only environment in which creativity is enhanced and learning takes place, or that the teacher is the sole agent of such achievements."[7]

3. Another task force item cites the June, 1971, report of the Education Commission of the States, which says in part:

It is not recommended that states establish formal classroom pre-school programs for all three- and four-year-olds because there is no

90

evidence that all children need a structured group experience if they are receiving some kind of systematic training and because there are viable, less expensive alternatives.[8]

4. The report calls for "at least one adult to every ten children"[9] in educating four-year-olds. Yet every experiment quoted in the report in which adult-child ratios were given (six out of eleven examples) the adult-to-child ratio was 1:5 *or less*, or a need for at least four to six times the number of adults required for a standard kindergarten-primary grade ratio of 1:20 to 1:30. Although the California cost proposals are still in the formative stages, Superintendent Wilson Riles is counting on a per-child annual cost of about $500 to $600. Yet one of the documents quoted in the report (*Preschool Breakthrough*[10]) notes that the pre-kindergarten experience of New York State sees an annual $1,800-per-child cost as necessary for "adequate day care" and "much more if the program reaches a desirable standard."

In view of such examples as this, it is difficult to understand how the task force concludes that all four-year-olds should be provided academic schooling. And the discrepancy between research and projected implementation goes much farther. Unfortunately, California's proposal is not an isolated illustration of such disparity, as Earl Schaefer, one of the nation's leading early childhood education specialists, notes:

> ... Although much of this [ECD] research data has been generated during the last decade, earlier studies of intellectual development have motivated the current volume of research. Unfortunately, interpretations of the significance of this data, although they have guided the course of research, have as yet had minimal impact on educational planning. ...[11]

This may be one of the reasons for the findings of William Rohwer (University of California, Berkeley) and others that "the research and development phases of early childhood programs have succeeded but the implementation phases, thus far, have largely failed."[12]

While there is evidence of some desirable effects

of ES programs for disadvantaged children, the assessment of failure of large-scale programs is related primarily to academic or cognitive achievement, a goal strongly stressed in the California report.[13] Referring to a number of large-scale ES programs it studied, the U.S. Commission on Civil Rights concluded that "A principal objective of each was to raise academic achievement of disadvantaged children. Judged by this standard the programs did not show evidence of much success."[14] The Westinghouse/Ohio University study found Head Start to have been "ineffective in producing any [lasting] gains in cognitive and affective development" and stressed the present "limited state of knowledge" about what would constitute effective intervention.[15]

What Systematic Research Says

For the purposes of this report, key factors in three types of studies will be considered among many on which there is substantial research evidence: 1) studies comparing early and later school entrants; 2) neurophysiological research, including brain changes which affect vision, hearing, cognition, etc.; and 3) maternal deprivation studies.

These will be followed by a brief review of research on family attitudes toward children and comparisons between the home and the school as alternatives for early childhood development.

Early and Late School Entry. Most academic schooling, it will be assumed, eventually rests upon an ability to read. In turn, Nila Smith points out, "Dozens of investigations indicate that reading maturation accompanies physical growth, mental growth, emotional and social maturity, experiential background, and language development."[16] Willard Olson found that "children of the same age and the same grade location are regularly found to differ by as much as four or five years in their maturation and their readiness to perform tasks."[17]

The question then is not only, Is the child *ready* for school? but even more important, Does he demonstrate his readiness by sufficient maturity to *sustain* learning? and, Will the early starter be *as well or better motivated and less frustrated and anxiety-ridden* than the one who starts later? A wide variety of studies provides the answers.

Inez King[19] reports an Oak Ridge, Tennessee, study of two groups totaling 54 children who were five years and eight months to five years and 11 months old when they started school. They were compared with 50 children who started at six years and three months to six years and eight months of age. Stanford Achievement Tests at the end of grade six showed a distinct difference, strongly in favor of the older group. In this study, of the 11 children who were retained, only one had started after six years of age; 19 boys and 16 girls of the younger group appeared to be maladjusted in some way, while only three boys and three girls from the older group were considered maladjusted.

ECD studies involving retention of learning have been done at virtually all grade and socioeconomic status (SES) levels, with remarkably uniform results. B. U. Keister[20] reported that five-year-olds could often develop enough skills to get through first-grade reading, but the learning was generally not retained through the summer vacation. Other comparisons of reading achievement of early and late starters were made by Marian Carroll[21] in the third grade, Joseph Halliwell and Belle Stein[22] in the fourth and fifth grades, and Richard Hampleman[23] in the sixth. All found generally that later entrants significantly excelled those who started earlier. Similar studies with similar results have also been reported by Elizabeth Bigelow,[24] Inez King,[25] Lowell Carter,[26] Clyde Baer,[27] Donald Green and Sadie Simmons,[28] and Margaret Gott.[29] There are many more.

John Forrester[30] did a vertical study of 500 grade 1-12 children in the Montclair, New Jersey, public schools. The very bright but very young pupils at the time of school entrance did not realize their school success potential. From junior high on, 50% of them earned only C grades. However, the very bright but older group excelled generally throughout their school careers.

While many of these studies were undertaken with a combination of low and middle SES children, higher SES groups perform similarly. Paul Mawhinny[31] reports how children from Detroit's elite Grosse Pointe, Michigan, families were selected by psychologists because they were considered mature enough or of sufficient potential to be admitted to kindergarten before age five. But after 14 years an evaluation was made. More than one-fourth of the selected group were below average or had repeated a grade.

Arnold Gesell and Frances Ilg, after extensive research and clinical analyses, found that school tasks such as reading, writing, and arithmetic "depend upon motor skills which are subject to the same laws of growth which govern creeping, walking, grasping." The resulting awkwardness and immaturity "are often sadly overlooked by teachers and parents":

> When the school child was a baby the adult attitudes tended to be more reasonable. One did not say he should walk at this or that age. Feeling confident that he would walk at the most seasonable time, one was more interested to observe the stage and degree of his preliminary development. If reading readiness and walking readiness are appraised on similar grounds, more justice is done the child.[32]

Neurophysiology and Cognition. The findings of neurophysiologists, psychologists, and medical personnel are remarkably similar in their timing of stages at which children are normally ready to think abstractly, or organize facts, and to sustain and retain learning without undue damage or strain. Many neurophysiological studies demonstrate significant changes in brain patterns which occur between ages seven and eleven. These include impressive experiments which lead one to question if children should be required to participate in regular academic instruction until they are at least eight years old. Some researchers and scholars suggest even until adolescence, e.g., Rohwer[33] and Fisher.[34]

A number of studies of the young child's brain, including Penuel Corbin's, Jean Nicholson's, G. C. Lairy's, W. E. Nelson's, and very recent studies by David Metcalf and Kent Jordan,[35] show that appreciable brain changes take place from birth into adolescence, including the shifting of control from the emotional centers to the reasoning centers. They point to ages seven to eleven or twelve as this important period during which a child eventually develops the ability to sustain high cortical thought.

A. Davis[36] records Paul Yakovlev's findings that the child's brain is not fully insulated or completely developed until after seven years, and sometimes not until age ten or later. H. G. Birch and M. Bortner[37] and M. Bortner and H. G. Birch[38] found that until these ages young children and brain-damaged adults were inaccurate in the perception of shapes and grossly inaccurate in attempts to reproduce them.

The findings of cognitive psychologist Jean Piaget coincide remarkably with those of the neurophysiologists. Willis Overton summarizes Piaget's four major steps in the development of the child:

> ... (a) the sensory motor period – birth to two years; (b) the preoperational period – two years to seven years; (c) the period of concrete operations – seven to eleven years; and (d) the period of formal operations between eleven and fifteen years.[39]

Overton notes that the change from preoperational to concrete operational periods of childhood finds the very young child involved in direct perception relationships with a minimum of reasoning. So this child relates quantity to shape and form of objects, but if the shape or form is changed he is confused. He must also change the quantity. For instance, he cannot understand how a low, wide glass can hold as much water as a tall, narrow one. It is not until he is seven or eight or later that he becomes a fully "reasonable" creature. As he goes through this transition he begins to reason abstractly instead of limiting himself to direct relationships.[40]

Millie Almy's replication of Piaget's work demonstrated "that only 48% of the second-grade children in the middle class school, with a mean chronological age of seven years and four months, were able to conserve in all three of the [Piagetian] tasks"[41] which were designed to measure cognitive maturity in terms of abstract thinking normally required for primary grades. Almy concludes that "failure to begin to conserve [Piaget's term for ability to understand certain problems] at an early age may be associated with a failure to grasp much that goes on in the classroom and elsewhere."[42]

William Rohwer sees schooling as an intrusion on the child's freedom to learn associatively during his preoperational years. He found "little evidence to support the rationale for progressively lowering the age of required school entrance if by evidence one requires data demonstrating a positive effect of early school entrance on later school achievement." He suggested that schooling, as commonly understood, be delayed "several years."[43]

Psychiatrist J. T. Fisher supports this thesis from clinical observation and affirms a need for a primary effort in behalf of the home. Speaking for greater initial freedom for developing a strong affective base for later stability in cognition, and incidentally for nongradedness, he says:

> Psychologists have demonstrated that a normal child commencing his education in adolescence can soon reach the same point of progress he would have achieved by starting to school at five or six years of age. I have often thought that if a child could be assured a wholesome home life and proper physical development, this might be the answer to a growing problem of inadequate classroom space and a shortage of qualified teachers — and the instinctive reluctance of all of us to hand over tax dollars for anything that doesn't fire bullets.[44]

William Rohwer (12) in doing rank correlations on the findings from Torsten Husen's international study(45), found a strong negative correlation between early entry age and attitudes toward school.

D. Elkind[46] found no support for "the claims of lastingness of pre-school instruction, [but] ... evidence in the opposite direction. ... The longer we delay formal instruction, up to certain limits, the greater the period of plasticity and the higher the ultimate level of achievement." He sees frustrated, anxiety-ridden, "intellectually burned" children who lose motivation for intellectual success which they deserve.

Visual Maturity. Findings on the child's visual system are highly similar to those of his brain: The processing of visual stimuli in the brain traces the same electrical path as do the impulses involved with cognitive activity that occur between the thalamus and the cortex. Therefore, if these connections are not completed in their development, the visual signals will not be interpreted clearly, according to James Chalfant and Margaret Scheffelin. These authors add that

The processing of visual stimuli at the higher cortical levels involves: (a) visual analysis, the separation of the whole into its component parts; (b) visual integration, the coordination of mental processes; and (c) visual synthesis, the incorporation or combination of elements into a recognizable whole. A review of literature reveals a variety of cognitive tasks requiring the analysis, integration, and synthesis of visual information.[47]

Luella Cole[48] observed that some children are unable to fixate on objects at close range until age seven or eight or later. Stanley Krippner[49] notes how hard it is to explain to parents that it is not the child's eye that reads but his brain. Chalfant and Scheffelin[50] confirm that "the retina is an outward extension of the cerebral cortex." Thus the visual system is not ready for reading until the brain is relatively mature.

An interesting longitudinal illustration of this relative maturity is provided by Moselle Boland's report of a paper presented by a Texas ophthamologist at the 1963 meeting of the Texas Medical Association:

> Dr. Henry L. Hilgartner said there has been a tremendous increase in nearsightedness in [Texas] school children in the past 30 years. . . . He blames use of their eyes for close school work at an early age. . . . The constant pull of the eye muscles to do close work, he said, causes the eyeball to become larger. This is the basic defect in nearsightedness. . . . Prior to 1930, he said, 7.7 children were farsighted to every one nearsighted. . . . In 1930, Texas compulsory school age was lowered from seven to six years. Today, he added, five children are nearsighted for every one farsighted. . . . "I believe the chief cause is children being required to start school at the early age of six instead of being allowed to grow for another year or two," Dr. Hilgartner commented.[51]

Ruth Strang[52] and Homer Carter and Dorothy McGinnis[53] note that when children cannot adjust to the difficulties and discomforts of tasks requiring close vision, they simply give up trying to read.

Carter and McGinnis explain how the six small muscles of each eye must coordinate precisely to focus on near objects and produce only a single mental image. At six years the "visual mechanism" is still "unstable."[54]

Luella Cole[55] and others report also that not more than 10% of five-year-olds can see any difference between "d" and "b" or "p" and "q." Not until children are eight years old can one "be perfectly certain the eyes are mature enough to avoid such confusions."

Auditory Maturity and Other Factors. As a child matures there is a progressive increase in sound discrimination. According to Carter and McGinnis,[56] this ability to differentiate similar speech sounds is considered by many investigators to be of prime importance in successful reading. If a child is unable to hear the difference in sounds, he will be unable to reproduce the sound correctly in speaking. This would also handicap him in recognizing written words, since improper pronunciation would lead him to expect a different spelling of the word. Luella Cole[57] notes specifically: "If he has normal six-year-old ears he will still be unable to distinguish consistently between the sounds of 'g' and 'k' and 'm' and 'n,' 'p' and 'b' or any other pair of related sounds."

H. G. Birch and A. Lefford[58] did not find intersensory maturity emerging until the children are at least seven or eight years of age. Joseph Wepman[59] found that in some children the combination of auditory discrimination and memory — "ability to retain and recall speech sounds" — is not well developed until the age of nine.

Maternal Deprivation. When a child is taken from home for early schooling or remains at home without loving care from someone he trusts, research says to expect mental and emotional problems which affect his learning, motivation, and behavior. John Bowlby presented evidence, formulated a statement of principle, and defined maternal deprivation in his 1951 report to the World Health Organization:

> . . . the infant and young child should experience a warm, intimate, and continuous relationship with his mother (or permanent mother-substitute) in which both find satisfaction and enjoyment. . . .
> A state of affairs in which the child does not have this relationship is termed "maternal

deprivation." This is a general term covering a number of different situations. Thus a child is deprived even though living at home if his mother (or permanent mother-substitute) is unable to give him the loving care small children need. Again, a child is deprived if for any reason he is removed from his mother's care.[60]

He reiterated this view nearly 20 years later, reporting that in the Western world much the commonest disturbances of attachment "are the results of too little mothering, or of mothering coming from a succession of different people." And these disturbances "can continue for weeks, months, or years" — or may be permanent.[61]

Many ES proponents believe that the young child needs social contact outside the home. There are a number of reasons to doubt that he does. Research is specific. Marcel Geber's work in Uganda demonstrates, much like Harold Skeels's, that such attention or deprivation reaches beyond the emotional responses of young children.[62] Using tests standardized by Arnold Gesell, Geber tested over 300 Uganda babies during their first year. The babies for the most part were from low-SES, tribal-oriented families in which mothers were child-centered, continually caressing, cuddling, and talking to their little ones. He found these infants to be superior to Western children in physiological maturation and coordination, adaptability and sociability, and language skills. It may be observed that African children often do mature earlier than Westerners. Yet Geber reports that in his sampling those babies from relatively high-SES Uganda families with less maternal contact but more involvement in formal training were much less mature in the above qualities than the babies of the low-SES mothers.

L. J. Yarrow also reports that "besides the retardation of development caused through emotional factors, maturation in adjustment is markedly slowed by deprivation of sensory, social, and affective stimulation when a child cannot be with his mother."[63] Bowlby adds that even partial deprivation "brings in its train acute anxiety, excessive need for love, powerful feelings of revenge, and . . . guilt and depression."[64]

The Mother's Attitude. The mother's acceptance of her role is of greatest importance in the child's development. Mary Ainsworth found

> . . . significant differences . . . when the
> mothers were grouped in terms of satisfaction
> with their role, whether the homemaker or
> the worker role. Dissatisfied mothers, both
> working and nonworking, reported undesir-
> able child-rearing practices and attitudes more
> frequently than mothers who were satisfied
> with their role.[65]

Education and reassurance of parents thus become a
vital concomitant of any ECD program, whether in
the home or in school, whether the mother works or
not, but particularly with the mother who does not
have a wholesome appreciation of her role. Thus,
says Bowlby, numerous direct studies

> make it plain that, when deprived of maternal
> care, the child's development is almost always
> retarded — physically, intellectually, and
> socially — and that symptoms of physical and
> mental illness may appear . . . and that some
> children are gravely damaged for life.[66]

Some educators believe that parents are either
too ignorant or obsessed with a desire for freedom
to be willing to give their children the care they
need for optimum development. A number of
studies demonstrate that this is not necessarily so.
Louise Daugherty,[67] Robert Hess and Virginia
Shipman,[68] Mildred Smith,[69] Hylan Lewis,[70] and
Phyllis Levenstein[71] found that parents are concerned, regardless of socioeconomic status. When
Mildred Smith took study-help materials to homes
and induced parental help, 90% of the homes
responded, and of these 99% of the parents asked
that the program be continued.

Levenstein[72] not only found generally that if
approached rightly, disadvantaged mothers "take
seriously the family's responsibility to lay ground-
work for school learning," but also noted that their
"aspirations for their children are very similar to
those of middle-income mothers." The fact that the
mother saw the practical teacher as less effective
than she, yet sensed her own inadequacies, suggests
as the more urgent role of the state the development
of home education programs for adequate parenthood.

School vs. *Home*. Then should the young child be taken from home to be trained in a school? There may be cases of acute or extreme deprivation where this is necessary. Yet Bowlby insists, on the basis of many investigations, that "children thrive better in bad homes than in good institutions," and children "apparently unreasonably" are even attached to bad parents. "It must never be forgotten," Bowlby observes,

> ... that even the bad parent who neglects her child is nonetheless providing much for him. ... Except in the worst cases, she is giving him food and shelter, comforting him in distress, teaching him simple skills, and above all is providing him with that continuity of human care on which his sense of security rests.[73]

Burton Blatt and Frank Garfunkel found it necessary to reject the research hypothesis of their own study involving low-SES children who "were at least two years away from entering the first grade." They concluded that (a) the home is more influential than the school, (b) the school can do little without strong home support, (c) disadvantaged parents "are often anxious to cooperate," and (d) school organization and requirements are often "foreign" to these parents who in turn are blamed by the school for not readily accepting them.[74]

Special education would certainly appear to be indicated for many specific cases of disability such as speech, vision, hearing, cerebral palsy, severe mental retardation, and certain neuroses, psychoses and advanced emotional problems. Yet it is difficult to find research support for *generalized* early schooling as described in the California Task Force report. In fact it is difficult to understand, in the face of substantial evidence to the contrary, how educators can justify existing generalized schooling down to ages five and six, or compulsory education below age eight.

On the other hand, certain child-care needs must be met. These are not generalized needs, but are specific problems growing out of parents' inability to care for their young children, e.g., physical or psychological handicaps, ineptness, immaturity, or severe economic stress requiring the mother to work. Any lesser reason which simply accommodates a growing demand for parental "freedom" must, in terms of research findings, be considered parental dereliction. And while research may not yet always be definitive in placing the blame, there is considerable evidence that points toward maternal deprivation and early schooling as primary reasons for childhood maladjustment, motivational loss, poor retention, deterioration of attitudes, visual handicaps, and a wide variety of other physical and behavioral problems, including minimal brain dysfunction.

In summary, research and comparisons of school entry ages clearly point to the need 1) to delay any type of educational program that proposes or permits sustained high cortical effort, or strain on the visual or auditory systems, before the child is seven or eight, and for 2) a warm, continuous mother or mother-surrogate relationship (without a succession of different people) until the child is at least seven or eight.

Investigators (Daugherty, Hess and Shipman, Levenstein, Lewis, Smith, *et al.*) have shown that parents, when clearly shown their children's needs, overwhelmingly respond to them. Likewise, other researchers (Rohwer, Elkind, Husén, *et al.*) make clear that the earlier children go to school the more likely they are to develop negative attitudes toward school.

Some Practical Solutions from Research

So the closer the child's early environment can be kept to his home (or other home with a low adult-to-child ratio) which may provide a continuous warm and free growing place, the more likely his maximum development will be. And this home should neither propose nor permit such learning as violates the child's normal developmental crescendo.

Parent Education. With some of these principles in mind, Susan Gray,[75] Phyllis Levenstein,[76] David Weikart,[77] Ira Gordon,[78] and others have been experimenting with home schooling. While research does *not* indicate the need for schooling as such, there is much to be learned from these researchers toward effective parent education which can lead to appropriate pre-school environments regardless of cultural background or socioeconomic status. And indeed, if as psychiatrist J. T. Fisher infers, the state desires to save money, one of the most effective ways may be to help in the development of "wholesome home life."[79]

Home Schools. Both Susan Gray and Phyllis Levenstein experimented with home schools. Levenstein describes her successful experience with such a program which she calls the "Mother-Child Home Program."[80] Because of the resistance of some mothers, particularly of low-SES families, to *teacher* visitation, she calls the professional visiting personnel "toy demonstrators." Gray notes that "the potential [of the home] is sometimes difficult to tap but it is there."[81]

Such programs may well provide a *modus operandi* for such child care as is really necessary and avoid heavy capital and operating costs which California's present proposal is certain to bring.

There is now a sufficient research base to suggest several procedures in lieu of early schooling as commonly conceived. The state should:

1. Carefully restudy the needs of its children in the light of research. It should realize that research provides no more reason for early schooling for all four-year-olds simply because they have intelligence than it does for early sex for twelve-year-olds simply because they have generated reproductive equipment. They must await the development of balancing factors. Great damage may be avoided.

2. Embark upon a massive parent education program, assisting first those who are in greatest need, but educating all parents, by all media available, concerning the developmental needs of their children. Parents who are neither handicapped nor forced to work should be helped to better understand their privileges and responsibilities as parents, to see that "freedom" sacrificed now will bring larger benefits later.

3. Make such provisions as are necessary for all exceptional children: the severely handicapped or disabled or others requiring special education. Even here research indicates that programs should be kept as close to the home as practicable.

4. Take an interest in providing care for the relatively normal children of handicapped parents or those forced to work, by selecting homes nearby, if possible, as home-schools. Those homes and mothers (or other adults) who are qualified would be selected for their warmth, continuity, aptness for children, and dedication to their welfare. These may

well be operated as enlightened care centers on a small adult-to-child ratio (normally not more than 1:4 or 1:5), and might be subsidized by the state where parents cannot meet the costs. Traveling teachers on state or local payroll could monitor these home-schools to see that they were provided adequate materials and equipment and to coordinate them with existing ADC and other social service programs.

Conclusion

It would be hard to find an area of educational research more definitive than that on child development and school entry age. It is difficult to see how planners can review this evidence and conclude that four- or five-year-olds generally should be in school, much less three-year-olds.

Goals of maximum development of the child are generally sound, but research says that California's proposed way to reach them can only lead to greater trouble. In short, it appears that California's planners, and others with similar plans, have either overlooked or ignored or seriously misinterpreted responsible research. If such evidence is questioned, then further research should be undertaken before legislating in areas so delicate as the young child's mind. Meanwhile, scientific evidence comparing the validity of the home and the school as early childhood environments clearly favors the home.

It is hoped that the California legislature and the State Board of Education will ponder these facts and that other legislators and educators — federal, state, and local — will also consider carefully the dangers of veering from the guidelines which re; search has supplied.

1. Benjamin S. Bloom, *Stability and Change in Human Characteristics*. New York: John Wiley & Sons, 1964, p. 88.

2. "Report of the Task Force on Early Childhood Education." Sacramento, Calif.: Wilson Riles, State Superintendent of Public Instruction, and the State Board of Education, November 26, 1971, p. 29.

3. *Ibid.*, p. 1.

4. *Ibid.*, p. 1.

5. *Ibid.*, p. 10.

6. Harold M. Skeels, *Adult Status of Children with Contrasting Early Life Experiences: A Follow-Up Study*. Monograph of the Society for Research in Child Development, No. 105. Chicago: University of Chicago Press, 1966, pp. 1-68.

7. White House Conference on Children and Youth, 1970, *Report to the President*. Washington, D.C.: U.S. Government Printing Office, 1970, pp. 97-98.

8. Education Commission of the States, *Early Childhood Development, Alternatives for Program Development in the States.* Denver, Colo.: The Commission, 1971.

9. *Ibid.,* p. 3.

10. *Ibid.,* p. 40.

11. Earl S. Schaefer, "Toward a Revolution in Education: A Perspective from Child Development Research," *The National Elementary Principal,* September, 1971, p. 18.

12. William D. Rohwer, Jr., "On Attaining the Goals of Early Childhood Education." (Paper presented at OEO Conference on Research in Early Childhood Education, Washington, D.C., 1970.)

13. *Ibid.,* pp. 1-5, 17-19.

14. U.S. Commission on Civil Rights, *Racial Isolation in the Public Schools,* Vol. 1. Washington, D.C.: Government Printing Office, 1967, p. 138.

15. Westinghouse and Ohio University, "The Impact of Head Start: An Evaluation of the Effects of Head Start on Children's Cognitive and Affective Development," in *The Disadvantaged Child,* Joe L. Frost and Glenn R. Hawkes, editors. Boston: Houghton Mifflin, 1970, pp. 197-201.

16. Nila B. Smith, "Early Reading: Viewpoints," in *Early Childhood Crucial Years for Learning,* Margaret Rasmussen, editor. Washington, D.C.: Association for Childhood Education International, 1966, pp. 61-62.

17. Willard C. Olson, *NEA Journal,* October, 1947, pp. 502-03.

18. H. M. Davis, "Don't Push Your School Beginners," *Parent's Magazine,* October, 1952, pp. 140-41.

19. Inez B. King, "Effect of Age of Entrance into Grade 1 Upon Achievement in Elementary School," *Elementary School Journal,* February, 1955, pp. 331-36.

20. B. U. Keister, "Reading Skills Acquired by Five-Year Old Children," *Elementary School Journal,* April, 1941, pp. 587-96.

21. Marion Carroll, "Academic Achievement and Adjustment of Underage and Overage Third-Graders," *The Journal of Educational Research,* February, 1964, p. 290.

22. Joseph W. Halliwell and Belle W. Stein, "A Comparison of the Achievement of Early and Late Starters in Reading Related and Non-Reading Related Areas in Fourth and Fifth Grades," *Elementary English,* October, 1964, pp. 631-39, 658.

23. Richard S. Hampleman, "A Study of the Comparative Reading Achievements of Early and Late School Starters," *Elementary English,* May, 1959, pp. 331-34.

24. Elizabeth Bigelow, "School Progress of Underage Children," *Elementary School Journal,* November, 1934, pp. 186-92.

25. King, *op. cit.*

26. Lowell Burney Carter, "The Effect of Early School Entrance on the Scholastic Achievement of Elementary School Children in the Austin Public Schools," *Journal of Educational Research,* October, 1956, pp. 91-103.

27. Clyde J. Baer, "The School Progress and Adjustment of Underage and Overage Students," *Journal of Educational Psychology,* February, 1958, pp. 17-19.

28. Donald Ross Green and Sadie Vee Simmons, "Chronological Age and School Entrance," *Elementary School Journal,* October, 1962, pp. 41-47.

29. Margaret Ellen Gott, *The Effect of Age Differences at Kindergarten Entrance on Achievement and Adjustment in Elementary School.* (Doctoral dissertation, University of Colorado, 1963.)

30. John J. Forrester, "At What Age Should Children Start School?," *The School Executive,* March, 1955, pp. 80-81.

31. Paul E. Mawhinny, "We Gave Up on Early Entrance," *Michigan Education Journal,* May, 1964, p. 25.

32. Arnold Gesell and Frances L. Ilg, *The Child from Five to Ten.* New York: Harper and Brothers, 1946, pp. 388-89.

33. Rohwer, *op. cit.,* p. 37.

34. James T. Fisher and Lowell S. Hawley, *A Few Buttons Missing.* Philadelphia: J.B. Lippincott Company, 1951, pp. 13-14.

35. Penuel H. Corbin (master's thesis in pediatrics, University of Minnesota, 1951. NA Med Library, W4A, 9C791F, 1951, C1); Jean M. Nicholson *et al., EEG and Clinical Neurophysiology,* Vol. 8, 1956, p. 342; G. C. Lairy *et al., EEG and Clinical Neurophysiology,* Vol. 14, 1962, pp. 778-79; W. E. Nelson, *Textbook of Pediatrics.* Chicago: Saunders Co., 1967, p. 1088; David Metcalf and Kent Jordan, "EEG Ontogenesis in Normal Children," in *Drugs, Development, and Cerebral Function,* W. Lynn Smith, editor. Springfield, Ill.: Charles C. Thomas, 1972, pp. 127-28.

36. A. Davis, *Regional Development of the Brain in Early Life.* Cambridge, Mass.: Harvard University Press, 1964.

37. M. Bortner and H. G. Birch, "Perceptual and Perceptual Motor Dissociation in Cerebral Palsied Children," *Journal of Nervous and Mental Diseases,* 1960, pp. 103-8.

38. H. G. Birch and M. Bortner, "Perceptual and Perceptual Motor Dissociation in Brain-damaged Patients," *Journal of Nervous and Mental Diseases,* 1960, p. 49.

39. Willis F. Overton, "Piaget's Theory of Intellectual Development and Progressive Education," in *Yearbook of the Association for Supervision and Curriculum Development, 1972.* Washington, D.C.: The Association, pp. 95-103.

40. *Ibid.,* p. 103.

41. Millie Almy, Edward Chittenden, and Paula Miller, *Young Children's Thinking.* New York: Teachers College Press, Columbia University, 1966.

42. *Ibid.,* p. 99.

43. Rohwer, *op. cit.*, pp. 7-8.

44. Fisher, *loc. cit.*

45. Torsten Husen, *International Study of Achievement in Mathematics,* Vol. II. Uppsala: Almquist and Wiksells, 1967.

46. D. Elkind, "Piagetian and Psychometric Conceptions of Intelligence," *Harvard Educational Review,* 1969, pp. 319-37.

47. James C. Chalfant and Margaret A. Scheffelin, *Central Processing Dysfunctions in Children: A Review of Research* (Ninds Monograph 9). Washington, D.C.: U.S. Department of Health, Education, and Welfare, 1969.

48. Luella Cole, *The Improvement of Reading, with Special Reference to Remedial Instruction.* New York: Farrar and Rinehart, Inc., 1938.

49. Stanley Krippner, "On Research in Visual Training and Reading Disability," *Journal of Learning Disabilities,* February, 1971, p. 16.

50. Chalfant and Scheffelin, *op. cit.,* p. 23.

51. Moselle Boland, "Going to School Too Soon Blamed for Eye Troubles," *Houston Chronicle* (Texas), April 30, 1963.

52. Ruth Strang, *Diagnostic Teaching of Reading.* New York: McGraw Hill, 1964, pp. 164-65.

53. Homer L. J. Carter and Dorothy J. McGinnis, *Diagnosis and Treatment of the Disabled Reader.* London: MacMillan, Collier-MacMillan Ltd., 1970.

54. *Ibid.,* p. 48.

55. Cole, *op. cit.,* p. 284.

56. Carter and McGinnis, *op. cit.,* pp. 51-52.

57. Cole, *op. cit.,* p. 282.

58. H. G. Birch and A. Lefford, "Intersensory Development in Children," *Monographs of the Society for Research in Child Development,* No. 89, 1963.

59. Joseph M. Wepman, "The Modality Concept — Including a Statement of the Perceptual and Conceptual Levels of Learning," in *Perception and Reading,* Proceedings of the Twelfth Annual Convention, International Reading Association, Vol. 12, Part 4, pp. 1-6. Newark, Dela.: The Association, 1968.

60. John Bowlby, *Maternal Care and Mental Health.* Geneva: World Health Organization, 1952.

61. John Bowlby, *Attachment and Loss,* Vol. I. New York: Attachment Basic Books, 1969.

62. Marcel Geber, "The Psycho-Motor Development of African Children in the First Year, and the Influence of Maternal Behavior," *Journal of Social Psychology,* 1958, pp. 185-95.

63. L. J. Yarrow, "Separation from Parents During Early Childhood," in *Child Development Research* I, Martin and Lois Hoffman, editors. New York: Russell Sage Foundation, 1964, p. 127.

64. Bowlby, *op. cit.* p. 12.

65. Mary D. Ainsworth *et al.,* "The Effects of Maternal Deprivation: A Review of Findings and Controversy in the Context of Research Strategy," in *Deprivation of Maternal Care, a Reassessment of Its Effects.* New York: Schocken Books, 1966, p. 117.

66. Bowlby, *op. cit.,* p. 15.

67. Louise G. Daugherty, *NEA Journal,* December, 1963, pp. 18-20.

68. Robert D. Hess and Virginia C. Shipman, "Maternal Attitudes Toward the School and the Role of Pupil: Some Social Class Comparisons," in *Developing Programs for the Educationally Disadvantaged,* A. Harry Passow, editor. New York: Teachers College Press, Columbia University, 1968, pp. 127-28.

69. Mildred Beatty Smith, "School and Home: Focus on Achievement," in *Developing Programs for the Educationally Disadvantaged,* A. Harry Passow, editor. New York: Teachers College Press, Columbia University, 1968, pp. 106-7.

70. Hylan Lewis, "Culture, Class, Poverty, and Urban Schooling," in *Reaching the Disadvantaged Learner,* A. Harry Passow, editor. New York: Teachers College Press, Columbia University, 1970, p. 24.

71. Phyllis Levenstein, "Learning Through (and From) Mothers," *Childhood Education,* December, 1971, pp. 130-34.

72. *Ibid.,* p. 132.

73. Bowlby, *op. cit.* (fn. 60), pp. 67-68.

74. Burton Blatt and Frank Garfunkel, *The Education of Intelligence.* Washington, D.C.: The Council for Exceptional Children, 1969.

75. Susan W. Gray, "The Child's First Teacher," *Childhood Education,* December, 1971, pp. 127-29.

76. Levenstein, *op. cit.*

77. David P. Weikart, "Learning Through Parents: Lessons for Teachers," *Childhood Education,* December, 1971, pp. 135-37.

78. Ira J. Gordon, "The Beginnings of the Self: The Problem of the Nurturing Environment," *Phi Delta Kappan,* March, 1969, pp. 375-78.

79. Fisher, *op. cit.,* pp. 13-14.

80. Levenstein, *op. cit.,* p. 134.

81. *Ibid.,* p. 127.

PRESSURE IN THE NURSERY

by HELEN BECK

I should like to explore critically some current trends in early childhood education and in the handling of young children. I shall consider the tendency to push cognitive learning and mechanical memory training among ever younger age groups and the effect this tendency is likely to have on the development of young children.

A recent ad for a popular series of children's books asserts: "Now that your little one is walking and talking, he is ready to start reading." An illustration shows a very "little one" indeed. These early reading attempts are meant, the text states, for 2-6-year-olds! Many nursery schools are also falling into line by making reading readiness and other "school subjects" priority items in their programs.

Television, too, is directing much of its program efforts to the teaching of the three R's to 3- and 4-year-olds, with endlessly repeated isolated letters and numbers for memorization and rote learning. Even those programs that

have served young children well for a long time with carefully selected, quietly presented material that engaged the young child's interest and stimulated his curiosity now find it necessary to slip unconnected segments of information on numbers, letters and shapes into their programming.

Pressure for early acquisition of academics may assuage adult anxieties about time passing, but it deprives young children of appropriate activities, unhurried time for affect development and opportunities for real learning. Thus it depletes the life of the young child and fosters the same kind of anxieties in the young which the adult tries to calm in himself.

Adults' feeling of "time running out" apparently gives rise to the wish that the next generation should be better equipped for mastery of our unwieldy environment. This, some experts think, can best be accomplished by cutting down on time "wasted" in play. (See the experiments of Carl Bereiter and Siegfried Engelmann).[1] However,

CHILDREN TODAY, Sept./Oct. 1972, pp. 20-24.

hurrying young children through their stages of growth is likely to create disorder in their development and to decrease rather than increase their ability to cope with stress. Forced development and premature inappropriate independence are likely to foster greater dependency needs and undercut the child's security and his trust in adults and in his own abilities.

The nursery years are important ones in the development of children. These are the years in which the child develops the roots of his human qualities and of his relationships to others—positive or negative, spontaneous or artificial. They are the years in which the child first conceives of himself as an entity, worthwhile or unimportant, in reaction to the people around him. Through endless repetition of actual experiences in his play activities, a child learns to cope with the world within and the world outside himself. Playing, he recreates the pleasures of enjoyable experiences and attempts to gain mastery over unpleasant occurrences as he actively recreates what he had at first passively endured. In this way a child tries out more effective solutions for unsatisfactorily resolved experiences. As he plays out experiences, he is testing and retesting solutions so that he can act differently when similar situations recur.

The nursery years are busy years, full of tasks that have their own specific seasons and can be fully mastered best at this point in time. Never again at a later stage can this mastery be striven for with quite the same urgency. Never again can it be obtained with quite the same feeling of achieve-ment and satisfaction. Early experiences in mastering tasks form the model for later approaches and for expectation of success or failure.

A Time for Learning

Acquisition of academic knowledge arouses pleasure, satisfaction and curiosity—once the child is mature enough to apply what he is learning and to retain the knowledge. What application a 3-year-old has for the letters and numbers he is taught in isolation is hard to imagine. What content does he have at this stage for reading? What value is there, for example, in his parrotting numbers if he lacks any kind of number concept?

The pleasure that a preschooler derives from academic achievement is likely to be only a reaction to adult approval. Although adult approval is important to children as an impetus to learning and should not be underrated, we must be aware when achievement is mechanical and not accompanied by an inner readiness in the child. To pre-empt the nursery years with tasks for which the child lacks neurological, physiological and emotional readiness may create hybrid successes that have little real meaning to the child as he acquires them, and cheat him of the excitement experienced when the time is ripe—excitement that provides drive for further learning.

Rote learning does not arouse curiosity and memorization does not lead to understanding. Studies indicate that the curve of knowledge thus acquired is likely to flatten out and that children who achieve this kind of learning do not maintain their advantage. As a matter of fact, they are likely to be disappointed when they are no longer admired for displaying special knowledge, once its possession has become appropriate to their age.

An experienced school counselor once remarked: "Many 'fast moving' children who have gone through accelerated programs rebel at the high school level. Being in an accelerated program, the children report, always means that 'as soon as I finish this, I *must* push on.'" Such children are not allowed time to linger or to enjoy their prowess. She described several children she knew who had been able to read such books as *Alice in Wonderland* before they entered kindergarten, but who, now that they were in the 6th grade, were "uninspired and uninspiring."

One of the theories developed to push disadvantaged young children ahead is concerned with what is called "stress teaching." The very name should make us suspicious. Stress does not promote greater application to a task or the development of ability. On the contrary, stress creates resistance, break-down and a tendency toward "copping out."

The defenders of the stress theory believe that since many poverty level children are so far behind their more fortunate contemporaries there is no time for them to finger-paint or play with blocks. Bereiter and Engelmann, as well as Jean Osborn of the University of Illinois, describe their program for 4-year-olds as structured along the lines of a "high school schedule," consisting of 20- to 30-minute periods of "pattern drills" in language (mechanical repetition of sentences, often in unison), in arithmetic and

in reading. Classroom equipment and schedule are described as follows: "There is no rest time, no outdoor play, and there are no toys." That the children are considered little more than learning machines who can be programmed at will becomes apparent when one notes under the heading, "Teacher Responsibility," the sentence: "The teacher is held responsible for what the child has or has not learned."

Play thus becomes an activity that only the more fortunate child of affluent parents may be permitted to enjoy. However, the child who is allowed time for absorption of what is presented to him benefits from carefully selected stimulation. The deprived child, on the other hand, is being doubly deprived if he no longer finds in nursery school or day care that which his own home cannot offer.

Among the children of the poor are many who have to cope with much pressure. Often they are exposed early to adult experiences and must take on adult responsibilities long before they can handle them. Such children do not need further exploitation but protection. They need a place where they can be their age—silly and serious—according to the dictates of their inclination and their stage of development. Whether they come from slums or more affluent homes, children need to have a place where they are appreciated for what they are, not for what they have learned.

Of course, a young child can manage a certain amount of instruction but he also has great need for being mothered and for an environment where he is allowed to experience and express feelings, and

109

where he can learn to cope with both positive and negative feelings.

Television

Pressure for academic, cognitive and memory training now reaches all ages and all economic groups in the very center of the privacy of the young child's home through a new vehicle—television. For instance, *Sesame Street,* a program whose quality is more relative than real, is setting a fashion in the approach to young children. However, its choppy, fragmented presentation of material, its jumpiness of segments, do not encourage the development of attention span in children. A young viewer would not have time to try to figure out what it all means, even if he were old enough to suspect that there is meaning behind this madness. Aldous Huxley's *Brave New World* seems indeed to have attained reality in our living rooms as the young are being drugged into a semi-waking stage by the onslaught of visual and auditory stimuli of questionable value. The program abounds in oral aggression: letters and numbers that seem to jump out of the screen to grab at the child are devoured by pseudo-sophisticated puppets. The cast is subject to constant pratfalls. Why this should be an advanced method to teach children is hard to understand. Basically, it creates only the same pleasure-fear reaction in children that is prompted by some commercials and cartoons which, although they have met with less approval, at least state their purpose openly.

The program often delights adults and older children who enjoy somewhat condescendingly the confusion created for the very young child under the guise of "teaching him concepts." A young teacher, for instance, spoke to me about his enjoyment of one segment, which purported to teach the concept of "here and there." He was amused by the confusion of the puppet who acted out the concept, for the puppet conceived himself as being "here" while the others told him that he was "there." This confusion, it seems, was never really clarified for the young viewer. Another program, teaching the concept "near-far," was so vague and fast paced that I doubt that the children got more than an impression of a cute pony trotting back and forth.

There are, of course, TV shows which are providing good entertainment and stimulation for young children, such as "Mister Rogers" and "Hodgepodge Lodge."

But since *Sesame Street* is promoted as a pattern of good programming for preschoolers and has invaded day care centers, one has to consider its pertinence as a model for teachers of young children and for parents. It is important in our contacts with young children that we respond to them, their questions and their ideas. However, the children who appear on *Sesame Street* seem more like props than live children who have their own fascinating ideas and logic and the adults on screen do not seem to respond to children's remarks if they do not follow the prepared lesson, however valid or pertinent the remarks may be. Independent thinking by children is thus constricted rather than encouraged. Moreover, questions asked of the children are usually of the "answer yes or no" variety

110

and responded to in unison, while feelings are explored on the program like academic dissertations without immediacy or relevancy to the young child.

Part of the program of day care centers should be to enrich children's experiences, and it is hoped that centers will offer programs and activities that the children's own homes cannot supply because they lack space for vigorous physical activity, equipment for stimulating play and adults who are not preoccupied with other pressing problems. Now, not only are children settled quietly before the television screen when they should be developing muscle skills, but their parents are being encouraged to let them watch the program again when they return home.

Until recently, the reasonable parent was inclined to feel guilty if his child spent too much time squatting before the TV set, and would insist on activities and outdoor play. Now he is beginning to feel guilty if the child is not watching and "learning." I recently interviewed a young mother. To my question about what the 3½-year-old liked to do, she answered, "If I would let him, he would just run out to play. I tell him he will have time enough to play—he ought to learn something." She was somewhat startled when I asked her when she thought the time for play would come if there was already no time at age 3½. This is frightening indeed.

Time, opportunity and assistance are needed to help children develop depth of feeling and the ability to cope with stress. Battering them with ever-changing stimuli that they cannot absorb makes for superficiality. It would be worthwhile to explore what relationship there may be between early saturation with overwhelming stimuli and young people's feelings of inability to involve themselves. It might be valuable to know whether the young people who are now troubled by a feeling of emptiness and who sometimes seek excitement through chemical means are the same ones who were snowed under by stimuli and early, ever-changing excitation, the same ones who lacked actual adult involvement in their development.

Growing Up Fast

"Growing up fast" is becoming so important in our culture that we cannot permit children to be children at the right chronological age. They are then likely to remain children ever after, trying to make up for lost time. "Be your age" is a singularly American phrase, peculiar to a country where it is unusually difficult to be one's age. We frown at the "immaturity" of the 2-year-old and promote all kinds of premature experiences of early "learning." We ridicule play activities which are still serving appropriate purposes, and promote early adult appearance in dress and make-up. Little boys are pressured into adult-like competitiveness in ball games, when games at their age should provide just fun, activity and opportunity to develop coordination and understanding of game structure. Doll play of little girls is discouraged early in many ways, last not least by commercially profitable doll creations that are for "show" rather than for providing the emotional satisfaction of cuddling and mothering.

After we have passed our teens, we remain "girls" and "boys" for the rest of our lives. Some part of the severity of the "generation gap" struggle may stem from young people's feelings that there is unfair competition for spaces that rightfully belong to them. Today's children too often are de-facto orphans. They have buddies, therapists and teachers, but no parents.

Maybe instead of spending so much money and good effort on some current TV and other "teaching" programs, we might provide better, more realistic programs that help parents to involve themselves more in the task of being parents. This could be done—not by making them ever more unsure about their handling of their children—but by helping them find concrete, realistic approaches to everyday problems. We could help parents establish realistic discipline and outlets and provide them with child-rearing techniques that would preserve the "natural" ingredients for growing up.

Maria Piers, in *Wages of Neglect*,[2] for instance, discusses a fascinating project of "teaching" mothers along with their children in preschool centers. The aim is, in a way, to achieve a change of attitudes of the parents toward themselves and their children's future.

There have been many attempts to assist parents in the rearing of their children. Among federally-supported programs, Project Head Start has involved parents in its activities from its inception, while its recently initiated new program, Home Start, focuses on parental involvement as the major means of helping the child.

Neighborhood groups under skilled leadership could also go a long way in giving practical help to parents. Such groups would have to be simply structured and not geared to exploration of the deeper springs of parent-child relationships or personality problems. Simple activities that the parents could enjoy themselves and with their children should be provided. There could be role play and there could be sessions engaging both parents and children to demonstrate management and constructive activity. Parents could find that a child can "learn" coordination and "staying within the line" by spreading peanut butter on a piece of bread as well as by "coloring the square red."

Television and radio could be used quite effectively in working with parents. One approach might be to give the kind of practical demonstration suggested above, through use of a spontaneous, unrehearsed meeting with a group of parents. Closed circuit television could be used to make neighborhood sessions available to larger groups and to encourage more hesitant parents to participate.

Although the media are here to stay, they cannot and should not become substitutes for the immediacy of human contact. Real emotional experiences between parent and child cannot be created through electronics. The child who has had natural "encounter" at home may not need an encounter group when he is grown. Children need to learn from close, appropriate, deeply emotional contact with people. Let us not push them out of the nursery before they have developed real, enduring values and can fend for themselves.

---

[1] An Academically-Oriented Preschool for Disadvantaged Children: Results from the Initial Experimental Group conducted at the University of Illinois. Carl Bereiter and Siegfried Engelmann.

[2] *Wages of Neglect*—Robert Coles and Maria Piers, Quadrangle Books, Chicago, 1969.

Helen L. Beck, ACSW, is a school social worker, Department of Special Education, Westport Board of Education, Westport, Conn. From 1957 to 1967, Miss Beck served as chief psychiatric social worker with the special project for neurologically handicapped children at St. Christopher's Hospital for Children, Philadelphia, Pa.

GISELA THOMAS O'NEIL

READING DISABILITY,
A PRODUCT OF THE AGE

PROBLEMS, PITFALLS, OUTLOOK

READING, THE KEY TOOL

Not too long ago, going to school meant for most children acquiring the basic three R's. We may smile at these humble goals of the past; yet in our modern reading-centered education, the first R has become the one dominant tool. With the expansion of the text-book industry and prescribed curricula, most learning now takes place via reading. Either a young child learns to read, or his daily trip to school may turn into a road that leads nowhere.

Today the QUALITY of a school system is measured by the achievement level of reading-scores in relation to a national norm. The oft-repeated demand for QUALITY-EDUCATION for minorities is synonymous with "higher reading scores in slum schools".

This emphasis on reading has infiltrated the life of the preschool child. The Kindergarten, once conceived as a carefree 'garden for children', has become the training ground for "reading readiness skills." Nationwide attempts have been made to teach this one skill EVER EARLIER, even to the incredible notion of mothers' teaching their infants how to read before they are able to speak.

EDUCATION AS AN ART, Fall/Winter 1972-73, pp. 1-27.

THE WAYSIDERS

At present in this country, the high school diploma is considered to be the minimum requirement for a productive adult. Yet our nationwide school drop-out rate is between 30 and 40 per cent. The most common factor in school difficulties is poor ability in reading. A 1971 survey by the Louis Harris polling organisation reported that 15 per cent of the American public, 16 years and older, or about 21 million persons, are lacking some or all of the practical reading skills needed "to deal successfully with even the most simple everyday experiences in modern life".[1] The most critical phase on this road to failure in the child's life is the early schooling in the primary grades.

DIAGNOSIS OF THE PAST: "THE EMOTIONAL BLOCK"

Until recently, the diagnosis for children not learning to read, despite adequate classroom exposure, offered two crude choices:
either the child was too dull to learn,
or if he seemed to have normal intelligence, there was a psychological disturbance, stemming probably from his home environment, that resulted in an "emotional block". Parents were told by school personnel, psychologists, physicians, and psychiatrists, that the problem was largely emotional in origin. The language was laden with derivations of Freudian terminology. To parents this implied that the difficulty was their fault, that something was wrong in their relationship with the child. This interpretation brought about feelings of guilt and failure as parents due to their child's learning-difficulty.

THE CHANGE IN FOCUS: FROM PSYCHOLOGY TO PHYSIOLOGY

During the last decade a revolution has taken place in the educational philosophy of this country. With the reading crisis permeating the schools, in spite of early schooling, headstart programs, and mechanized remedial efforts, the interest has shifted to the physical functions of that part of the human organism which is supposed to do the reading. The former "emotional block" theory has given way to the new diagnosis of "dyslexia" or simply "reading disability". The voice of authority now stems from the physiologist, the neurologist, the neurosurgeon, or the ophthalmologist, with the ancillary professions carrying out extensive testing programs.

There is a burst of new literature with varied theories, and a new technical language has arisen. Clinics have sprung up for testing and reading. New programs have proliferated.

THE NEW TERMINOLOGY

The earliest term used for describing the inability to read, during the first half of our century was WORD-BLINDNESS. STREPHOSYMBOLIA (twisted symbols) occurs also in the early literature (Orton). In 1950 Hallgren, a Swede, introduced the formulation DYSLEXIA. This term was adopted widely to connote poor reading ability. SPECIFIC DYSLEXIA was applied to children showing this weakness in reading skills only, while the slow learner suffers from dyslexia plus other learning difficulties.—Dyslexia varies from illiteracy in that the illiterate person has been deprived of learning situations, while the dyslexic child has been sufficiently exposed but has remained to a large extent unresponsive.—However, there is no uniform definition, each author on the subject seeming to define his own meaning. It can mean a severe handicap, total inability, or mere backwardness.

Later authors introduced new terms, or modifications of the existing ones, such as: DEVELOPMENTAL, or GENETIC dyslexia, in contrast to acquired dyslexia (loss of ability in later life). PERCEPTUAL DIFFICULTIES, NEUROLOGICAL LEARNING DISORDER, or DYSFUNCTION OF THE CENTRAL NERVOUS SYSTEM, are formulations that clearly point to the profession of the authors.

READING DISABILITY, as a general term, has been widely adopted since Knud Hermann used it as a title for his book on word-blindness in 1959. It plainly states a fact: "Can't read!"

THE SPECTRUM OF INTERPRETATIONS

Some investigators have observed that poor readers run in families, and have therefore stressed the aspect of INHERITANCE. Others have simply called it CONGENITAL, or inborn. Then there are those who postulate a MINIMAL BRAIN-DAMAGE, due to early childhood illness or to slight oxygen-deprivation before or during birth. Others reject the label of "damage" and speak of DYSFUNCTION OF THE CENTRAL NERVOUS SYSTEM, due to unknown or known causes. Theories on LEFTHANDEDNESS or DOMINANCE fall into this group.

Another school of thought emphasizes DEVELOPMENTAL DISCREPANCIES or LAG IN MATURATION; for instance, the correlation between delayed walking or delayed speech in early childhood, and reading difficulties.

Frequent findings in comparative age studies have led some authors to the conclusion that the school-entrance age of six (or even six-minus) is arbitrary, and for many children too early, and that the MATURATION OF THE SENSE ORGANS, especially the eye, has not proceeded in many children to the point where they can cope with the complicated process of reading. This view is strengthened by the fact that many more boys (who mature somewhat slower than girls) suffer from reading difficulties.— There is empirical evidence that in many children dyslexia or reading disability is of a TRANSIENT NATURE. Many children who have perceptual difficulties at the age of six show considerable improvement at ten or twelve.

THE DEMANDS OF READING

Reading-readiness skills are usually practiced in Kindergarten. Often pre-primers or primers are introduced. In the first grade the printed page has to be mastered. No concern for differences in development is possible. The demands have to be met or the road to failure begins. — I would like to quote here what is asked of the six year old child at the beginning of his schooling.[2]

117

"Many factors are involved in this early school learning. The child must be able to sit still, attend the incoming stimuli, and to sort visual, auditory and tactile-kinesthetic stimuli from the background of distracting sight, noise and movement of the average primary classroom. He must also be able to maintain some measure of impulse control, tolerate some frustration, and wait a reasonable time for gratification. In addition, the child must be able to:

1) perceive small differences in two-dimensional visual symbols (visual perception);
2) adequately understand word meanings when he hears a word;
3) pronounce the word clearly;
4) perceive small differences in sounds (auditory discrimination) i.e. "pin" vs "pen", "bass" vs "bath";
5) orient himself in space, be aware of small changes in position, and have awareness of left-right direction of symbol sequences;
6) have the necessary motor coordination to reproduce these symbol sequences on paper;
7) have the ability to integrate visual, auditory, and tactile-kinesthetic sequences;
8) store these associations in the form of visual, and/or auditory, and/or tactile-kinesthetic memories."

THE MATURATION OF THE CHILD—
PERCEPTUAL DEVELOPMENT

A newborn horse may get up on its four legs and run, and chicks may break the egg shell and search for food, but the newborn child is helpless and totally dependent. An article in SCIENTIFIC AMERICAN (July 1972, by Lytt I. Gardner) on "Deprivation Dwarfism" documents the fact that for the child to prosper, physical care is not enough. It needs love, or the organism will not develop. It will become dwarfed, skinny and sickly, the development stunted. Therefore what we call ordinary development is the result of physical care and human love bestowed on the unfolding organism.

In the first three years man surpasses the animal by achieving the vertical position and speech. But while most animals are already reproducing by this age, man has still a long way to go to reach maturity.

This path to maturity unfolds in ordered sequence. In the first seven years, until the change of teeth and school-readiness, this development is primarily bodily: the directed use of the motor organism, the use of the speech organs, the maturation of the senses, the development of the brain functions, and the interrelation of all sense avenues.

The body of the newborn child is fully formed; the sense organs, nervous system, and all the brain cells are organically present. The child has to make this body his own, learn to use it as his instrument, activate and direct its various functions.

Much has been written on this systematic acquisition of bodily skills. Since the details would go beyond the scope of this article, I would like to quote the major steps from the widely used Frostig manual[3] :

"From birth to the age of approximately two years is the period of maximum sensory motor development. Between 1½ or 2 and 3 or 3½ years is the period of maximum language development. Between 3½ and 7½ years is the period of maximum perceptual development. Perceptual development is followed by the maximum development of higher thought processes after 7½ years."

This outline seems in sharp contrast with the demands of our modern education, where perceptual skills are expected to have been fully achieved with school entrance age.

Since "perceptual difficulty" is so often cited in reading disability, we will have to take a closer look at the development of the eye functions.

The vision of the infant is totally different from that of the adult. To begin with, it is peripheral, that is, the visual sensations arise from the visual sense cells lying outside the central or foveal area of the retina. Control and precision, necessary for reading of the printed page, have to be achieved in the course of development.

"Some children will be found to have great difficulty establishing control of the eye. In the first place, the muscle systems involved in this control are among the most complex in the body. Their innervation comes from both the voluntary and the involuntary systems; three pairs of muscles must work together in perfect synchrony; and two separate systems, the right eye system and the left eye system, must be perfectly congruent. Therefore, the sheer problem of coordination is staggering.

In the second place, the precision required in eye movements is among the most demanding in the organism. The fovea is only about two millimeters in diameter. Upon this minute area the image of the target must be accurately projected. This projection must be sufficiently precise to permit the child to sort out this one target for central fixation from among an intricate network of adjacent targets. Such precision is extremely demanding and it must be maintained over long periods of time."[4]

How does the child learn to control the eye? In the earliest stage the infant learns to control his hand, to grasp, to reach, to touch, to move. He then watches his hand as it moves, teaching the eye to follow the hand. At this stage the hand is dominant and guides the eye. "The eye learns under the tutelage of the hand" (Gesell). Eventually, the eye can explore on its own without the help of the hand and control is supplied by the body of visual information.

This natural sequence in the development is crucial. It is important that the exploring, manipulating hand teaches the eye, that toys are not watched or looked at, but handled, moved, played with, their forms felt; that perception is matched to motor, and not the reverse.

"Particularly in our modern civilization, where we put so much stress on the early interpretation of perceptual data in books, pictures and the like, children frequently make the perceptual motor match in the wrong direction. They assign primary importance to perception and match motor data to perceptual data. Such children develop a very tight perceptual control of the motor responses. These children are frequently seen in the classroom. If asked to draw a geometric form, the child keeps the eye exactly on the point of the pencil. Movements are tight and inflexible and follow the eye precisely. The child visually controls his movement, he does not visually monitor it . . . He does not maintain awareness of the total form; he concentrates on the control of the immediate movement. Such a reversed perceptual-motor match leaves the child at the mercy of perceptual distortions."[4]

Another aspect of maturation is the shift in dominant sense-avenues through which the child is learning. The child proceeds from TACTILE DOMINANCE, where everything has to be touched, handled, or even brought to the mouth, to AUDITORY DOMINANCE. He becomes receptive to language, learns to speak and sing through imitation, and acquires a sizable vocabulary. He loves to listen to stories, wants to hear them over and over again. Young children of the primary grades still learn foreign languages through imitation, that is, through auditory perception, a task almost impossible to a VISUALLY DOMINANT person.

"Numerous studies have revealed how children's learning is first more effective on an auditory level. Gradually, after passing through the transitional stages in grades 4 and 5, children become more proficient learners, using their eyes rather than their ears."[5]

Therefore, from a development aspect, reckoning with the nature of the child in the primary grades, the purely visual approach to learning seems contraindicated.

THE VISUAL CLASSROOM APPROACH: SILENT READING, LOOK-SAY LEARNING

During a large part of the average school day, the primary classroom takes on the air of hushed silence that we experience in a library for adults. The child is instructed not to move his lips, but to read for meaning only.

But even the silent library for reading adults is a modern innovation. Medieval monks needed individual reading booths or carrels, because they spoke what they read; reading was not separated from speech.

> "They read with their lips, pronouncing what they saw, and with their ears, listening to the words pronounced, hearing what is called the 'voices of the pages'. It was a real accoustical reading, an activity which, like chant and writing, required the participation of the whole body and the whole mind."[6]

The result was more than a visual memory of the written words. It was an aural memory of the words heard, as well as a muscular memory of the words pronounced.

Throughout antiquity and long thereafter, even private readers regularly pronounced the words of their texts aloud. Silent reading was such an anomaly that St. Augustine found Ambrose's habit remarkable: "When he was reading his eyes glided over the pages and his heart searched out the sense, but his voice and tongue were at rest." Visitors came to watch this prodigy.

In the past "reading" meant reading aloud. The hushing-up of the readers has been a gradual process. It is only today that we are commanded by the speed-reading institutes to divorce eye and speech in the act of reading. The fact that in reading from left to right we make incipient word formations with our throat muscles was discovered to be the principal cause of "slow" reading. Lip movements and mutterings from a reader have been associated with semi-literacy, hence the American stress on a merely visual approach to reading in elementary learning.

But is so-called vocalization or sub-vocalization such an unusual phenomenon? Experiments with electronic devices attached to the throat muscles have indicated that sub-vocalization takes place in practically every reader, no matter how rapid and skillful he may be.

And should this emphasis on silent scholarly reading as the ideal method be applied to beginning readers in the primary grades? It seems alien to the nature of the young child. Most of these children will never become scholars. Many are burdened with inarticulate speech, impoverished vocabulary, inability to sustain concentration, or lack motivation for scholarly pursuits. These children need to be activated, not to be toned down! And from a developmental aspect, most children are not as yet so visually dominant that they can learn effectively through this single sensory avenue.

The earlier, more concrete steps to reading, namely translating symbols into sounds and then sounds into meaning, are simply left out in the effort to get meaning from the printed page, where the eye becomes divorced from speech.

The second aspect concerns the teaching of reading. English is an ALPHABETICAL language. The writing consists of 26 graphic symbols. Each character, or combination of characters, represents a sound in the English language. It can also be used for other languages, such as Latin, Spanish, French, Italian, German, Norwegian, Danish, Swedish, etc.

The American Indians used a PICTOGRAPHIC language for writing. Simplified pictures were drawn to represent a concept, such as the sun for fair weather or lightning for a storm.

Then there are IDEOGRAPHIC languages in which symbols or characters represent ideas or concepts. They are not pictorial, but abstract. Chinese is such a language and is said to be very difficult to learn to read, and it cannot be used for other languages.

The English alphabet is a great advantage to us. We should not abandon it. But we are in danger of doing so when the whole word, or look-say method is taught. The child does not learn an alphabetic language, that is alphabetic characters which stand for sounds, but graphic symbols standing for a whole word or concept. He is urged to learn the visual configuration of the word as a Gestalt. This is the essence of teaching an ideographic language, a technique much more akin to Chinese than to English.

The whole word, or look-say method, was developed in the first half of the nineteenth century. Horace Mann is generally considered its father and originator. In 1837 he set out the theory and practice of the word-method in use today:

"In speaking the word apple, for instance, young children think no more of the Roman letters which spell it than in eating the fruit, they think of the chemical ingredients which compose it; hence, presenting them with the alphabet is giving them what they never saw, heard or thought of before. It is as new as algebra and to the eye, not very unlike it; but printed names of known things are the signs of sounds which the ears have become accustomed to hear and their organs of speech to utter and which may excite agreeable feelings and associations. When put to learning the names of the alphabet first, the child has no acquaintance with them, but if put to learning familiar words first, he already knows them by ear, the tongue, and the mind, while his eyes are only unacquainted with them. It can hardly be doubted, therefore, that a child would learn to name twenty-six familiar words much sooner than the unknown, unheard, and unthought-of letters of the alphabet."[7]

This may sound reasonable, but the only way to make the words stick is through endless repetition. The first-grader learns to read about 300 words by repeating each one hundreds of times. In the first three grades, a child using the Macmillan series of basal readers learns 1,342 words by repeating them 28,000 times. By that time, the "agreeable feelings and associations" Horace Mann anticipated, may well have evaporated.

Yet in spite of the endless silent repetitions, many children do not learn. To many of them the words remain meaningless jumbles of details. They cannot perceive and remember the Gestalt with its intricate details, to say nothing of connecting it with a thought. Knud Hermann reports in his book READING DISABILITY that the exclusive use of the word-picture method, which prevailed for a period in Danish schools, was virtually catastrophic for word-blind children.

Katrina De Hirsch, in "Specific Dyslexia or Strephosymbolia"[8] states that for

"children who have trouble with the organisation of visual patterns this method does not work at all; it is, as a matter of fact, one of the causes of their difficulty."

It is hard to see how a method could be more vigorously condemned. It is unsound in theory and it has been ruinous in practice.

THE STRESS ON PARENT AND CHILD

The complaint of school difficulty places great strain on the most stable family. For the unstable family, the stress can become disastrous, with parents disagreeing over handling of the problem.

In the early grades, when the child first encounters difficulty, the parents are usually told "not to worry, he'll catch up". Or "he'll learn to read when he is ready." Later they may try to help him at home, with the homework sessions resulting in agony for both parents and child. When with their efforts the child does not improve, when after much struggle he learns to spell or read a word, and then cannot recognize it again a sentence later, the parents frequently interpret this as a stubborn disinterest and become exasperated. – As the child's learning difficulty continues, the anxiety sets in that he must be mentally retarded or unbalanced. In school the child may be ridiculed by classmates as being "stupid". Many of these children may worry secretly, yet at the same time present to the parents and teachers the defensive behavior of "not caring", "being the happy-go-lucky class clown", or "being rebellious and defiant". They may even develop psychosomatic symptoms, such as abdominal pain or headache, and avoid school attendance.

THE COMPLEX OF SYMPTOMS

While reading difficulty or disability is the universal symptom, there is a whole list of sub-symptoms that have been observed in individuals, and as the most common factors in large groups of poor readers.

The most striking are reversal of letters—so-called mirror reading and mirror writing, such as b for d, saw for was, etc. – and translocations of letters within a word in reading and writing.

"Those errors are notoriously common among all beginners in reading and writing . . . the dyslexic individual is not unique in making reversals and translocations, but he is unique in making so many of them and for so long a time."[9]

Almost always present among younger dyslexics is directional confusion, the inability to differentiate between right and left; they are unable to carry out directional commands, to touch various body parts with either the right or left hand.

They are usually left-handers (or come from families in which there are left-handers), or are ambidextrous, or have mixed motor choices, e.g. right-handed and left-eyed (or left-footed), or were late in establishing dominance.

Boys are affected more often than girls. (Edward H. Senz, gives the ratio as ten to one in "Neurologic Correlates in the Reading process"[8])

There are often delays in maturation, such as late walking or speaking.

Many have poor articulation, have a poor ear for words, cannot differentiate between finer shades of sounds, or may not be able to carry a tune.

They are usually awkward in motor functions, their movements are uncoordinated and jerky.

They cannot sustain rhythm and are therefore inept in rhythmic motor action like skipping rope or swimming.

They are usually clumsy with their fingers.

They have poor Gestalt perception, show difficulty in reproducing geometric forms, and cannot remember whole-word patterns.

They usually have a low frustration level.

They are often described as "young for their age", babyish in behavior and looks. Soft features around mouth and chin are often pronounced.

Any of these subsymptoms may occur also in good readers, while the dyslexic may not have all of them. But he will have many of these telltale signs, because his disability is not an isolated defect but part of his holistic development.

HANDEDNESS AND CEREBRAL DOMINANCE

The skeleton, the nervous system and brain, the sense organs and limbs are built symmetrically. To begin with, the child has no internal awareness of the two sides of the body, it uses its left and right arms and legs simultaneously. Later on it begins to favor one hand, one foot, one eye, and one ear. This is a gradual process, beginning at two years of age, and often extending into early grade-school years. Once it is fully established we speak of handedness and dominance. The majority of people are right-handed, and the right side becomes the active, more conscious, and more skillful side.

With the development of speech, cerebral dominance occurs. One side of the brain takes the lead in the control of articulate speech and manual skills. In the right-handed person this will be the left hemisphere. Once this dominance has been fully established, a cerebral insult to the left hemisphere will result in loss of speech (and paralysis of the right-side motor functions).

In the past it was assumed that the opposite process was taking place in left-handed people. But this seems to occur only in a small percentage, while the remaining group of left-handers appear to fail in establishing fully cerebral dominance. A stroke on either side of the hemisphere may result in loss of speech, or only temporary loss, due to the fact that both sides of the brain may have been engaged in serving the speech functions.

What does this have to do with reading disability? There is evidence that a large percentage of children with specific reading disability are either left-handed, or show weak, mixed, or inconsistent lateral preferences.

A. Silver, in "Diagnostic Considerations in Children with Reading Disability"[8] recommends using the Schilder extension test to discern cerebral dominance. It has been observed that on extension of the arms, with the eyes closed and the fingers spread, one hand tends to be slightly higher than the other. The elevated hand is the one with the greater muscle tone and indicative of the dominant hemisphere. Right-arm elevation suggests left cerebral dominance, and vice versa, while arms at equal height show that dominance has not been established. This cannot be proven, but interesting evidence turned up in comparing the elevated hand and that used in writing. In those cases where the results did not agree with the "writing hand", a test distinguished 85 per cent of the children with reading disabilities in normal third and fourth grade groups, while in good readers this discrepancy between elevated hand and "writing hand" did not occur.

R.M.N. Crosby,[7] a pediatric neurologist and neurosurgeon, suggests that an early switch in handedness may have occurred through a minimal or transient dysfunction that corrected itself due to the plasticity of the brain in the earliest years. He believes that a permanent record is found in the measurement of the nails of thumbs and of great toes. Both are larger on the dominant side, and this is not the result of greater use because a significant percentage of individuals have larger thumbnails on their nondominant hand.

Observation and measurement of nail size in children with reading disability will show that roughly one-half of them have discrepancy between nail-size and handedness. The thumbnail on the dominant hand is either smaller or of equal size compared to the one of the nondominant hand. The same is true of the great toenail.

The area that affects the change in growth of body extremities in the brain is in proximity to other areas affecting motor, speech, reading, and other abilities. It is hypothesized that whatever caused the shift in handedness also caused the problems connected with dyslexia, such as disordered dominance, perceptual difficulties, speech disorders, impairment in motor ability, or slow maturation.

This view—that the failure to establish a dominant hemisphere is the result and not the cause of congenital abnormalities of brain functions, which also express themselves in disabilities of speech, reading, and writing — is shared by other leading neurologists.

Psychologist O. L. Zangwill[9] offers three explanations for dyslexia in the same direction:

1. A partial transfer of speech to the right hemisphere may have taken place.
2. A certain proportion of children with ill-defined laterality have in addition a constitutional weakness in maturation.
3. Individuals lacking strong and consistent lateral preferences (and perhaps also those with sinistral antecedents) are particularly vulnerable to the effects of stress.

These explanations strongly suggest that children with ill-defined laterality should be protected rather than pushed ahead in their early years of schooling, being allowed to mature before the demands of an intellectual schooling press in upon them. A school entrance age of seven rather than six for such a child seems reasonable. It could prevent many of the hardships and stresses resulting from early failure due to slower maturation.

CORRECTIVE APPROACHES

Library shelves abound with literature on REMEDIAL READING. Specially trained personnel are employed by school systems to help remedy the failures of children to learn by customary methods. They provide extra drill in sight words, the alphabet, and phonics. Often this proves successful, especially if the previous teaching exposure had been inadequate or one-sided. However, for a large percentage of children this implies doing more of what they cannot do in the first place, and the more does not help!

PROGRAMMED READING MATERIALS AND COMPUTERIZED TEACHING MACHINES, once hailed as solutions to the reading problem besetting our schools, have led to disenchantment. In fact, relying too much on them was quoted in TIME[10] as a major cause of failure in "performance contracting". This was a year-long experiment (1970-71), organized by the Office of Economic Opportunity and conducted in eighteen school districts by six educational firms. The failure was particularly painful because the experiment cost $7.2 million and was expected to revolutionize teaching.

Another approach in vogue for some time has been VISUAL TRAINING, consisting mainly in the use of the tachistoscope, an apparatus for exposing figures or other visual stimuli for one-tenth or one-hundredth of a second. It is used individually or for groups in order to develop perceptual "intake" skills. Since visual accuracy and visual retention are often lacking in the beginning reader, the principal aim is to accelerate visual maturation. When used in kindergarten or first grade, it is supposed to make the children visually dominant. – Professionals do not agree on either usefulness or results.

The most recent therapeutic approach is called PERCEPTUAL MOTOR TRAINING, or BODY MANAGEMENT SKILLS. It is based on a developmental view, resulting from detailed observation of the bodily learning steps of the preschool child; how the child achieves motor control, body awareness, laterality, directionality, how he can relate to three-dimensional space and coordination of hand-eye function.–Many modern children (from either affluent or deprived environments) are lacking in early game and play experiences. The dyslexic child and the slow learner in the classroom are deficient in coordination and control. Through perceptual motor training they are helped to catch up on the steps that have been omitted or distorted, so as to restore the developmental course. – The balancing board, the jump rope, the ball for bouncing or catching are part of the regular equipment. – As an illustration, the school system of Dayton, Ohio, introduced such a program in the fall of 1965 as a preventive measure for all children in Kindergarten and First Grade. In addition, children with problems in gross motor skills, hand-eye coordination, or form perception, receive additional therapeutic help. Screening of more than 5000 children showed that 50 to 60 per cent are in need of extra help in body management area.

THE CHILD BEFORE SCHOOL AGE IN THE PAST

The child of the past–before the affluent society–walked, ran, skipped, hopped, jumped. There were ring games with singing rhythm, skipping rope, hop-scotch, etc. There was play, lots of it, with sand, mud, water or snow, and simple crude toys. The hands were active, explored, manipulated, became skillful in the doing. The imagination lived in the make-believe world. Ball play, marble games, catching, and tossing brought about the integration between hand and eye. Speech developed through imitation of human voices, through conversing, listening to bedtime stories. There was singing and even live music in the cultured home. The

130

child followed the mother around the house and imitated human work.

In brief a healthy sense-organism was developed naturally, which brought about the integration of all the senses and the maturation of the brain function.

Translated into technical language:

Gross Motor system development: Rhythm, balance, and coordination were achieved through running, hopping, skipping, games, etc.

Small Motor skills: Nimbleness and finger dexterity were developed through play, manipulation and exploration of simple toys and objects and materials of nature, and through imitation of human work.

Auditory Perception: Human voices, singing, music fostered and refined the hearing apparatus.

Perceptual Motor Match: The eye followed the exploring hand. Ball play, catching, tossing, etc. established interrelationship.

This was achieved in a natural way, before the child went to school.

THE OVERSTIMULATED CHILD OF THE AFFLUENT SOCIETY

Rare is the child today that is not exposed to the infernal noise of the average American home: the washing machine, the dishwasher, the vacuum cleaner, etc., and the blaring entertainment machines: radio, records, television. The onslaught of mechanical sounds has become the daily fare for the tender growing organism.

The infant already is hauled to the shopping center or supermarket, and exposed to a deluge of bewildering sense impressions – the loud music, the glaring lights, the pushcarts, the rushing adults, the thousands of objects.

The nursery is packed full with playthings, from the expensive mechanical toy that performs when a button is pushed, to the plastic junk from the drugstore, – Again a multitude of impressions and over-stimulation of the senses, inviting boredom and aimless wandering amid affluence. Most children cannot play any more.

Most of the hours that used to be spent in childhood games and imaginative play are now taken up watching TV. One-third to one-half of the waking hours would be a modest estimate for the majority of infants.

What does the child DO during this time? The body is limp, the hands are idle. The eyes and ears are overwhelmed by a continuous stream of pictures and sounds. Ears are deluged by noise and become desensitized. They may hear, but they do not listen; they have learned to "shut off". Eyes stare passively for hours while the camera lens does all the focusing, from distance to nearness, from left to right, from up to down. This orientation in three-dimensional space is done for the child artificially on the screen, but it is no part of HIS learning process.

The awkward body, the clumsy fingers, the lack of coordination, the inability to orient in three-dimensional space, the sluggish eye-mechanism, the tone-deaf ears, are all symptoms of the overstimulated child who has been deprived of the natural simplicity of a human environment, of childhood games and play. — But they are also the symptoms of children with reading disability.

THE TASK OF PRESCHOOL AND KINDERGARTEN

Since modern life deprives children of so much that is essential to health, well-being and organic ripening, the Preschool and Kindergarten should foster these very qualities. They should provide a peaceful human environment and not add to the dilemma of our technical age.

There should be childhood games, singing and ring games, rhythmic nursery rhymes, story telling, live music, skipping, hopping, outdoor play with sand, mud, sticks, and simple toys to foster exploration and imagination. They should cultivate in children the lost art of how to play, to use the body to establish coordination, rhythm, and balance; to restore the capacity to listen, to converse, to sing. Ordinary common sense dictates this direction for therapeutic work.

TV and record players, so common in preschools, only add to the detrimental overstimulation of the senses.

Why should infants learn to read? All evidence points to the simple fact that five-year-olds cannot distinguish directions, have not yet reached Gestalt perception. To force reading programs on the immature organism is to ignore the process of maturation. Besides, children that are exposed to a learning task before they are ready for it, not only fail to learn the task, but also learn from the experience of failure to fear, dislike, and avoid it.

Let us have artistic, imaginative, kindly, and motherly adults for our young, and protect them from the reading instructors.

The young child before school does not need a "headstart", it needs a "body start"! It needs rhythm, balance, coordination, finger skills, articulate speech, and perceptive eyes and ears!

The preschool years are most important years. They lay the foundation for health, happiness, and successful learning.

Much of the agony of failure, the drudgery and expense of remedial work later on, could be prevented if only we paid attention to the needs of the developing child.

We have to re-evaluate our priorities and stop the myopic too-much-too-soon syndrome, before the damage becomes irreparable.

READING IN A WALDORF OR RUDOLF STEINER SCHOOL: THE ROLE OF THE CREATIVE TEACHER

It would be abstract to describe our methods of teaching without taking into account the role of the teacher in our schools. Since we use no textbooks, no primers, no basal readers, no ready-made visual aids, the teacher himself and his training is of utmost importance.

After college years and the acquisition of degrees, the adult, wanting to teach, must first overcome the impoverished, juiceless, intellectual, abstract adult approach which is a side effect of his schooling. He must learn to see again with the richness of a child's eyes, the power of a child's imagination, and to be able to speak to these needs.

He must be trained in blackboard skills, to be able to conjure up an illustrative picture in colored chalk in front of the children. Since he is also a performing artist, the appealing colorful telling of stories, of describing things and events, the art of communicating to children must be learned. The monotony of the classroom drone is prime target of attack!

Our training of teachers is essentially an artistic one; speech, gesture, painting and drawing, modeling. and music take up a large proportion. Learning to observe and to work with the phases of child development, and practical skills make up the rest.

A teacher must be able to excite a class, but have also the skills to quiet it down again. He must be able to reach the visile and the audile child, the precocious one and the slow bloomer, the active and the passive one, the damaged child, or the shy one.

He must learn to observe and to know intimately each child entrusted to his care, the strength and talents, but also the weaknesses. He will have no test scores to rely on. Through parent evenings, interviews, and visits in the child's home he will become acquainted with each child's background.

This total involvement of the creative teacher with his responding group (and the children do respond with attachment and love) is not broken up at the end of the school year.

No responsible adult could possibly do the same limited work over and over again and maintain the original commitment, interest, and enthusiasm. It does not work in industry at the assembly line, where employees and workers suffer from the deadly monotony of small sections of routine work. In order to overcome the disinterest and carelessness, the frequent absenteeism, the restlessness and change of jobs, industries all over the world are trying new approaches at giving up the assembly-line, widening the scope, interest and participation of the workers.

In our schools the homeroom teacher stays with the same group of children, ideally through all the years of elementary schooling. He does not start all over again every year. He becomes a specialist with one group of children, not one small section of the educational process. He is responsible and accountable for his work. With this responsibility comes also the freedom from an authority figure hovering over him or telling him what to do. The teachers in our schools are autonomous.

METHODS: FROM THE CONCRETE TO THE ABSTRACT

The capacity to read fluently, that is to read any book with suitable content, is a skill achieved by children at individual moments in their lives. A few may reach it already in the first grade, others in 5th or 6th grade, with the majority attaining it in between. When it happens, if it happens organically, nothing can stop them. They would rather read than go out for recess, and the book may be their secret absorption during lessons or homework assignments.

If it occurs too early, when the vocabulary is not rich enough to master good prose, there is the danger that the child may run out of enthusiasm and become a reader who does not want to read.

The Waldorf schools are not reading-centered in the younger grades, that is, reading is NOT the avenue to learning. We never teach it as an isolated skill but as integral part of the language arts, together with subject matter, speaking, recitation, and writing. It is not divorced from speech. The slow bloomer, the late reader, the audile child, are not deprived but aided in their development.

We use no primers, no basal readers. All visual aids are created by the teacher with colored chalk on the blackboard. The children make their own manuscript readers. They use large bound notebooks (9x12) with unlined white paper and broad beeswax crayons both for writing and for illustrations. These carefully created notebooks become treasured possessions of the children.

We lead from the concrete to the abstract,
from large to small,
from speaking and recitation to writing and then to reading,
from involvement of the whole organism to the sole use of the eye muscles,
from all sensory avenues to the visual one alone.

This organic sequence corresponds to the nature of the young child, and it seems utterly natural to anyone who has ever taught this way, or has even pondered it.

Now to the individual steps in the primary grades.

We first teach the capital letters of the alphabet and their phonetic sounds. We do not begin with the abstract symbols, but derive each letter from a concrete picture: we treat the letter pictographically. The teacher will tell an absorbing story and then draw a concrete illustration from this story on the blackboard; the children will draw this also in their books, usually simultaneously. Out of this picture one figure emerges, a swan, a fish, or a dragon. The next drawing would be a stylized swan which then becomes almost abstracted into the capital S, perhaps a colored beak being left as a memory-aid. The children learn to connect the first sound of "swan" with the abstracted symbol. They will find other words that begin with the S-sound. In this way the symbol is married to a sound, not to a letter name. They may walk the form of the letter on the floor, write it in the air, draw it on the blackboard, and then finally copy it in large size into their books, with one letter filling a whole page. Usually the teacher makes an alliterative rhythmical sentence or verse for recitation in connection with this sound and symbol. This may become part of a growing daily repertoire of speech exercises, which are recited vigorously. The children may draw large S forms into the air while reciting. – If a consonant has several sound values, as happens in English, this is also carefully included in the story, in the abstracted symbol, and in the speech exercise. (Many teachers have found that the vowel sound and symbol introduction in the first grade is sufficient, and have left their more intricate variations in English for second and third grade work in phonics and spelling.)

Later on, after all the letters with their sounds have been carefully introduced and vigorously practiced in speech and "reading" (daily brief practice in translating the symbols into sounds), the alliterative rhythmic speech-exercises and familiar brief songs or poems are used as first written sentences or poems. First on the blackboard in colored chalk and then read in chorus.

136

This is always a very joyful experience. Young children love to "read" things they know already, and at this stage rhythm and rhyme are more appealing than prose. The children then copy it from the blackboard into their manuscript readers, usually separating the individual words by small yellow stars (spacing has to be learned). The manuscript readers with growing content are used over and over again, with the children vying for turns in oral reading. They are encouraged to follow the words with their fingers, and to enunciate vigorously.

Alongside with speech, recitation, form in space, gesture, and symbol, there is regular practice in AUDITORY PERCEPTION. This can be done in the form of delightful games that the children love. They may all stand on their chairs and earn their seats through individual answers. The teacher says a word and each child has to enunciate the first sound or initial consonant. With practice, every child becomes surefooted (or sure-eared!). This is then applied to the last sound, or final consonant of a word. Later it is extended to the first and the last sound, then to words beginning with two consonants, and finally to as many sounds as they can distinguish in a word, which then leads to the writing of words. They can print (we are still in the capital phase) the names of all the children in the classroom, the names of animals, plants, and trees. There are endless possibilities for active (sometimes a bit noisy) work of translating sounds and words into symbols.

On this level, the reversal problems that plague the young child with the traditional method do not exist. Among the capital letters it is mostly M and W that could cause confusion; but if the teacher chooses a wavy form for W (out of wave, water, wind), there will be no reversals.

During the second grade, colored pencils replace the crayons for writing. Now the small letters are introduced. Again, not as abstract symbols, but metamorphosed out of the capitals. As children resemble their parents, sometimes a lot, sometimes a little, and some not at all, thus it is with the small letters in relation to their capitals. Some are just half-size: such as O-o, S-s, W-w, C-c, etc. Others resemble them; "b" has dropped one wing of the Butterfly (or whatever the original picture was). How did a

"G" have a child that looks like "g"? If the "G" was originally a Golden Goose, the baby "g" made a clockwise somersault, with the head under water and the tail sticking out. This may be hard to see for adults, but it is obvious to children. — Humor, active participation, imagination, and joy, are vital to learning. They also aid the memory, much more so than the neutral experience through a printed reader.

Phonic drill can be the dullest drudgery, with disinterested children making minimal efforts. But if it is done through writing, which is much easier for children than reading, and if the teacher has imagination and ingenuity, the drudgery turns into joy and lively participation. Children love to be called out to write on the blackboard, or to write words into the air. Who can change hat into mat? into cat? into fat? into rat? At this stage, nonsense rhymes delight children.

Aesop's fables are brief, humorous, relevant, and of moral substance. They form the main content for telling, discussing, illustrating, writing, and reading. — Towards the end of the second year the children are sufficiently far along to retell them in writing on their own. Most will do it still phonetically, with the teacher as authority as to the final form of spelling (after the individual attempts, not before!). Then the pupils read out loud to the class their individual versions.

In the third grade the stories of the Old Testament are told, retold, written, and then read orally. Some of the beautiful passages are copied from the blackboard and are later read daily in chorus, or individually (orally) from their own books. — Script is metamorphosed out of the printed letters. — Grammar is taught, with verbs, adjectives, nouns, etc: e.g. the verb as an action word: what can stones do? what can plants do? what can animals do? what can I do? with the feet? with the hands? with the head? Discussion and action precede the writing, which precedes the reading. — Spelling of new words is carefully practiced, because they are needed for writing. At this stage, the longer the word, the more loved. After they have been written on the board, analysed, their regularity or their spelling peculiarity duly noted, the children like to cover their eyes and rattle off the letter sequence.

To strengthen the visual memory, they can be spelled backwards in the same manner. The children do this with enthusiasm, always favoring the longest words.

These are the highlights from the course of teaching language arts, of which reading is one aspect, in the primary grades. And to emphasize it again: reading is the most difficult, the most abstract, and therefore the last one in the learning sequence.

From the viewpoint of DEVELOPMENT AND READINESS SKILLS, mention should be made of some of the other subjects that are taught alongside the language arts, beginning with the first grade.

Every boy and girl learns how to KNIT, with large needles and colorful wool. They knit scarves (and some even sweaters) in the first grade. Clumsy fingers are made skillful in a beloved, meaningful activity. In the second grade they crochet, and later on they learn to sew and embroider. — Besides lots of singing, every child learns to PLAY A MUSICAL INSTRUMENT. In the first grade we teach the wooden recorder or block-flute to all children, first through imitation of the teacher's fingers, then through their own musical memory, that is, by ear. Most children will take up a second, more complicated instrument later on. — A favorite subject for all children is FORM DRAWING; geometric forms are created with radiantly colored beeswax crayons. Children are eager to draw stars, 5, 6, 7, 8, or even 10-pointed ones. The basic freehand constructions have to be shown and learned gradually, but then there are endless possibilities for individual skills and artistic variations. Children will work for hours, creating colored stars, introducing all kinds of intricate design elements to fill the whole page. Or again, turning a small star in the center of a page into an ever-expanding flower form. If these children were given Gestalt-perception tests, most of them would bring in outstanding scores. The talents vary greatly, but all children are aided in their development through Gestalt-creation! — Also beginning with first grade, all children are taught EURYTHMY, a new form of movement, where to the accompaniment of live music, children practice rhythm, balance, and coordination. They may form geometric shapes in space, circles, triangles, squares, spirals or stars, whereby orientation in three-dimensional space is greatly aided. — TWO FOREIGN LANGUAGES (French and German in most schools) are taught from first grade on, first through imitation of songs, singing games, rhymes, poems and conversation.

In the fourth grade, besides reading their mother tongue, all students learn to read music (through writing) and two foreign languages.

The path to reading is slower than in other schools, but it is infinitely broader, richer, and more vital.

Giving children time to mature at individual rates of development, engaging them in varied activities of learning, unfolding other human skills besides reading, providing a rich curriculum, is the path of an education that uses and furthers creative childhood forces, — instead of working against them.

1 National Observer, Nov. 4, 1972; "Companies Teach Workers Reading"

2 Jerome Hellmuth, ed., EDUCATIONAL THERAPY, Special Child Publications of the Seattle Sequin School, 1966, vol. I, p. 63.

3 Marianne Frostig, THE DEVELOPMENTAL PROGRAM IN VISUAL PERCEPTION, Follett Educational Co., Chicago 1966.

4 Newell C. Kephart, THE SLOW LEARNER IN THE CLASSROOM, Charles E. Merrit Publishing Co., 1971.

5 Harold A. Solan, "PERCEPTUAL TESTING AND TRAINING METHODS USED IN THE PRIMARY GRADES", N. J. Journal of Optometry, May-June, 1968.

6 Marshall McLuhan, THE GUTENBERG GALAXY, University of Toronto Press, 1962.

7 In R. Crosby, THE WAYSIDER, Delacorte Press, New York, 1968.

8 In CHILDREN WITH READING PROBLEMS, G. Natchez, ed., Basic Books, N.Y. 1968.

9 John Money, ed., READING DISABILITY, Johns Hopkins Press, 1962.

10 Time, Feb. 14, 1972: "Result of a Test: F."

The Socially Disadvantaged
A Rationale And New Concept Of Human Development

Earl J. Ogletree

Volumes have been written on the socially disadvantaged. The literature has adequately described their
familial and socio-economic mileau and the efforts of
poverty and deprivation on their experiences, language
and cognitive development. Two theories related to the
disadvantaged have evolved: The first is the "deprivation
theory" which stresses the importance of an enriched
environment, during the early years, on the cognitive
and emotional development of the child. " The second is
"the cumulative intellectual deficit theory, which points
out that the child's (emotional and intellectual) deficit
increases as he passes from grade to grade. "[1]
Many of these children are found to be functionally
retarded in language and the ability to do the abstract
thinking required to read, write and count. Allen states,
"These children and adults are, in the main, at the
borderline and mildly retarded levels of deviation in
measured intelligence".[2] This "...deficit tends to
increase cumulatively and to lead to permanent retardation".[3]
However, no one has been able to fully explain "how"
and "why" (the cause for) the diminishing organismic
development of the disadvantaged child from a restricted,
impoverished environment. The author will attempt to
provide such a rationale as to the "how" and "why" of
the resulting influence of deprivation by means of a
theory of human development which includes the new concept of bioplasmic forces, etheric or growth forces on
which the Russians and others have been doing a great
deal of research.[4,5] Prior to this we must establish a
theoretical foundation in child development, an examination of normal growth patterns. The author will attempt
to explicate the stages in child growth by means of the
concept of controlled-movement over locomotive, speech
and cognitive development.

ORIGINAL MANUSCRIPT, 1973.

Controlled-Movement

Motor control: The first premise we begin with is that human development is a process by which the human being gains greater and greater voluntary control over himself, i. e., his motor, speech and cognitive development. For example, the new born baby has no voluntary controlled movements; his movements are chaotic. Soon after birth, control of movement develop in a descending order from the head downward.

The growing child begins with movement control of the eyes, the mount, the entire face, descending over the neck, which gradually allows the child to turn and lift its head. Then voluntary control of movement gradually descends further to the arms and hands; here the child develops the ability to co-ordinate eye-and-hand movement (hold hands), and by the third month to reach for objects. By the third month, the child rolls over, by the fifth month pulls to sit, and at five and a half month sits without support. By the first year of life voluntary movement control has descended yet further enabling the child to stand alone and walk well. In a period of a year, he has developed a minimal level of voluntary control over his motor system. [6,7]

Language control: Accompanying this descent in movement-control of motor development is the development of language. Lennenberg states:

> Since motor development is one of the
> most important indices of maturation,
> it is not unreasonable to assume that
> language development too, is related
> to physical growth and development.
> It is also interesting that language
> development correlates better with
> motor development than it doew with
> chronological age. [8]

The child gains gradual mastery over the finer muscles of mouth, lips tongue and larynx. From the first months he increasingly gains control over his speech organization through the stages of cooing, babbling, saying(imitation of words), naming, then speech or talking.

Just as there is a descent of voluntary control of movement during the first year of life from the head through the trunk to the limbs, there is also a descent of language development of grammatical sequence, from the cognitive through the affective (emotional) to the active limbs or psychomotor realm. The noun corresponds to the head (cognitive) the adjective to the feeling realm - the heart etc., (affective) and the verb to the active limbs (psychomotor). Table I indicates this sequence of language or grammatical sequential development. [9]

Table I

	Age	Nouns	Adjectives	Verbs
Cognitive	1.3	100%		
Affective	1.8	78%	22%	
Psychomotor	2.0	63%	14%	23%

At each level of motor development the child reaches a certain level of motor-movement control or maturation before language develops. It is a kind of controlled motor readiness. It is also known that when the child is struggling for motor-movement control, there is a temporary retardation in language development. Once the child masters a certain phase of motor development the rate of language development accelerates. There is a transformation of voluntary motor control, i.e., from the movement control of locomotion to an extension and perfection of these movements into the more refined and differentiated movements of speaking.

Cognitive: Locomotion and speech are control motor movements. Speaking is a more subtle and finer control of the muscels of the speech organization than is motor locomotion. Thinking or cognition can be though of as a kind of control over one's mind, as the mind shifts from one cognitive level to the next. Piaget has shown that children exhibit stages of mental abilities as they mature. Their minds evolve through a series of intellectual stages as they progress from early childhood through adolescence. Piaget has classified these into four main stages: [10]

I.   Sensory-Motor Stage (0-2 years)
II. Preoperational Stage (2-7 years)
III. Concrete Operational (7-12 years)
IV. Formal Operational Stage (12-15 & over)

This transition is the result of the child mastering his locomotion and speech organization to a certain level of maturity, i.e., gaining experiences. As the child gains voluntary movement control over locomotion and speech, he also gains control over his cognitive processes. Therefore, could not thinking be considered a more refined and subtle form of movement? Unlike locomotion ans speech there are no muscles involved..., but movement from percept, mental image and fantasy, to concept and idea. Modern psychological and neurological theories consider the brain to be a kind of muscle, to develop it must be exercised. There are certain maturational indices (65% physical maturity) of the development of the brain when learning of a language is optimal. After the brain has reached physical maturation, language acquisition becomes more difficult.[11] (This may not be a casual correlation, but it does indicate the dynamic nature and optimal developmental characteristics of the brain in relation to language development).

Another indication of the dynamic aspects of thinking as movement is the functional basis of the electroencephalograph, which is used to measure noise levels and electro-wave patterns of the brain. The electroencephalograph electrodes placed on the scalp of the subject measures $1/1,000,000$ of a volt. The recorded noise level of the brain is about 100 times that potential.[12] The brain also has different rhythms, measured in cycles per second--delta waves (deep sleep), .5 to 3.5 cycles; theta waves (dominant in younger children), 4 to 7 cycles; alpha waves (dominant in adults) 8-13 cycles; and beta waves (exist in states of anxiety and psychological instability), 14-30 cycles.[13,14] Recent research in biofeedback and autogenic training has shown that a person can control the rhythms of the brain, muscle tension, temperature of body, headaches, hypertension/(blood pressure), etc.[15]

To explicate this point further, let us examine the act or process of cognition. For example, when we are attempting to find a solution to a problem we are searching for the correct concept or idea out of the rather vast storehouse of concepts, ideas and experiences we already possess. We labor cognitively to find the proper connection or link between our knowledge and the solution. We sort, select, reshuffle our old concepts. We seek new ideas from other sources to reinforce and refine our knowledge. And the conditions we want for thinking or the sorting out process are quiet and solitude. This type of concentrative thinking does not take place automatically nor effortlessly, but it requires contemplative effort and cognitive energy. Mental fatigue is just as real as physical fatigue. In both cases energy is expended. In physical energy is expended through covert activity or movement. This hypothesis that thinking is movement is confirmed by Piaget's stages of cognitive development. Piaget's three major stages of development are preoperational, concrete and formal operational and can be summarized as follows:

Table II

Piaget's Stages of Development
    Pre-operational (2-7 years)
1. Cannot conserve or hold mental images.
2. Thinking is non-reversible.
3. Thinking is perceptual bound (bound to physical body - the senses).
4. Cannot deal with variables or changes.
5. Little voluntary control over thinking (non-operational).

    Concrete-Operational (7-14 years)
1. Can conserve or hold mental images.
2. Thinking is reversible.
3. Thinking bound to inner-life, emotionally affectively oriented.
4. Thinking is imagery and pictorial, not symbolic.
5. Needs concrete props to support thinking, such as solving.
6. Can solve problems with transformations, variables or changes.

7. Has greater voluntary control thinking-
(thinking is semi-operational).

Formal Operational (14-... years)

1. Solve problems using symbols and pure concepts, without outer concrete props.
2. He can hypothesize solutions using propositional logic.
3. Thinking is more objective, free of emotional life.
4. Thinking is abstract, flexible and mobile-grouping classification, etc.
5. He can think about his own thinking for the first time.
6. He has greater voluntary control over his thinking processes. (Thinking is fully operational.)

The theme of increased voluntary control over cognitive processes is the thread of transmutation through the three stages. Each succeeding stage depicts an increased independent and higher level of cognition, a greater and greater manipulative power and control over thinking. The terms pre-operational and operational signify this. The terms are cogent and relevant; they accurately describe the cognitive abilities at the different levels. Pre-operational means the inability to operate one's thinking. It is nonoperational, and noncontrollable. His physical and experiential maturity are not developed sufficiently at the preoperational level to give him the power to control his own thinking processes. As shown, at this stage, the child cannot conserve, reverse his thinking or deal with variables. Whereas at the concrete operational level, his thinking is operational, i.e., he can control it to a certain degree in terms of conservation and reversibility and the ability to handle variables. The same pattern applies to the formal operational level when the youngster's thinking is more abstract, symbolic, logical, and most importantly more mobile, flexible and free. He can hypothesize.

Piaget also alludes to thinking as movement, when he

speaks of operations. He states:

> Learning is possible only when there
> is active assimilation... To under-
> stand the development of knowledge,
> we must start with an idea which is
> central...the idea is operations...
> to know an object is to act on it. To
> know is to modify, to transform the
> object, and to understand the process
> of this transformation... An operation
> is thus the essence of knowledge; it
> is an interiorized action which modifies
> the object of knowledge... In other
> words, it is a set of actions (mental
> movements) modifying the object and
> enabling the knower to get at the
> structures of the transformation. [16]

Summary of Controlled Movement

The author has advanced the theory of voluntary control of movement through the stages of locomotive, speech
and cognitive development. Thinking is a more subtle
form of movement. One could say that the child's mental
maturity and acquisition of experiences are dependent on
his ability to gain voluntary control over his movements
(in all realms of development) and hence his environment.
Voluntary-control of movement is an integral part of
learning. In essence, voluntary control over thinking
processes is the definition of readiness.

Ilg and Ames have done extensive studies on the
maturational readiness of children. [17] They have discovered, as have others, that there is an orderly pattern
of developmental maturation out of which certain kinds of
learning and performance fall along an age-readiness
scale. This included the capacity to write names, letters,
addresses; numbers one-twenty, complete "Incomplete
man figure, " naming of animals in 60 seconds, and
copying geometric patterns (horizontal lines, circle, cross,
square, triangle, divided rectangle and a diamond). [18]
Their most interesting task was the geometric test in

that the ability to copy geometric figures fell along a age-readiness scale in the foregoing sequence. This development depends upon maturation, not experience. [19] For example, some children who can easily draw a cross (age 3), or copy a circle (age 2 1/2 or square (age 4), cannot draw a diamond (age 7), but the reverse is not true. Also a child cannot be trained or forced to copy a particular geometric figure prior to the stage of readiness to do so. The intensive training of a five year old in the specific act of drawing a diamond will not only be difficult but ineffective. But at age seven, no training is necessary. This developmental sequence of performance capacities, which are transitional stages and not distinct steps, emerge as a form instinctive motoric development --reflected in evolutionary geometric patterns or forms. The following is an outline of geometric patterns copied at sequential age levels.

Table I

Age in yrs	Geometric Pattern	Physiological or Psychological Characteristics
10 mo. or less	horizontal scribble	child lies in horizontal position
1.2	selective horizontal isolated strokes	begins to stand and walk
1.6-	vertical lines and	
2.0	struggles with circle, scribbling, experimenting	mastering climbing and walking (transition from sensory-motor to pre-operational thinking.)
2.3	draws distinct horizontal line	walk, running, speech development
2.6	draws two or more parallel strokes	continuous motoric and speech development
3.0	draws a cross draws a single distinct circle for the first time, but not mastered	child says"I"-first person, becomes aware of self as apart from his environment

4	draws square	hops, skips, jumps, etc.
5	draws a triangle and oblique lines	continued mastery over locomotion
6	rectangle and diagonal	continued mastery over locomotion
7	draws or copies diamond	change of teeth, enhanced mental capacities (pre-operational to concrete)

Piaget's study of geometric operations in young children showed they draw topological structures before the projective and the projective forms before the metric. He says the geometric sequence corresponds "... to something in the natural thought of children."[20] In light of the voluntary movement-control theory--the child needs less control to draw topological forms (circular) than projective forms. The metric forms require the greatest amount of intellectual movement-control. The phenomenon of controlled-movement, which can be extended into other performance spheres, is dependent on the maturation of the whole organism.

Maturation: Maturational-readiness is based on the phenomenon of organismic growth (a coined phrase for all available growth ages at a given point in the child's development); the growth patterns such as height, age, mental age, dental age, etc. of a child tend to cluster around a mean.

> ...i.e., that the various attributes in an individual tend to cluster about a center of gravity of growth of that individual and that the freedom to vary is restricted. This detailed support has been worked out, but the manuscript has not been printed.[21]

Therefore, maturation is a complex organismic pattern which reaches levels or plateaus of development. It is from this orderly sequence of maturation that natural development and the capacity for certain kinds of learning and performance unfold and fall along an age or performance scale. Learning is integrally related to organismic growth patterns. Piaget states, the unfoldment of learning capacities are:

> ...tied to the whole process of
> embryogenesis... (which)ends in
> adulthood... In other words,
> development is the essential pro-
> cess and each element of learning
> occurs as a function of total
> development. [22]

Studies and research in child development have long known the simultaneous relationship between physical maturation and intellectual development. Few researchers have ventured to ascribe a cause-effect relationship between these two phenomena. The characteristics of the stages of physical development and the stages of cognitive development such as those developed by Piaget have been fully described. But we do not know how physical maturation, cognitive development, and readiness are related and unfold.

Let us examine the physical-mental development correlation as it occurs at the pre-operational - concrete operational transitional period at age seven years. Ilg and Ames conducted a study on the rate of teething in relation to school readiness with first grade children. [23] They found that those children (96%) who were ahead of schedule in teething were definitely ready for and could profit from academic school experiences. Those children who were behind schedule in teething (54%) should have repeated (22% did repeat) the first grade. Of those whose teething was both ahead and behind schedule 64% would have benefited by repeating the grade (14% did repeat). Ilg and Ames reported that subsequent to teething the children seemed to have reached a higher level of mental development. They ascribe an indirect cause and effect relationship between teeting and mental development.

What does this mean in terms of the transition between the pre-operational and concrete operational cognitive stages? Teething signifies that the brain has reached about 95% of its development, the head about two-thirds adult proportion, and now the child is ready for academic learning. He has had a change in mental development; he has crossed the bridge from the preoperational to the concrete levels of thinking. He now has greater control over his thinking, it is free; it is less sense bound.

At the transitional period between the concrete and formal operational, ages 13 - 15 years. Nisbet found that the attainment of puberty correlated with increased achievement on intellectual and academic achievement tests. [24] That is, adolescents who had attained puberty performed better on intellectual tests than adolescents who were still at the pre-puberty stage, although the subjects were the same ages.

Implications for the Socially Disadvantaged

Socially disadvantaged: One of the most cogent conse-quences of the environment on the socially disadvantaged child is his slower rate of transition from the pre-opera-tional to the concrete and from the concrete to formal operational. Almy tested the conservation ability of inner city second graders using Piaget's liquid test ("the establishment of identity when he sees the liquid in one vessel poured into another of a different shape"). [25] She found that "... only 23% of the second graders were able to conserve consistently," an indication that the transi-tion rate from the preoperational to the concrete opera-tional transpired at a slower rate. Ausubel thinks that the transition rate takes place more slowly and hence com-pletely at both transitional levels. [26] These findings were confirmed by the author who studied one-hundred first and second grade inner-city children in terms of teething, age level and conservation. The author found that their average age was 6.7 years and 80% had begun teething, only 19% were able to conserve. [27] This would indicate a general retardation in maturational and organismic devel-opment. In terms of school readiness, Ilg and Ames call these children "reality-bound."

> Such children abstract poorly and
> find it difficult to learn through
> the more usual methods of teaching. [28]

The existing intellectual deficit is compounded by the fact that they are less able to profit from new experiences. They are intellectually overwhelmed by the exposure to new learning which exceeds their experiential background and level of cognitive readiness.

Jenson defines educability to mean "... the ability to learn school subjects by means of classroom instruction."[29] To be educable the child must possess such cognitive skills as,

1) Voluntary control of attention,
2) The perception of order,
3) Self-initiated rehearsal of newly acquired behavior,
4) Self-reinforcement for successful performance.

In short, learning is possible only where there is active assimilation. The child must act upon knowledge to experience it.

> Learning is not a passive absorption
> but an active response ... content
> acquired through manipulation
> (cognitive manipulation - self-rehearsal)
> does not seem to evaporate so rapidly,
> he experiences it).[30]

The socially disadvantaged child seems to lack these operations. He is unable to act upon the intellectual learnings, hence the cumulative deficit is a result of the slower rate of organismic growth.

Organismic growth-rate patterns exist in varying degrees. The rate of development can be forced or coerced. A positive, propitious environment is required to attain full organismic growth. Anderson states,

> Man is not only a product of his
> environment, for in a real sense
> man is also a victim of the environment.[31]

In the case of the socially disadvantaged, the environment dominates and presses the child, so to speak. In fact, it suppresses his development. The environmental press can be such a dominating force in terms of dissonante, hyperstimulation, chaos, poor nutrition, lack of social or human intercourse, or love, etc., that in extreme cases simulated idiopathic hypopituitarism (physical, emotional and cognitive entropism) can result.[32, 33, 34]

Powell, et. al. found that emotional disturbances in children as a result of abnormal home environments resulted in growth failure.[35] When these children were removed from the home and placed in a convalescent hospital, they demonstrated remarkable growth acceleration without receiving growth hormones or agents. The height ages of the 13 children, ranging from age 3.3 to 11.5 years, were 30 to 66 percent of the chronological age. In all but three cases their bone age was commensurate with their height age, both were underdeveloped. The social responses of the children were immature; some were withdrawn and exhibited little verbal communication. The authors indicated emotional factors, malabsorption, malnutrition and a poor parent-child relationship as possible causes of the retarded growth. The authors add:

> The behavior of these institutionalized children... appears to be an abberation of the normal developmental pattern, which usually make their appearance at one or two years of age--, i.e., speech, feeding oneself, toilet training and imitation of interpersonal relations. The onset of symptoms and growth retardation began at the same time (in those 13 children). The first two years of life appear to be the most critical in establishing a proper parent-child relationship.[36]

As a result of change of environment there was a consistent improvement in personality and speech development. They appeared happier, less withdrawn and more open for interpersonal relationships. Growth - rate in height ranged 0.5 to 0.8 inches per month, averaging 0.65 inches per month. (The average normal rate of growth is 0.2 inches per month.) This study showed that accelerated growth can be achieved without the administration of exogenous growth hormones when children are placed in compatible and propitious environments. The authors stated:

> Therapy in the present study consisted of placement in a good convalescent hospital (with no special medication, medical or psychiatric therapy). This improvement during hospitalization again points up the adverse effect of the home environment... The results suggest that treatment of this type for short stature requires removal from the home until the abnormal parent-child relationship can be improved. [37]

In England they found that working class (lower-socio-economic) youngsters twelve years of age were as much as 1 1/4 inches shorter than their middle class peer at age fourteen. This difference applied to other physiological and psychological measurements as well. [38]

As shown, the environment plays an important role in the growth process. Anderson makes a comparison with plants:

> Given a cotton seed from the same stock, the environment plays a determining role in the growth process. In Minnesota with its cool nights and short seasons, one cannot bring out the best there is in cotton no matter how good the seed. [39]

However, we know that the morphological development of man is less effected by the environment than plants. Nevertheless the potential of the genotype is expressed through the phenotype which is influenced by the quality of the environment. Hence, growth is based on the phenotype. Ausubel states:

> New growth... always proceeds from the existing phenotype... from the actualized capacity rather than from potentialities inherent in the genotype... If as a result of a consistently deprived environment during the early formative years, superior intellectual endowment is not actualized, the attained deficit in functional capacity

significantly limits the extent to which
later environment stimulation, even if
normal in quantity, can increase the
rate of cognitive growth. (The relative
growth rate of intelligence remains
constant). [40]

Of course, there are different levels of environmental
domination; each youngster will respond differently and
be effected differently. It is evident that a low quality
environment will affect the rate and quality of the organismic patterns of growth. Anderson sees this phenomena
as psychological and physiological entropy, the degradation of psychological/biological energy levels. The result
is a slowing down in organismic growth because of the
decrease in biological energy. In this same light Ausubel
points out that the plasticity of human intelligence
decreases with age, and with the socially disadvantaged
the plasticity of development diminishes at a faster rate,
compared with children raised in more propitious environments. The disadvantaged child seems to become fixed
in a cognitive or learning pattern earlier, and is less
flexible and open for new experiences. In other words,
his development is incomplete in terms of his full potential. He is retarded, his development arrested prematurely.

How and why does the environment have such a deliterious effect? Let us now examine several theories of
human development and as well as a new theory or model
of development.

Bioplasmic-Organismic Theory of Development

It is quite clear that our conventional theories and
views of human development offer little explanation as to
why and how the environment effects human developmental
process. Kagan's article on the isolation effects on
Guatemalan children and Kaspar Hauser's article, included
in this volume, seem to contradict all the known rules of
human development. We have volumes of information on
the characteristics (definitions, facts) on the growing
child at the various age and developmental levels. However, we are little aware of the process of human develop-

ment, e. g. , how the child acquires speech, how thinking
develops, what is thinking, etc. We have little knowledge
of the process of development. We don't have a wholistic
view of human development, e. g. , in the same way we
have a working theory of how the automobile engine functions or how the electrical motor operates.

We need to view the complexities of human growth as
wholistic processes, and physical and mental development
in a cause and effect relationship. We need a more comprehensive theory.   A number of theories have evolved
to explicate man's biological and mental nature. There
is the mechanistic theory in which life is explained in
terms of operations of the laws of chemistry and physics.[41]
The mind is a function of the environmental forces acting
upon it. An opposite view is the vitalistic theory.[42] Here
the physiological organism is operated by an invisible
force - a vital force. The life force, or "elan vital" is
nonmaterial, nonmechanical and nonchemical. Vital force
theory is regarded as old fashion because of its inability
to explain the full range of the behaviors of man and to
rationalize how the nonmaterial mind can affect a material
body and vise versa. This theory wandered too far into the
realm of philosophy to be a viable scientific explanation of
human development. The theory does not go far enough.
Neither of the foregoing theories provides an adequate
explanation of the life processes of human development.
(The intent here is to give a view of the various positions,
not to explicate the criticisms of each theory.) A third
theory is the organismic theory or the biological theory.
The biologist's view of human processes or the organismic theory focuses on the life forms of wholes--total
growth of the organism and it interacts with the environment.[43]   The study of physical and mental development and
their relationship are basic tenets of this theory. However, the organismic theory rejects the mechanistic view
because of its reliance on a cumulative-functional theory
of external causes and reflex arcs. The vitalistic theory
is rejected because of its nebulous, invisible life forces.
Like the other theories, the organismic model also fails
to indicate the how and why of human processes. None of

the mentioned models appear to offer a rational and practical explanation of human development.

One of the problems appears to be the attempt to use and apply natural scientific theories which explain inorganic life very well to organic life--the world of the living. It is becoming increasingly clear that the forces that are operative in the inanimate world cannot explain the phenomena of life. What is needed is a different model or theory of human development, based on more dynamic and living concepts, processes found in the human being. Therefore, the purpose here is to offer a viable rationale for a cause-effect relationship between physical and mental development as it unfolds in the growing child based on the newly, rediscovered phenomena of bioplasmic forces by Russian scientist and the vital or life forces undergirding the Chinese art of medicine--acupuncture. Let us now examine such a theory or model of human development.

Models or hypotheses are merely perceptual aids to explain phenomenological relationships, to gain a fuller understanding. As the models become more refined and differentiated, they become the criteria by which we test and judge the accuracy of our reasoning and comprehension. The primary purpose of the model is to provide a sufficient comprehension of the subject to facilitate inquiry and investigation as well as the possible validation of the model. This approach has been used to develop theories and laws about the physical world. After all we have the atomic theory or model to explain our chemical-physical world, the law of gravity and the laws of electricity (Ohm's law), to explain physical phenomena. These laws were once models. Once they consistently explicate a wider and wider range of phenomena, they become laws. The author will use the same approach to explicate his model--the bioplasmic-organismic model.

Nature of Growth or Energy Forces:

Let us look at a phenonmenon that we see and experience, but of which we are not fully cognizant. That phenomenon is the process of growth. Organisms grow and develop. We know the child grows from the head downwards; plants grow upward. Each germinates from a sperm 'beta body', 'conter body', 'pre-physical body', to name a few.[44]

They further report that Russian scientists announced their discovery in 1969, based upon scores of experiments done on living plants, animals and human beings using sophisticated electronic equipment. They concluded that the energy, etheric or biological-plasma body consisted of,

> Some sort of elementary plasma like
> constellation made of ionized, excited
> electrons, protons and possibly other
> particles. But at the same time, this
> energy body is not just particles. It is
> not a chaotic system. It is a whole
> unified organism in itself. It acts as a
> unit...and as a unit gives off its own
> electromagnetic fields and is the basis
> of biological fields.[45]

Ostrander and Schroeder comment that their investigations showed:

> Within the last few years, may scientists
> in many countries* have postulated that
> there is some kind of matrix, some kind of
> invisible organizing pattern inherent
> in living things.[46]

American biologists have been aware of a type of electrical system in animals, known as the electrometabolic field. The organism is considered to be a field of forces, with overlapping and interacting subfields. They found an association, not necessarily cause and effect relationship, between changes in metabolism and electrical field changes in the body.[47] This is as far as the theory was developed.

However, according to Russian research, the bioplasmic body or growth body contains energy levels that sustain the development and replacement of cells in the body.

---

* Scientists at Stanford University and private research foundations, such as the Academy of Parapsychology and Medicine in California have been replicating the Russian's research and pioneering research on the bioplasmic body and in acupuncture.

It changes the minerals of the body from an inert to an active state. For example, the etheric body maintains magnesium levels in the blood as a screen between the activities of calcium, potassium, phosphorous and sodium, maintains the level of iron in the hemoglobin of blood cells and makes possible the transfer of oxygen to the tissue cells. It maintains the proper proportion of minerals in the body. It is the dynamic current that facilitates the reproduction of organ and body cells. It is in continuous motion and metamorphosis, and is responsible for maintenance of all the elements that are necessary to keep the organism going and healthy.

Steiner stated:

> The life - (bioplasmic) body works in a
> formative way upon the substances and
> forces of the physical body, thus bringing
> about the phenomena of growth, repro-
> duction, and inner movement of the saps
> and fluids. It is therefore the builder
> and moulder of the physical body, its
> inhabitant and architect. The physical
> body may even be spoken of as an image
> or expression of the life-body. [48]

Ostrander and Schroeder reported research on a photographic process developed by the Russian scientist Kirlian by which the energy or bioplasmic body can be photographed:

> ...the energy body didn't seem to be
> merely a radiation of the physical
> body. The physical appeared somehow
> to mirror what was happening in the
> energy. [49]

It was reported that the Kirlian process was used to photograph the moment of death in plants and animals. Slowly as the plant or physical body died,

> ...Russians saw sparks and flares of
> the bioplasmic body shooting out into space
> swimming away and dissappearing from
> sight. Gradually there was no luminescence
> at all coming from the dead plant or
> animal. [50]

They hypothesized the energy coming from the dying physical body to be the dispersing bioplasmic body.

Sieweke described the bioplasmic forces as following definite laws of development. He explains that during the embryonic and early periods of childhood, the bioplasmic or etheric forces are occupied with physical growth. During the process of physical maturity and growing up, the etheric or formative forces gradually turn away from physical development to concentrate on the processes of emotional and cognitive development, a metamorphosis of the formative forces from outward (physical) development to inward soul (affective and cognitive) development. Sieweke emphasized,

> Any disturbance or change in the etheric forces during the formative years of childhood will have an impact on the emotional and intellectual constitution of the child. That is, the metamorphosis of the etheric forces from physical development to emotional-cognitive development can be accelerated or retarded. There is a delicate balance between these two functions of the etheric forces. On the other hand, the etheric forces dissolve themselves step by step in different regions of the body at different strengths out of the bodily functions. Those forces which turn away from physical development, become the material for emotional and intellectual development. [51]

In other words, the etheric forces have duel task: the development of the physical body and the unfoldment of the emotional and intellectual life. The bioplasmic forces are continuously renewing themselves under this double pressure. Sieweke stated that there is a dynamic liveliness, fluctuation and interaction of the bioplasmic forces between the processes or organ building and that of psychological development. [52]

Mann, an acupuncture physician, agrees that the growth

or bioplasmic energy is the basis for cognition:

The capacity for the regeneration of
the tissue in the human being must be
taken into account when judging the
possibility of a cure. It must be
remembered that the human has less
power of regeneration than any animal,
and vastly less than the lower animal.
A flat worm will completely regenerate
itself if it is cut in half longitudinally
or transversely (so that two flat worms
are made out of one); if the tail of a
rainworm is cut off, it will partially
regrow; the fin of a lung fish will grow
again if it has been broken off; similarly
the limbs of an amphibia.. The human
being has not the same regenerative
power. His creative energy has been
transferred to the power of thought. [53]

Russian research on the bioplasmic body or forces has
given visible proof to the premises of acupuncture and
homeopathy, both of which are medically based on the
rebalancing of the bioplasmic or vital forces. Both acupuncture and homeopathic medicine are based on empirical
not authoritative knowledge. [54,55]

As indicated, Russian scientists found the etheric body
to be a mirror image of bioplasmic body. Similarly,
Chinese physicians view the physical body as a temporal
materialism of the etheric or vital forces. As indicated
Russian scientists discovered a method of observing and
photographing living substance using high frequency elec-
tric fields. After a number of years of research they
concluded that all organic matter, plants and animals,
have both a physical body and an energy (etheric) body.
They also found that any imbalance in the etheric body or
forces has a reciprocating effect on the physical body.
The energy forces are affected drastically by illness,
emotions, moods, thoughts, drugs. When a person is
tired, tense and irritable the energy forces leave.
Because of the intimately related dual task of the etheric
forces, a dependent mind-body relationship is created.

The psychological constitution can affect the physical constitution and vise-versa. Therefore, the condition of both the physical body and the mind are dependent upon the vitality and condition of the etheric or formative forces, and the various physical organs are in reality a temporal deposit of these dynamic, metamorphosing bioplasmic currents, moving at various speeds throughout the body.

Let us now examine acupuncture-and its use of bioplasmic forces. Acupuncture is an ancient Chinese method of healing by the placement of fine needles in the skin at certain acupoints. The stimulation of any of these 800 or more acupoints causes the flow of nerve impulses or energies in the body. This traditional Chinese art of healing, which is being researched in this country, is based on years of empirical findings,

> ... that in good health there is free and
> unimpeded circulation of energy--the
> life forces--flowing from organ to organ
> along an invisible network of inter-
> communicating channels (14 meridians). [56]

The blockage of one or more of these 14 meridians or channels brings on illness--an imbalance in the organism. These life forces which flow along meridians or channels effect the flow of blood to effected tissues. However, these meridians are not the same as nor do they follow the nervous, blood or lymph systems in man. The bioplasmic energy meridians, which have their own pathways and physiological functions, are foreign to American and western medical and scientific knowledge. The concept of bioplasmic energy or current flow stems from ancient Asiatic theory or knowledge that the physical organs are the end products of the bioplasmic currents which move continuously at various speeds throughout the body. It is known that the substance of the liver is changed in the course of ten days, the tongue can regenerate itself, whereas the substance of the brain takes much longer, and it is almost six months before new tissues appear in the bones. To the acupuncturist, pathological conditions of both mind and of body result from an imbalance and blockage of these etheric current movements. Stimulation of the appropriate acupoints restores harmonious etheric balance in the organism. A number of American scientists have been investigating the theoretical and medical basis and function of acupuncture and the various methods of stimulating etheric flow in the body. Dr. William Tiller, Stanford University, writes:

> There are several ways in which one can produce acupuncture stimulation. It appears all one needs to do is stimulate, sufficiently, the acupuncture points. This can be done by chemical stimulation. This is the weakest method. It can be done via the acupuncture needles. This is the next best. Likewise it can be done by the injection of electrical energy. That is the next best, but it requires sophisticated understanding. The next best is to use a laser beam which, again, requires sophisticated equipment and understanding. Finally, the very best is the psychic energy, spiritual (healing), energy, injection. This seems to be the best procedure for bringing out the bodily balance.[57]

A number of sophisticated instruments have been developed to locate acupoints and to measure the intensity and balance of the bioplasmic or etheric energy.

Homeopathy, also based on the bioplasmic energy theory, uses microdiluted elements or trace elements as medicine instead of external physical stimulation to establish a balance in the organism.[58] Homeopathy is widely practiced in Europe, Russia and India. This form of medicine, which is over 150 years old, was also relatively popular in the United States in the early decades of the twentieth century. Because of it being based on the invisible vital forces, including other factors, it fell into disrepute in medical circles. It is now being revived. (The author refers the reader to the book by Coulter for additional information.)

Another piece of evidence that seems to confirm the existence of an etheric or bioplasmic body is the phenomenon of the phantom limb. Persons who have a missing limb often continue to sense the missing arm or leg as if it were still there. [59] Research by Weinstein and others has shown that among 101 born with missing limbs, 18 had clear perception of phantom limbs. [60] In the development of body-schemes in children it was found that there was no difference between blind and normal children in the development of the body scheme with respect to hand-perception. This indicates the child's visual perception of its own physical body and of the body of others had no influence on the development of his own body scheme or image. The same phenomena is true of children born with missing limbs. These children showed body-scheme perception of all limbs. [61] Since the development of the body-scheme is not dependent upon the physical limbs, therefore, the phantom (bioplasmic) limb must be the basis for the development of the body scheme. That is to say, the phantom or bioplasmic limb contains the dynamic process or energy forces of growth, which facilitate the physical limb, when present. The phantom limb grows and develops just like the physical limb, except it is non-material, invisible. The child grows into a body scheme. This perhaps is what the Russian scientists meant by "...the physical (body) appeared to somehow mirror what was happening in the energy (bioplasmic) body". [62] Steiner referred to the bioplasmic body, the phantom limb as the functional gestalt, the ether body or the body of the formative creative forces of growth. [49] He asserted that human development and the accompanying development of a body-scheme in childhood is the birth of the freeing of the child's formative or etheric forces of growth. When the child reaches certain levels of physiological or biological maturity (e.g. at age seven, teething and ages 12-16, puberty) the forces of growth are then released for the new, but more subtle and higher functions of memory and thinking.

As indicated, at age seven (teething) there is a shift in thinking from the preoperational to the concrete operational. The same relationship applies to the onset of puberty and the child's change from the concrete operational to the formal operational level of cognition as

mentioned. Nisbit found that those adolescents who
attained puberty scored higher on intellectual and academic achievement tests than youngster who were still at
the prepuberty stage of development. During this time
there is a growth spurt; the teenager is reaching adult
proportions. The growth or energy forces are then released to be used for the higher level of formal operational thinking. There has not been much research on this
age level. However, there are indications that there is a
delay in the attainment of the formal operational level of
thinking even after the attainment of puberty. Physical
maturation seems to have raced ahead of mental development at this later stage. No one really knows the reason;
further research is needed.

Before going on to the implications of the bioplasmic-
organismic theory, it would be apropo to mention an
addition dynamic feature of the bioplasmic forces, i.e.,
the dynamic, regenerative and recovery powers they
possess. Mann has indicated the regenerative powers to
regrow part of the physical body in lower animals. And
man does not possess this power, except in the recupera-
tion from illnesses; etc. However, it is seen in nature
that seeds that are 100 to a 1,000 years old can germinate
into a plant by the application of water and soil. In other
words, the physical effects of the bioplasmic or growth
forces can be almost entirely withdrawn or temporarily
suspended. For example, Kagan observed the effects of
isolation of Guatemalan infants in dark huts, cut off from
human intercourse and environmental stimulation, except
for nursing by the mother for the first two to three years
of their life. [63] He found the 2 and 3 year olds to be
retarded in everyway -- motorically, intellectually and
socially. He then observed and tested the nine and ten
year old children in the village, who had gone through the
same rearing practice, and found them to be normal,
socially well adjusted, happy and highly intelligent children. Although Kagan was puzzled by his findings because
it contradicted traditional findings in and information on
child development, it is apparent that the isolated, low
stimulating environment merely served to suspend the
actions of the bioplasmic forces or growth forces. When

the children were later released to interact with the
human and social-culture mileau of the village, the bioplasmic forces, which had been dormant, were activated.
Using an analogy, just as "... soil, moisture and warmth
call forth the plant seed into germination, ...", so a
social-human environment calls forth the birth and development of the human personality, speech and thinking.[64]

Summary:
     The bioplasmic forces are the basis of physical and
psychological development. During the early years of
development, the bioplasmic forces concentrate on the
physical growth, and gradually as the child reaches plateaus of physical maturity, the growth forces are released
and transmutted into the forces for cognition at about age
seven and fourteen. The physical body is a mirror or
reflection of the bioplasmic body or forces which can be
effected by physical, mental and environmental conditions.
The bioplasmic-organismic model indicates a mind-body
relationship. It also indicates definition and sequence of
readiness, i.e., physiological maturation preceeds mental maturation and it is the organismic maturity of the
organism that determines readiness, not the external
influences of cumulative learnings and experiences. However, when the organism has reached a plateau of organismic readiness, then it is the external stimuli, social and
intellectual experiences, etc., that will build on and bring
to fruitation that which the organism has developed. The
experiences, external stimuli must be compatible with the
child's stages of physical, emotional and cognitive development. Let us examine the educational implications of the
bioplasmiac-organismic model for the disadvantaged child.

Implications for the Disadvantaged:

It is well known that the public schools have never been able to educate the poor. Compensatory and Head Start programs have been a failure, despite the momentous effort and the millions of dollars expended. As a result of the poor environment, the deprived child begins school with a handicap. The theory of transmuted bioplasmic forces offers an explanation for the retardation phenomenon of socially disadvantaged children. Let us review the two theories; deprivation theory and the cumulative deficit theory.

The effects of a deliterious environment can result in various degrees of physical, emotional and intellectual entrophy. For optimal development a harmonous, compatible, propitious environment is needed. The rate of development is affected. Disadvantaged children proceed through the developmental stages at a slower and less complete rate than their middle class peers. The transition from the concrete to the formal operational levels of cognition is slower and less complete.

The deprived child has cumulative deficits in growth incurred from past deprivation.

> The child who has an existing deficit
> in growth incurred from past deprivation
> is less able to profit developmentally
> from new and more advanced levels of
> environmental stimulation... his
> deficit lend to increase cumulatively
> and to lead to permanent retardation. 65

The phenomenon of environmental press, domination and disorganization results in psychological entropy, and hence the degradation of psychological and biological energy. The end result is physical and mental entropy. The plasticity of intelligence tends to decrease with age, limiting the organism's degree of plasticity or freedom to respond developmentally in a certain direction compatible to the environmental stimulation. The decrease in plasticity in intelligence is in proportion to the decreased rate of transition from the concrete to the formal operational levels of cognition which is directly proportional to the strength or amount of bioplasmic forces available to the child at the transitional period of cognition.

Retardation is the result of the inadequate development and sustenance of the child's bioplasmic forces during the early formative years. As a result of the restricted and chaotic, stimulated environment, there is a degradation of the child's psychological and biological energy--resulting in psychological and physical entrophy. The environment dominates the child's growth processes, rather than sustaining them. His energy forces are dissipated. There is a loss of bioplasmic energy. This degradation and dissipation of energy in the human body has been confirmed by the high frequency photography of the bioplasmic body or forces by Russian scientists;

> Illness, emotion, states of mind,
> thoughts, fatigue, all make their
> distinctive imprint on the pattern
> of energy which seemed to circulate
> continuously through the human body.
> (In the pictures, you can see the
> fingertip of a normal, healthy person,
> photographed by Kirlian process. The
> second picture shows the same finger-
> tip of the same person, this time he is
> fatigued and overstrained. More energy
> appears to pour out of the body when tired.)[66]

One could infer from this that an extremely deleterious environment causes extreme degradation of bioplasmic energy levels. Extreme forms of environment press, etc. during the early critical years of childhood can be responsible for growth retardation, causing in some cases simulated idiopathic hypopituitarism.[67] The depletion of bioplasmic forces during these formative years leaves little energy or growth forces left to be transmuted into cognitive processes later on. Perhaps this is the reason why many inner-city children are not getting beyond the concrete operational level of cognition. The deficit is partly irreversible. The plasticity or forming power of the organism decreases with age. Intelligence becomes prematurely differentiated and fixed, compounded by limited experiences and environment and decreased experiences. How are the bioplasmic forces and human development affected?

It has been indicated that the bioplasmic forces are dynamic and in continuous motion throughout the body. The organs, the physical body, etc., are the temporal deposits of these forces or currents moving at various speeds throughout the body in the building up and regenerative processes. As indicated, when there is an imbalance or distortion in the bioplasmic or formative forces flow illness and pathology result. The human being is a dynamic being, ever interacting with his environment-- motorically, emotionally, and psychologically; he is in movement (remember the author hypothesized the theory of voluntary control of movement in all three realms). Sieweke indicated an interweaving and interaction of the etheric or formative forces for physical, affective and cognitive development, from outer to inner development. Hence, it is the child's intercourse with and reaction (movement) to the quality and quantity of the environment that effect and interweave with the movement and flow of etheric or formative forces of growth. It is this invisible liveliness and fluctuation of the formative forces in conjunction with the movements of the organism that nurture or entrophize its development, depending upon the quality of the environment. It would also follow that in order to prevent pathological conditions, such as retardation of development, the movements have to be altered or removed. Then one could go a step further and assume that conducive movements could be implemented to have a healthy and nurturing effect on the formative or etheric forces of growth. This change in movement would include a change in environmental living and life style, etc. as well as remedial programs in physical and motor development. The essential point is the very intimate relationship of the developing human being to his environment that determines and, in a sense, predicts his future development (cumulative deficit). As indicated, any disturbance in the developing etheric or growth forces is imprinted into his physical and psychological constitution.

The socially disadvantaged child's problems are compounded further by the fact that he begins school with these deficits. He is therefore less able than his middle-class peer to profit from new experiences. He is cognitively immature. In short, he is environmentally retarded, which affects his mental and academic capacities. Here, too, the environment has depleted his bioplasmic growth forces. He therefore begins schooling with weakened and insufficient growth forces. When the child matures enough to shift from a lower stage of mental development to a higher (preoperational to concrete) he does not possess enough growth forces to be changed into forces for thinking to make the transition complete. He is neither out of the preoperational stage nor in the concrete operational stage. He hovers in between. His rate of development is retarded. When these developmental problems are compounded by forced, premature learning, the result can only be further retardation, perhaps permanent retardation.

Most of the research shows the preschool academic-readiness programs for the disadvantages, such as head-start, have been "ineffective in producing any (lasting) gains in cognitive development.[67, 68] Moore, Moon and Moore's article cites a number of studies in which children who began reading a year or so later than their peers, surpassed the earlier reading children in reading ability later on in their school career.[69] Cases were cited in which preschool age children who were exposed to academic learning exhibited a greater number of incidents of maladjustment than children who began their school career at a later age. They also show that the full maturity of the senses does not occur until age 8 or 9 years. Also the skill and knowledge retention level of preschoolers or cognitively immature learners was much less as compared to later school entrants. It is known that children who are forced into intellectual learning beyond their present capacity or maturation level become "turned off".[70] Jensen states that readiness is a matter of cognitive control, the ability to integrate subskills. He points out;

> It is the child's progressing ability
> to integrate the component subskills
> that the phenomenon called readiness
> is most apparent. It is the integrative
> process, the development of a higher
> order 'master plan' that depends most

upon the maturation of brain structure.[71]

Jensen demonstrated this point when he attempted to teach his five year old daughter to play chess. She readily learned the names of the six chess pieces, the placement of pieces on the board and the rules for moving each piece. She was highly motivated, and her learning proceeded smoothly through a cumulative-associative approach. However, when it came to playing a game, putting together all that she had learner "... a game did not emerge."[72] A year later, age six, she had no trouble in playing chess. She had reached a level of maturation and cognitive development where the subskills were integrated into an organized whole. Based on the bioplasmic theory one could state that the child had thus reached a level of physical maturation, releasing the growth forces for thinking. The child now had more power or energy for greater cognitive control, for manipulation and integration of subskills and learning. The child now possessed the cognitive energies, transmuted forces of growth to control her own thinking. It is as if the shepherd appeared to amongst the flock and establish peace and order.

Early learning seems not only to be inefficient, but there are indications that it results in a lower plateau of learning proficiency. Premature learning may create a mental block, resulting perhaps in a permanent handicap, a lower ceiling for the subsequent development of a particular skill, e.g. reading. It may even result in permanent cognitive and academic retardation.[73] Research has found negative correlations between early schooling and school success and attitudes toward school.[74,75] Elkind states, "The longer we delay formal instruction, up to certain limits, the greater the period of plasticity and the higher the ultimate level of achievement."[76]

Let us examine these problems in light of the theory of transmuted growth forces for thinking. Cognitive readiness is a matter of the organism reaching a certain level of physical maturation at which time the growth forces can be released to become the energy for thinking processes. Therefore, the preschool child (pre-operational)

does not have enough cognitive energy available to cognitively act on the learning so as to fully experience
intellectual learning, making it a part of his own being.
Almy refers to these learnings as pseudo-concepts. [77] The
child's learnings are non-transferable to new or different
situations. This also explains why later school entrants
become more efficient readers than early school entrants.
Since the preschool age learner has been burdened with
these pseudo-concepts (which are somewhat non-transferable) he is unable to use them as a foundation to build
or to integrate subsequent skills and learnings. He
doesn't have enough cognitive energy to manipulate the
concepts, to perceive order or self-rehearse the learning.
Hence, he cannot experience it. In fact it may condition
his style of learning and cognitive plasticity maybe reduced in this area of learning.

Looking at the effects of premature or forced learnings,
one could state that something never comes out of nothing.
To gain one thing, something else must be sacrificed. So
it is with accelerated or prematurely forced learning or
the attempt to speed up the stages of cognitive development,
there is an accompanying loss in quality of development.
Portman reports, "Whenever acceleration has occurred
there has been a noticeably increased susceptibility to
certain diseases especially those of psychological origin." [78]
Shortened processes of maturing cause maladjustment in
inner-city children and in early school entrants. Since
learning is hardly ever a purely cognitive process but
contains emotions (e. g. interest, motivation, preferences,
etc.) it could be that the stress on early intellectual
development entropizes emotional development.

From the point of view of Chinese medicine--particular-
ly acupuncture--there is little essential difference between
physical and mental illness. The mind and the body are
integrally related. Mann summarizes this relationship:
1. A physical dysfunction can cause
    a mental disease.
2. A mental dysfunction can cause a
    physical disease.
3. A physical dysfunction can cause a
    physical disease.

4. A mental dysfunction can cause
    mental disease.

Steiner also had a mind-body theory of development:

> For every thought-process there
> is a corresponding process within
> our organism; and the same is true
> of every emotional process which
> may be denoted as an 'impulse of
> will' (our actions). [80]

In short, "...whenever something takes place in our
psyche it produces a wave which repeats itself as far down
as the physical organism."[81] Steiner points out that
premature or forced intellectual learning may cause
prematuration of the physical organism.

> If we force intellectual powers in
> the child we arrest growth... certain
> organic processes (etheric forces
> are depleted) that tend inwardly to
> harden the body are brought into play. [82]

There is a premature use and misdirection of the bioplasmic forces in urging the young child to think for
himself. The bioplasmic forces are turned inward too
soon. Therefore the physical body is less plastic and
mobile in its formative potential. Physical maturity sets
in sooner. *

As the immature learner becomes frustrated and an-
ziety-ridden he loses motivation for intellectual success
later on. He becomes "intellectually burned out". In
becoming frustrated and psychologically disorganized,
the psychosomatic effect produces the entrophy of physiological energy and cognitive energy.

Something else is sacrificed; it is the full physiological
potential development of the organism. It has been stated
that energy forces for thinking are metamorphosed from
the same forces that facilitate physical growth. If the

---

*Perhaps this is one of the reasons that young people ma-
ture physically sooner than did their ancestors. An example is that 1850 girls reached menarche at age seventeen;
today it is age 13.5, a decrease of approximately four
years in a century. [83]

child is forced into intellectual learning prior to readiness, as determined by physical and experiential maturation, the child is prematurely using these forces for psuedo-intellectual thinking, which should be used to develop the physical organism. Hence, physical development must be sacrificed, to some degree. What ultimately may be sacrificed is the full development of the vehicle for thinking, the brain. Research has shown that gross brain changes take place from birth through adolescence, which entails the shifting of cognitive control from the emotional centers to the reasoning centers. [84] If these bioplasmic forces are wasted on premature attempts at accelerated cognition (this is what we attempt to do through compensatory programs) with immature children, not only is there an entropism of the brain but an inefficient use of these forces as well. The reason for the inefficiency is that the bioplasmic forces at this age level (pre-seven year old) are not totally free from the formative processes of physical development. Forced intellectual thinking at this period in the child's development prematurely drains off a certain portion of these bioplasmic forces (but not enough for effective cognitive processes) which should be utilized for physiological and emotional growth.

The consequence is that there are not enough trans-formed bioplasmic energy forces to effect the efficiency of thinking (e.g. pre-operational to concrete operational). On the other hand, perhaps the physical body (brain) is being robbed of its full growth potential. The overall effect may be total, affecting the young child's total growth pattern--physiological, emotional, and cognitive. The wasting of these bioplasmic forces leads to accumulative physiological and psychological entropy. The effect is cyclical. Therefore, it is important that these etheric or growth forces be sustained and developed in the growing child rather than being prematurely misused for intellectual learning.

Conclusion

It is obvious that the socially disadvantaged child is handicapped by the fact (according to this theory) his bioplasmic or etheric forces are weak--entrophied. This is a part of his cumulative deficiency. The schools only add to the deficit, inhibiting the child's natural development. Therefore, the popular educational approaches of today with their intellectual heavy-handedness will never allow children to develop and blossom naturally. They can only do damage, making children into premature unhappy adults. They will never be able to serve those children from different and less desirable economic environments. Our conventional approaches--pouring knowledge into the child, "fitting him into a curriculum" that is foreign to his nature--must cease. We must examine the needs of the child; how and why he develops as he does. Then what we need is to develop a curriculum and methods compatible with his unfolding and developing stages of growth. The bioplasmic or growth forces model provides a wholistic, rationale approach. It explains human growth, the development of thinking in children, the rationale for readiness and the basis of social deprivation. If the theory is correct, it implies that the educational process should help the child to sustain and develop his bioplasmic body, his forces of growth. A curriculum, extracurricular activities, etc., compatible with and supportive of these growth forces would have to be developed. The bioplasmic - organismic model may be the key to human and child development. It may be the road back to humanism for education. It could very well revolutionize education.

References

1. Ornstein, Allan C. , Urban Education, Columbus, Ohio: Merrill Publishing Company, 1972, p. 6.
2. Allan, Robert M. , "The Culturally Disadvantaged, " ed. Charles H. Carter, Handbook of Mental Retardation Syndromes, Springfield, Ill. : 1970, pp. 244-45.
3. Ausubel, David P. , "The Effects of Cultural Deprivation on Learning Patterns, " Audiovisual Instruction, Vol. 10, Jan. 1965, p. 11.
4. Ostrander, Sheila and Lynn Schroeder, Psychic Discoveries Behind the Iron Curtain, New Jersey: Prentice-Hall, 1971.
5. Sieweke, Herbert, Anthroposophsche Medizin, Dornach, Switzerland: Philosophisch - Anthroposophsches Verlag, 1959.
6. Frenhenburg, William K. and Dodds, Josiah B, "Denver Developmental Screening Test, " (Chart), Distributed by Mead Johnson Laboratories, 1969.
7. Weihs, Thomas J. , Children in Need of Special Care, London: Souvenir Press, 1971, pp. 22-32.
8. Lennenberg, Eric H. , "On Explaining Language", Science, Vol. 164, #3880, May, 1969, p. 636.
9. Konig, Karl, The First Three Years of Childhood. New York: Anthroposophical Press, 1969, p. 46.
10. Piaget, Jean, Piaget Rediscovered, ed. , R.E. Ripple and V.N. Rockcastle School of Education, Cornell University, March 1964, pp. 33-37.
11. Lennenberg Loc cit.
12. Ertl, John, "Goodby I. Q. Hellow EI (Ertl Index)", Phi Delta Kappan, October 1972, p. 91.
13. Konig, Karl, The Phenomena of Electo-Encepha-lography, Beitrage Zu einer Erweiterung der Heilkunst nach geisteswissenschaftlichen Erkenntnissen, 1954, trans. , P. Engel, Aberdeen, Scotland: November 1971, (monograph), pp. 4-7.
14. Smith, Anthony, Body, New York: Avon Books, 1969, pp. 379-380.
15. Karlins, Marvin and Lewis M. Andrews, Biofeedback, New York: Warner Paperback Library, 1973, p. 25.

16. Piaget, Loc. cit., pp. 8-9.
17. Ilg, Frances L. and Louise B. Ames, School Readiness. New York: Harper and Row, 1964.
18. Ibid, pp. 32-41.
19. Jensen, Arthur, Understanding Readiness: An Occasional Paper. University of Illinois Press, 1969, pp. 4-5.
20. Piaget, Loc cit., pp. 36-37.
21. Olsen, Willard and Byron Hughes, "Concept of Growth - Their Significance to Teachers", Childhood Education, XXI, October 1944, pp. 53-63.
22. Piaget, Loc cit., pp. 30-31.
23. Ilg Ames, Loc cit., pp. 238-39.
24. Nisbet, J. D., "Puberty and Test Performances", British Journal of Educational Psychological. Vol. 34, June 1964, pp. 202-203.
25. Almy, Milly, "New Views on Intellectual Development in Early Childhood Education" Intellectual Development: Another Look. ed., Harry Passow, ASCD Publications, 1964, p. 24.
26. Ausubel, Loc. cit.
27. Ogletree, Earl J., "Relationship of Teething, Puberty, SES, and I.Q. to the Piatet Tasks with Socially Disadvantaged Children," Unpublished Study, 1971.
28. Ilg and Ames, Loc cit., p. 20.
29. Jensen, Arthur R., Social Class, Race, Genetics: "Implications for Education," American Education Research Journal, Vol. V, No. 1, Jan. 1968, pp. 36-37.
30. Allport, Gordon, Personality and Social Encounter, Boston: Beacon Press, 1960, pp. 184-85.
31. Anderson, Harold and Gladys Anderson, "Social Development", Manual of Child Psychology. New York: John Wiley and Sons, Inc., 1954, pp. 1178-1180.
32. Powell, G. F., Brasel, J.A. and R.M. Blizzard, Emotional Deprivation and Growth Retardation Simulating Idiopathic Hypopituitarism: Clinical Evaluation of the Syndrome," The New England Journal of Medicine, June 8, 1967, Vol. 276, No. 23, pp. 1271-78.

33. Winick, Myron, "Nutrition and Intellectual
    Development in Children," Nutrition and Intellectual
    Growth in Children, The Association for Childhood
    Education International; Washington D. C.,
    1969, pp. 25-28.
34. Montagu, Ashley, "A Scientist Looks at Love,"
    Phi Delta Kappan, Vol. LI, No. 9, May 1970,
    pp. 463-67.
35. Powell, Loc. cit., pp. 1273-74.
36. Ibid.
37. Ibid., p. 1272.
38. Children and Their Primary Schools: Report of
    the Central Advisory Council for Education, London,
    England: Vol. I. H. M. S. O. 1967. pp. 10-12.
39. Anderson, Loc cit.
40. Ausubel, Loc. cit., p. 12.
41. Hebb, Donald, The Organization of Behavior:
    A Neuropsychological Theory, New York: Wiley
    and Sons, 1949.
42. Morris, Charles, Six Theories of Mind, Chicago:
    University of Chicago Press, 1932.
43. Bigge, Morris and Maurice Hunt, Psychological
    Foundations of Education. New York: Harper &
    Rowe, Publ., 1962, pp. 63-65.
44. Ostrander, Sheila and Lynn Schroeder, Loc cit.,
    p. 210.
45. Ibid., p. 213.
46. Ibid, p. 214.
47. Bigge and Hunt, Loc. Cit., p. 67.
48. Rudolf Steiner, The Education of the Child,
    London: Rudolf Steiner Publishing Co.,
    1955, pp. 8-9.
49. Ostrander, et. al., Ibid., p. 202
50. Ibid., p. 216.
51. Sieweke, Herbert, Anthroposophic Medizin,
    Dornach, Switzerland: Philosophisch-
    Anthroposophisches Verlag, 1959, pp. 142-144.
52. Ibid., pp. 153-154.
53. Mann, Felix, Acupuncture: The Ancient Chinese
    Art of Healing and How it Works Scientifically.
    New York: Random House, 1972, pp. 195-196.

54. Moss, Louis, Acupuncture and You, New York: Dell Publishing Co., 1972.

55. Coulter, Harris, Homeopathic Medicine, Washington, D. C.: American Institute of Homeopathy, 1973.

56. Moss, Loc. cit., p. 8.

57. Tiller, William A., "Energy Fields and the Human Body, Part I;" (Address to A.R.E. Medical Symposium on Mind-Body Relationship in the Disease Process), Phoenix, Arizona, January, 1972, p. 19.

58. Coulter, Loc. cit., pp. 3-5.

59. Gangale, J.P., "A Review of Phantom Sensation Phenomenon," Virginia Medical Monthly, Vol. 95, July 1968, pp. 425-429.

60. Weinstein, E., C. Sersen and R. Better, "Phantom and Somatic Sensations in Cases of Gongenital Aphasia", Cortex, Vol. 1, 1964, pp. 216-290.

61. Arnim, George Von, "Imitation and the body Scheme", The Cressent, Vol. 13, No. 4, October, 1967, pp. 21-22.

62. Ostrander and Schroeder, Loc. cit., p. 202.

63. "Do the First Two Years Matter? A Conversation With Jerome Kagan", Saturday Review, April, 1973, pp. 41-43.

64. Popplebaum, Hermann, The Etheric Body in Idea and Action, London: Anthroposophical Publishing Co., 1955, pp. 9-10.

65. Ausubel, Loc cit., p. 12.

66. Ostrander and Schroeder, Loc cit., p. 205.

67. Powell, et. al, Loc cit.

68. Westinghouse and Ohio University, "The Impact of Head Start: An Evaluation of the Effects of Head Start on Children's Cognitive and Affective Development", in The Disadvantaged Child. Joe L. Frost and Glen R. Hawkes, editors, Boston: Houghton-Mifflin, 1970, pp. 197-201.

69. Kolberg, Lawrence, "Early Education: A Cognitive-Developmental View", Educating the Disadvantaged. (1965-1969). Vol. 1, Parts 1 and 2, ed. Allan Ornstein, New York: AMS Press, pp. 73-122.

70. Moore, Raymond, Robert Moon and Dennis Moore, "The California Report: Early Schooling for All?", Phi Delta Kappan, June, 1972, p. 615.

71. Ibid.

72. Jensen, Loc cit., p. 12.

73. Ibid.

74. Elkind, David, "Piagetian and Psychometric Conceptions of Intelligence", Harvard Education Review, 1969, pp. 319-337.

75. Husen, Torsten, International Studies of Achievement in Mathematics. Vol. II, Uppsola: Almquist and Wiksells, 1967.

76. Elkind, Ibid.

77. Almy, Loc cit.

78. Portmann, A., "Umzuchtunk des Menschen? Aspekte Heutiger Biotechnik", Universitas 21, 1966, pp. 785-803.

79. Mann, Loc. cit., p. 196.

80. Steiner, Rudolf, An Occult Physiology, London: Rudolf Steiner Publishing Company, 1951, pp. 148-49.

81. Ibid.

82. Steiner, Rudolf, The New Art of Education, London: Anthroposophical Press, 1928, pp. 136-137.

83. Children and Their Primary Schools: Report of the Central Advisory Council for Education, England: Vol. I, H.M.S.O., 1967, pp. 8-12.

84. Metcalf, David and Kent Jordan, "EEG Onotgenesis in Normal Children", Drugs and Development and Cerebral Function. ed., Lynn Smith, Springfield, Ill.: Charles C. Thomas, 1972, pp. 127-128.

TEACHING THE DISADVANTAGED

Some Trends in Education for the Disadvantaged

Adelaide Jablonsky, Ed.D.

The entrance of the federal government into active financial assistance for educational research and service programs attempting to offer improved educational experiences for poor children precipitated a flood of experimentation and research literature. In 1965, Hess[1] and in 1966, Gordon and Wilkerson[2] compiled directories of existing programs for disadvantaged children and youth to summarize trends and to suggest possible directions for the future. Since the publication of the Hess directory and the Gordon and Wilkerson book, numerous additional references have been made to various groups of programs. Among these, the recently prepared indexes to Title I[3] and Title III[4] projects under the Elementary and Secondary Education Act of 1965[5, 5a] provide extensive information as to who is doing what and where. Supporting those inventories are thousands of reports prepared by the school systems and other related agencies. Attempts to alleviate educational deficiencies, however, are not limited to those programs supported by federal funds, since private foundations and local agencies have also turned their attention to the problems of slum schools. These latter efforts, however, tend to be more experimental and limited to small numbers of pupils. Given the size of the population we call disadvantaged, it is clear that only through adequate governmental support can we hope to establish programs of sufficient magnitude to make a difference in the development of most of these children.

Definition and Demography

If we define the disadvantaged primarily and realistically in terms of family income, we may be talking about 30,000,000 to 35,000,000 individuals of all ages. The Office of Economic

IRCD BULLETIN, ERIC Information Retrieval Center on the Disadvantaged, 1968, Vol. 4, No. 2, pp. 4-11.

Opportunity, OEO,[6] has taken both family size and urban and rural factors into consideration in establishing annual cash income thresholds to poverty. Some selective figures from their present criteria are:

FAMILY SIZE PERSONS	NON-FARM	FARM
2	$1,990	$1,390
5	$3,685	$2,580
7	$4,635	$3,245
10	$6,135	$4,295

Using these criteria, the OEO provides the following information for children and youth:

PERSONS IN POVERTY

AGE	MILLIONS	PERCENT OF NON-WHITE POOR	PERCENT OF POOR AND NON-POOR POOR BY AGE GROUP
Under 6	5.8	40	24
6 to 15	8.1	38	21
16 to 21	3.0	30	17

The total of almost 17 million children and youth, then, forms the hard core of the poverty group. It is patent, however, that the group of disadvantaged children and youth to whom the educational establishment is relating extends far beyond this number. Since these income figures are minimal, factors such as one-parent families, father absences, inadequate housing, physical malfunctions, malnutrition, and others are not taken into consideration. One-fourth to one-fifth of all young people are in the poverty group. Many others must be considered disadvantaged when we include educational criteria.

We have purposely eliminated from our statistical estimates criteria such as educational background of parents, housing conditions, and behavioral disorders because of difficulty in securing appropriate measures. Included in these projections is the small proportion of youngsters from backgrounds of poverty who nevertheless are making acceptable progress in school. Instruction must both compensate for deficiencies which exist and complement the assets of these pupils. We have not segmented the statistics by farm and non-farm populations or by white and non-white populations because we assume that compensatory education in the United States must serve all children who require it.

Taking 50 percent of the population at each age level as operating at or below grade level and reducing that by 10 percent, representing the mentally retarded and seriously physically handicapped or other children needing intensive professional attention, we can establish a 40 percent overall figure.

It would perhaps be justified if we were to include in the

target population most non-white children in the United States since their education is routinely retarded by factors of discrimination beyond the problems faced by the poor. Another group requiring special attention are children above the poverty level with language difficulties and/or cultural or social deficiencies resulting from geographic isolation or from limited resources of home and community. If we were to include these children and youth, we would need to add another 5 percent to each category of persons.

The following total population, then, requires compensatory education. We have rounded figures to represent the annual average for the period 1967-1970.

		TOTAL
Birth to 2 years of age	5,000,000	5,000,000
3 to 5 years of age	5,000,000	5,000,000
6 to 7 years of age	3,200,000	
8 to 9 years of age	3,200,000	
10 to 11 years of age	3,000,000	9,400,000
12 to 13 years of age	3,000,000	
14 to 15 years of age	2,500,000	
16 to 17 years of age	2,500,000	8,000,000
18 to 19 years of age.	3,000,000	3,000,000
		30,400,000

The Search for Answers

With the education of over 30 million children and youth involved, how and where would one find those programs which seem to have solutions to existing problems? *ERIC–IRCD* asked over 200 people from all sections of the country which programs they felt showed promise or demonstrated effectiveness based on the criteria of professional or community judgment or based on demonstrated improved academic achievement.

The responsible heads of school systems and programs observed were exceedingly cooperative in allowing the author free access to facilities, staff, and children. Our major regret is that the school systems observed for this report constitute only a limited sample and that expediency was, on occasion, a factor in selection. The author expects to continue observations in order to prepare an extended state-of-the-art paper describing programs in greater detail. It would be helpful if readers would submit to *IRCD* documents (in duplicate) delineating details of programs which have demonstrated effectiveness in educating poor children.

Most of the documents referred to in this report have been or are being processed through the *ERIC* computer system and will be available in microfiche or hard copy. (See information in the introduction to the bibliography on page 8.)

The Integration Debate

The controversy over the most direct and rewarding route to the solution of the complex problems of providing quality education for our poor and different children goes on and on at many levels and in all sections of the country. In an attempt to present the several positions on the question, we suggest reference to the two basic documents[7, 8] and to four papers presented at the November 17, 1967 National Conference on Equalizing Educational Opportunity in America's Cities: Problems and Programs for Change, sponsored by the U.S. Civil Rights Commission.[9, 10, 11, 12] The basic debate poses the question as compensatory education versus integration in education.

From our observations, it becomes clear that while both sides have some degree of validity, the reality of differing circumstances must dictate which are to be the first steps. We propose that integration with quality education for all children is the ultimate objective. However, where segregated housing, social decay, and a lag in education of many decades have stunted the development and growth of poor and minority group children and where geographic and bureaucratic strictures delay meaningful racial and economic integration, the immediate need is for massive attack on the problems of educating the disadvantaged where they are now.

It may have been a rocky road which White Plains, New York[13, 13a] traveled in integrating its schools, but the enlightened segment of the community identified the problem in the early phases of its development and proposed viable solutions. Today, this community could serve as a model for other school systems, particularly in small cities.

During the period when one of its elementary schools was growing in population from 40 to 65 percent Negro, the decision was reached to transfer the segregated school from housing elementary classes to utilizing the building for adult education and manpower training. Concurrently, the bussing program, which took no child further than four miles from his home, with all children from housing developments or blocks moving as a unit, distributed the children so that no school in White Plains had fewer than 10 percent nor more than 30 percent Negro children. What has resulted in this predominantly affluent community has been quality education for all children, with comfortable social interrelationships particularly at the primary grades. Since the program was initiated in 1964, its full potential impact has not yet reached through all secondary levels.

There is only one high school which has homogeneous grouping in its several basic curriculum areas and heterogeneous grouping in others, but the residual educational deficiencies of prior school patterns and a considerable immigration of students with poor educational experience and learning habits result in some separation of the races in the honors groups. The administration of the White Plains school system is aware of the need to correct this inequity through early identification and reinforcement of special talents among the Negro students. It should also be stated that a large percentage of the Negro population is represented by upwardly mobile families, and that there is very little abject poverty as in the slums of large cities.

Berkeley, California[14] proposes to integrate all of its schools in September 1968. Children from the lower grades in Negro schools will be bussed to the white schools, and the fourth, fifth, and sixth grade white students will be transferred to the prior all-Negro schools. Every school and every class is to have between 30 and 40 percent Negro pupils. The city has been divided into four parallel segments with a junior high school and its feeding elementary schools in each. There is one high school.

A token bussing program has for the last few years transported about 250 selected Negro children to four of the predominantly white schools. These children have been receiving very high quality education, similar to that found in cities and schools around the country where two to five poor Negro children are placed in classes with middle or upper class white children.

Unfortunately, in Berkeley, despite the use of federal funds in target area schools, the gap between the level of achievement of the poor Negro children and that of the many children of professionals, university staff, and other upper middle class families would seem to indicate the probability of serious dislocations for several years ahead. It will be an important test of the "integration first" position and will be watched with great interest by proponents of both sides of the integration-compensation issue.

Federal Funds Do Make a Difference

The ESEA Act of 1965[5] provided the first massive infusion of funds to assist communities in improving the education of their disadvantaged children. This was a breakthrough in the schism between the states and the federal government in relation to authority and responsibility for education. Some states, objecting to federal "control" through pursestrings, did not accept ESEA funds for one or two years after the approval of the act. As reluctant states observed other communities initiating programs with almost complete local autonomy, they became aware that the major controls, such as population to be served, were valid and, in fact, desirable, and they joined the program.

Early evaluation reports reflected very little effect due to factors intrinsic to all new efforts. Some results are hard to measure objectively; however, this does not detract from their importance. When absentee and dropout figures fall appreciably, it is measurable. When attitudes toward school and learning improve, or when self-concept is strengthened, these findings are subjective, but nonetheless important.

Projects were uneven in planning and performance. This led to the obscuring of positive effects by the weight of the problems and early defects in programs. In addition, the funds and resources to utilize them effectively were too little and too late in relation to the enormity of the task. More money and more time are imperatives.

It is very clear that federal funds have made a significant impact on the colossus. Looking back only three years, every one of the state and local administrators and teachers with whom I spoke emphatically stated that the seemingly hopeless task had begun to appear soluble through the financial assistance afforded by the act. In the overburdened large cities particularly, with the exodus of upper and middle class families, local assessments could not raise the level of education and, in fact, the level had been progressively lowered as school buildings grew older and were neglected, as teachers fled to the suburbs, as class size mounted closer and closer to 50, and as equipment and materials became inaccessible.

Alarm was expressed by many that federal funds might be withdrawn just as systems were beginning to find ways of solving educational and personal problems of their children in need. It is distressing to observe this alarm about delays in passing legislation or the possibility of withdrawal of funds rather than about the deficiencies in local funding and the defects patent in many programs.

Some Promising Programs and Their Implications

It should become clear that most, if not all, of the recommendations to follow apply to the education of all children, not only to the disadvantaged. Many are not new. In isolated, favored public and private schools across the country, they are standard practices. Now they must become a common pattern.

The programs which would assure quality education for all of our children would provide: 1, integrated schools affording differing social, economic, ethnic, racial, and religious groups with continuing and open opportunities to learn, work, and establish relationships across all boundaries; 2, the highest caliber of administrative leadership and instructional staff; 3, physical facilities which provide sufficient, pleasant, and appropriate space for study, health, recreation, and other school functions with commensurate equipment and supplies; 4, an education program which assumes responsibility for our young at a much earlier age for an extended school day, week, and year, thereby expanding the present limited function of the school; 5, modernization of curriculum and instruction to increase each individual's ability to learn independently that which has meaning for his present and future life; and, 6, return to the concept that education of our children is a community responsibility thereby involving parents and other appropriate adults in meaningful decision making, with the school and its staffs being held accountable for the quality and quantity of its students' learning.

This design is not new, but where in our cities can one find all of these elements essential to valid education for a democracy?

The Crucial Person

Given circumstances in which education can take place, the gifted and highly motivated teacher can overcome inordinate obstacles in educating children. But gifted teachers are rare, and someone higher in the organizational structure must create the favorable circumstances.

In some school systems, an isolated school will be identified as doing an exceptional job of educating disadvantaged children, as evidenced by community support, academic achievement, or other criteria. These objectives are achieved far beyond those attained by comparable schools without direct reference to special funds, although special funding is at times in evidence. In each of these schools, one finds a dynamic, determined, and competent principal who has inspired children, parents, and teachers to join in the successful venture. He has an idea which he knows will work. He is in every classroom every day. He knows almost every child, every teacher, many parents, and he cares about them all. He changes organization and provides services and inservice education to bring his idea to fruition. He holds his teachers accountable for the achievement of children. He works far beyond school closing time and expects his teachers to do likewise. He is informed and moves in the front ranks of educational progress. He is an instructional leader in distinct contrast to many of his peers who throw up their hands in despair or who hide from reality behind the excuse of too much paper work. Abdication of responsibility occurs too frequently with devastating effects on the children. Unfortunately, one finds too few of the competent breed in slum schools. We must again look to a higher power for an answer.

It is an interesting phenomenon one finds in a few school systems when almost everyone you meet refers to someone at the central education headquarters as the spearhead of progress. This top level administrator has been able to convince his school board that everyone would be better educated if certain clear changes were made in philosophy and practice. This intense focus permeates down to all staff people in the system since they are aware that they will be held accountable. This cannot happen or, rather, has not happened in the largest cities where the weight of numbers blocks direct contact and impact. Here is at least one good reason for decentralizing large school systems.

Planners at central headquarters and the principal are wisest when they realize that the point of contact is still within the classroom and when they involve teachers in all stages of planning and implementation of programs. Systems where teachers' committees on equalizing educational opportunity are active show greater morale and progress than those where teachers feel impotent in the face of administrative decision.

Creating Readiness

A quiet revolution is taking place in Head Start, Follow Through, and kindergarten programs. Prior emphasis on waiting for readiness in early childhood classes is beginning to give way to creating readiness. The Malabar Street School[15, 15a] in east Los Angeles, California serves a portion of the Mexican-American community. They propose that in order to make up for deficiencies, preschool experiences for three to five year olds should develop linguistic ability to the point of readiness for formal learning in kindergarten. In their belief that children at very young ages can be taught basic skills and concepts usually reserved for older grades, they begin formal instruction in handwriting of the child's name early in the kindergarten year. Patient assistance by parents and teachers on an individual basis helps the child to write his name correctly. Concurrently, the class is learning to recognize the letters of the alphabet, to write them and to understand their phonetic equivalents, and to read all the children's names and other words. By the end of the year, the children can count and write numbers to 20 and beyond. Simultaneously, each child receives individual language assistance (see page 6). It was refreshing to observe kindergarten children who have learned that they come to school to learn, not to play, and who participate enthusiastically in their individual learning tasks.

It was exciting to observe first grade children writing their own stories, participating in peer teaching, self-selecting activities, and reading. They turn to the teacher for assistance but feel responsible for their own progress. The relationship between teacher and child is a private one, with help given directly and promptly and with a minimum of correction and reprimand.

In first and second grades, a ratio of 30 children to one teacher is consistent with non-project classes, but the established behavior patterns make for a busy, positive classroom community. At these grade levels, curriculum focuses on basic language and arithmetic skills. The class is usually divided into three groups, with the teacher working directly with each child in rotation in one group while the other groups are busy with independent reading aloud or with skill building games. The Fernald technique of word tracing is used, with each child building his own file of words as he needs them. By the end of the second grade, despite the language difficulty, most of the children have a firm command of the standard language phonic and number tools needed for further learning. Most important, however, is the fact that each child has experienced for three years continuous opportunity for decision making, for self-direction, and for responsibility for his own growth. They glowed with the excitement of learning.

The introduction of correct handwriting in kindergarten and first grade classes in the Focus on Achievement program at the Ryan Elementary School in Houston, Texas[16] again proves that children can be taught appropriate and useful skills at very young ages and that this learning constructively influences their subsequent academic achievement. Intensive handwriting instruction continues through the sixth grade as a vehicle for learning spelling, improving reading, and for creative writing.

Individualizing Instruction

A new acronym, IPI, has emerged which represents individually prescribed instruction. Its antecedent is the old contract method refined and improved. In the past, many believed that only the "intellectually gifted" could learn to learn on their own. Now it is clear that with proper teacher preparation, sufficient and appropriate materials, and determination, almost all children, including many classified as mentally retarded, can be given the opportunity to prepare adequately to solve the problems they will face tomorrow in a world we cannot presently foresee.

Many components are involved, such as regrouping, redeployment of staff, restructuring of school buildings, employment of proven audio-visual equipment and its accompanying software. Elements are referred to as unitizing, discovery, process, sequential, individualizing; but they all add up to education which works with all children, and which has proved successful with the disadvantaged. Grouping for IPI also removes the stigma of being retained in grade—a practice still followed in most school systems which results in physical and social incongruities within classes.

In addition to the benefits indicated above, the one which strikes me most forcefully is the question of waste of time. Entering a classroom using IPI, one is impressed by the purposeful, ongoing activity. In sharp contrast, one sees the hours and hours of lost learning time in the traditional, self-contained, teacher-instructed classroom. "We will all wait for Jane to get on line." "We will begin after John has passed out the papers." "Wait until the others have finished," can be multiplied a thousandfold and still not spell out the tragedy of children who learn primarily to do what they are told, when they are told, and how. Discipline for the sake of discipline is nonsense. The only rational discipline is self-control evolving out of interest and industry. No child and no teacher with whom I spoke in IPI classes wanted to go back to the traditional format.

The Coleman Report[7] indicates that one of the prime factors influencing the learning patterns and pace of children is the degree to which they have learned that what they do has a direct influence on their present and future. IPI places them continually in the position of making decisions for themselves, with opportunities to learn from mistakes in less painful ways, with open opportunity to correct themselves.

Several isolated attempts to move toward individualizing instruction have been observed. The most comprehensive program was found in Duluth, Minnesota[17, 17a, 17b] where the movement began in the Franklin-Nettleton school in the inner city and is now planned for the entire system. Other programs include a limited continuous progress program at the high school level and one junior high school reading program in Seattle, Washington[18, 18a, 18b, 18c] and the James School in Kansas City, Missouri.[19] A federally funded Title V Higher Education Act Experienced Teacher Fellowship program at the University of Missouri prepared the faculty of the school for the change to IPI. The Differentiation of Instruction to Individualize Learning (DIIL) program at the Callum School in Omaha, Nebraska is another example of this trend. The School Improvement Program in Racine, Wisconsin[20] combines each two grade levels in its target schools with five to seven teachers responsible for each unit.[21, 21a, 21b, 21c, 21d, 21e, 21f]

Before any system contemplates moving in this direction, funds for paid inservice education must be provided so that teachers can learn needed techniques and select and design curriculum materials appropriate for the subject and levels of the class.

New Attitudes Toward the Problems of Adolescence

As schools have moved from the task of educating the elite to that of educating all children, the problem of the cast-out adolescent has emerged as a critical challenge to secondary schools. As the problems faced by adolescents have been complicated by a combination of the need for more education and the unavailability of employment for unskilled labor, the rejects from our schools have become a social problem of considerable proportion. Partly for humanitarian reasons and partly for self-protection, our society is establishing new centers for learning with new methods and new curriculums to meet the specific requirements of special groups of young men and women, including teenage pregnant girls and youth who are disruptive or who have left school.

One of the earliest comprehensive programs designed to provide continuing education for teenage pregnant girls was developed in Los Angeles.[22] Another is supported by the Syracuse, New York school system.[23] The Los Angeles program is directed by a medical doctor who initiated a pilot project in 1962. Expanded under Title I, there are now six centers for 145 girls. As soon as pregnancy is identified, the staff assumes social, medical, and educational responsibility until eight weeks post-partum. The curriculum provides for the continuation of the individual's formal coursework and adds sewing of layettes and maternity clothes. The nurses and social workers also help prepare the students for delivery and motherhood. The long term agenda is directed toward completion of high school, continuing education, and vocational preparation through intensive emotional, social, and educational support.

Satellite school facilities have been set up in several cities in order to remove the disruptive junior high school or high school student from the parent school. Others are designed to serve the returning or retrieved dropout. Education programs combined with active guidance and work programs have been developed to combine formal classwork with vocational and technical training, in some cases supported by local industry.[24, 25, 26] In almost all the centers, small class size, some curriculum revision leading to greater relevance, and acceptance by the staff brought remarkable changes in overt behavior. In most of the centers observed, there were evidences of changed attitudes toward school and learning with commensurate spurts in achievement.

The Roads to Literacy

A multiplicity of materials and techniques for teaching reading was in evidence at every site observed. Still the problem remains in most schools that desirable levels of reading skills and comprehension are not achieved. While we propose no pat solutions, several clear organizational patterns emerge. One is the off-site reading center, as utilized in Omaha,[27] Des Moines, Idaho,[28] Cheyenne, Wyoming,[29] and the Communications Skills Centers in Detroit, Michigan.[30] Another trend is toward reading specialists located in the schools working with small groups, as in P.S. 192M in New York City,[31] and in the newly constructed units built adjacent to target school buildings in Houston.[16] A third trend is toward the use of instructional paraprofessionals, student teachers, college tutors, community volunteers, and homework helpers, as in San Francisco, California.[32]

All of these programs, in order to be successful, must provide individual diagnosis and individual or small group instruction with all the resources available. Closets, coatrooms, halls, and basement corners have become reading centers for lack of sufficient space. Most effective appear to be systematic programs of instruction which provide each reluctant reader with the opportunity to read self-selected materials aloud in a supportive climate.

Progress is reported in many quarters. One noteworthy program has been instituted in Phoenix, Arizona[33] where all ninth grade students in the target area South Mountain High School receive individual and small group reading instruction one period a day for a whole year. Students who are not near their potential at the end of that year are scheduled for a second year. Title I funds were used to construct the facility and pay the staff of six. Results of the last year are impressive. In Kansas City, a reading staff of five specialists has established a center at the Lincoln Senior High School to overcome deficiencies in basic skills on all four grade levels. A program combining oral language development with individualized reading instruction has produced remarkable results at P.S. 129 in New York City.[34]

Language and Linguistics

Current thought and practice support the view that for children for whom bilingualism presents problems, basic skills and concepts should first be taught in their native tongues before or at least during the time that a second language is being learned. Awareness is also developing that some dialects can be deterrents to early mastery of effective reading and writing of standard English. American Indian, Mexican-American, Puerto Rican, and Oriental children, and children with myriad other native backgrounds, and the Negro child with a strong regional dialect face serious problems when placed under the usual pressures of our typical schools.

Many systems and schools have token programs to alleviate these problems. Some have moved to instruction in the native language. Others provide vestibule classes and/or speech therapists. Kansas City has developed a program in which all classes in target schools receive two to three half hour language development lessons a week combining instruction in articulation, projection, phonics, grammar, usage, posture, and etiquette.

The Malabar Street School in Los Angeles[15, 15a] studies the speech of each child in the preschool and kindergarten project groups. Every child's speech is taped for two hours every 20 days. The tapes are analyzed and are used for prescribing instructional emphases for the next and subsequent periods. Structured interviews are carried on with these children each term in the first and second grades. The speech of each child is analyzed to diagnose continuing difficulties, to study progress in speech production, in sentence complexity, and thought conveyance. Prescription of remediation is followed by instruction by the classroom teacher or by the specialist.

Libraries and Resource Centers

Libraries and librarians have been added to many schools at all levels with Title I funds, but the supply of competent librarians is extremely limited. In some schools, resource centers, or audio-visual sections of libraries, or curriculum supply repositories have been built, and supplies and equipment furnished. It appears that having extensive resources in each classroom for frequent and continuing use is effective and desirable. Some programs have built into their budgets funds to provide books to be given to students in order to help them acquire personal libraries in areas of their special interests.[35] This approach appears to reduce the rate of loss of library holdings while motivating reluctant learners to read.

The Parents' Role

Schools which have open doors to parents and community members have greater success in educating children. Among other reasons, parents can better understand the way in which a school functions and how learning takes place, and they frequently become aware of specific ways in which they can become more effective in helping their children to learn. In addition, strengthened positive parent attitudes toward the school function to motivate the children to approach schooling enthusiastically. The children seem to be direct beneficiaries of the change in perception on the part of their parents. Some systems employ parents as paraprofessionals, such as Minneapolis, Minnesota,[36] using 350 aides. That state is developing new certification requirements for several levels of education and function for these school employees. Kansas City employs 135 teacher aides in 17 target area schools. At P.S. 129M in New York City, a clearly designed program integrally involves parents in the day-to-day learning of their children.

Adult involvement takes different forms. Many Head Start and Follow Through programs require parents to participate, as in the Malabar Street School[15, 15a] and Berkeley.[37] Instructional and non-instructional paid aides from community groups or college student bodies can relieve teacher shortages. Women belonging to social groups acting as non-paid volunteers have proven an excellent instructional asset to those systems which encourage their use.

Caution should be indicated in regard to preservice and inservice preparation of aides for their special tasks. Adding adults to classrooms does not always raise the level of instruction unless they are prepared adequately for their roles.

Hardware and Software

Several school systems have utilized federal funds to create central audio-visual service units for all target area schools. Houston and Omaha[38, 38a] have demonstrated their usefulness in supplying teachers with tested materials so that no school and no teacher in those localities can excuse lack of accomplishment because of lack of needed units, charts, forms, film strips, films, etc. In addition, several systems have used secretaries or aides to prepare dittos and to coordinate equipment. Availability of these services tends to do away with the practice found in several systems of having all children buy their own workbooks and other instructional materials.

Educational television is developing rapidly. Some teachers report considerable use and positive results from viewing prepared programs, but this avenue leaves much to be desired, both in the programs themselves and in the way teachers use them. Programs are at times condescending to the children and on occasion have an impersonality which reduces impact on learning. Rigid schedules of TV programs control classroom use rather than being available when appropriate to the interest and progress of the children. In too many instances, teachers neither prepare the children for the unit nor provide meaningful follow-up activities. The performance proceeds beyond the control of the teacher, often after the class has been lost by confusion or lack of comprehension. Perhaps video-tapes will resolve some of these problems in the future since teachers will then be able to pace exposure to the level of the children and will be able to prescreen and select units.

Equipment and related instructional materials are essential to fruitful individualized instruction. Children can and do learn very quickly how to use most AV machines. When given the opportunity to self-pace their use, learning is facilitated.

While film strips and movie and opaque projectors were often in evidence, more complex equipment, such as instructional computers and talking typewriters, were not as yet introduced in the schools for disadvantaged students we observed. The most frequent reason given is the inadequacy of available instructional software.

Special Emphases

Since most of the documents in this report are available on microfiche or hard copy (see page 8), and since they will be spelled out in greater detail in the state-of-the-art paper being prepared, we will simply mention below some interesting and effective programs with special emphases. Programs which are carried on outside of established school instruction hours are not included in this report. However, their impact on the learning of children and on the community should not be underestimated.

P.S. 168M in New York City is a more effective More Effective School. In addition to a well defined drive utilizing all teaching staff for improving reading, this school has an outstanding industrial arts shop serving grades K-6. At the middle grades, all work is related to the basic curriculum. The staff has been organized so that a qualified industrial arts instructor is available to work with every class in the school. A shop has been fully equipped by discreet use of funds, gifts, and the work and skill of the instructor. Everything which is made from the kindergarten up is useful either to the person, the class, or the school. Expert quality is expected and achieved, with commensurate satisfaction and skill development. Large scale relief maps, dioramas, and displays are in evidence in many rooms. In a second grade class, the children's poems, which evolved out of a language arts unit, were typeset and printed by the children.[39]

Physical education specialists have been added at the elementary levels to develop fitness, agility, and gross and small motor dexterity, as in Berkeley[40] and Cheyenne, where swimming and team sports are also emphasized.

In social studies, a total submersion approach to visual learning has been developed in the EPOCH program at Berkeley,[41] funded for three years under Title III ESEA. After two years of planning and preparation, they are now beginning to bring classes to this center. The center provides a large round room with chairs for students around a low table on which has been plotted the history of man. The walls of the room are screens for projection of films augmenting the place, people, and time being studied. A second area provides resource materials and equipment for further individual study of the social sciences.

The Dropout Project in Des Moines [42] is designed to identify potential dropouts at the first, second, third, and seventh, eighth, and ninth grades. Class size is held to 15, and one teacher works with the class for three years. Positive results would suggest further projects with these elements.

A Saturday and summer program, Project Open Future,[43] for poor but academically qualified students in Los Angeles is conducted at Claremont Graduate School. A similar program is provided by Wheaton College for Chicago, Illinois students.

Two programs in the Chicago system are designed to improve Negro self-image. "Magnificent Seven Plus Two" focuses on prominent Negroes. "I, Too, Sing America" is a drama about the American black people. Performances by the students are presented, followed by a dialogue between the audience and the students at the end of the play.

Music, art, dance, and drama activities are included in many comprehensive programs. When they involve students as participants, they are more effective than when the children are involved only as spectators.

Some Problems

There is wide variance in the nature and extent of medical, psychological, and dental services. Free breakfast and lunch programs are available in systems which realize that a hungry child cannot concentrate on learning. This awareness is regretfully lacking in other situations where the need is as great. Community aides, when employed, try to help families in need. But how does one help the children who fall asleep at their desks because of inadequate home facilities and circumstances except by massive social and welfare assistance?

Those systems which utilize university personnel or departments in planning and implementing their programs appear to be better organized. One might also put greater reliance on information from systems which turn over evaluation to objective outsiders, either Research and Development (R & D) centers, regional laboratories, or universities. National Teacher Corps programs, student teaching placement, college tutors serving during observation semesters, and Title V Higher Education Act fellowship programs could help schools while providing better field work for future and inservice teachers. Still one finds many schools completely insulated from these potential sources of assistance even in communities where proximity is not a problem.

Leaders of Community Action Programs and other local agencies are frequently impatient with the school systems, and often when cooperation would have been of mutual benefit it was difficult or impossible to achieve. Several administrators have realized that this gap must be closed and have taken initiative to involve community in school affairs.

There is an insufficient supply of minority group teachers, especially males. Only a token number of qualified and competent minority group teachers have been elevated to supervisory positions, principalships, or to decision making positions at central headquarters. Disagreement between school administrators and staffs often results in work stoppages which retard effectiveness of educational programs. Other means, such as negotiation-arbitration, should be employed to their full potential to resolve differences.

In many communities, new school buildings are built for the more favored areas, with the slums waiting or settling for repainting jobs or minor additions to existing buildings.

Thefts of equipment and vandalism persist. Riots disrupt the process of education through development of fear, hate, and the destruction of material wealth and social channels of communication.

In Closing

Across the country there are hard working and well-motivated staffs trying, despite many limitations and obstacles, to fulfill their professional roles as educators. In almost all schools observed, an atmosphere conducive to learning has been established and children are, at least, compliant and well-behaved, and, at best, are actively involved in improving their skills and raising their academic competence. These schools were selected as models. Much is exemplary, but many leave much to be desired. If these are the best, what are the rest of slum schools like? Who will bear the guilt for relegating those children to years of nonlearning?

Most summer programs everywhere are reported as being "wonderful." The opportunity to select staff more carefully, the freedom from curriculum strictures, the closer teacher-student relationships, the use of trips and community resources, the individualizing of instruction, are all given as reasons for the success of these programs. No answers are as yet forthcoming as to why many of these elements are not built into the year round program.

It is proposed that a massive infusion of funds, perhaps an extra 100 billion dollars a year, is needed. Schools will need to assume responsibility for children's learning earlier, perhaps as early as the neonatal period. Several projects are in the early stages of exploring the effectiveness of earlier intervention. Schools will need to serve children and youth over longer periods of each day, each week, and each year.[10] Programs will be needed to educate young adults and, in fact, all adults desiring further learning experiences.

In order to insulate the child from many of the destructive elements in disorganized communities and families, educational services will need to be reinforced by medical and dental care, provisions of a fortified diet, welfare services, recreation, and other social assistance.

Given the dimensions of the problem and the importance of education for our general welfare, and indeed for the preservation of our democratic form of government, it is imperative that our government, our social scientists, and our educators arouse themselves to furnish the resources and the skills required for the task of providing for a nurturing multicultural society for all. In light of the presence in our country of several aroused minority groups, any alternative and each delay will, we fear, further complicate these problems.

A Teaching Strategy for Culturally Deprived Pupils: Cognitive and Motivational Considerations

DAVID P. AUSUBEL

The possibility of arresting and reversing the course of intellectual retardation in the culturally deprived pupil depends largely on providing him with an optimal learning environment as early as possible in the course of his educational career. If the limiting effects of prolonged cultural deprivation on the development of verbal intelligence and on the acquisition of verbal knowledge are to be at least partially overcome, better-than-average strategies of teaching are obviously necessary in terms of both general effectiveness and specific appropriateness for his particular learning situation. Yet precisely the opposite state of affairs typically prevails: the learning environment of the culturally deprived child is both generally inferior and specifically inappropriate. His cumulative intellectual deficit, therefore, almost invariably reflects, in part, the cumulative impact of a continuing and consistently deficient learning environment, as well as his emotional and motivational reaction to this environment. Thus, much of the lower-class child's alienation from the school is not so much a reflection of discriminatory or rejecting attitudes on the part of teachers and other school personnel—although the importance of this factor should not be underestimated; it is in greater measure a reflection of the cumulative effects of a curriculum that is too demanding of him, and of the resulting load of frustration, confusion, demoralization, resentment, and impaired self-confidence that he must bear.

THE SCHOOL REVIEW, Winter 1963, Vol. 71, pp. 454-463.

An effective and appropriate teaching strategy for the culturally deprived child must therefore emphasize these three considerations: (*a*) the selection of initial learning material geared to the learner's existing state of readiness; (*b*) mastery and consolidation of all ongoing learning tasks before new tasks are introduced, so as to provide the necessary foundation for successful sequential learning and to prevent unreadiness for future learning tasks; and (*c*) the use of structured learning materials optimally organized to facilitate efficient sequential learning. Attention to these three factors can go a long way toward insuring effective learning for the first time, and toward restoring the child's educational morale and confidence in his ability to learn. Later possible consequences are partial restoration of both intrinsic and extrinsic motivation for academic achievement, diminution of anti-intellectualism, and decreased alienation from the school to the point where his studies make sense and he sees some purpose in learning. In my opinion, of all the available teaching strategies, programmed instruction, minus the teaching-machine format, has the greatest potentialities for meeting the aforementioned three criteria of an effective and appropriate approach to the teaching of culturally deprived pupils.

Readiness.—A curriculum that takes the readiness of the culturally deprived child into account always takes as its starting point his existing knowledge and sophistication in the various subject-matter areas and intellectual skills, no matter how far down the scale this happens to be. This policy demands rigid elimination of all subject matter that he cannot economically assimilate on the basis of his current level of cognitive sophistication. It presupposes emphasis on his acquisition of the basic intellectual skills before any attempt is made to teach him algebra, geometry, literature, and foreign languages. However, in many urban high schools and junior high schools today, pupils who cannot read at a third-grade level and who cannot speak or write grammatically or perform simple arithmetical computations are subjected to irregular French verbs, Shakespearean drama, and geometrical theorems. Nothing more educationally futile or better calculated to destroy educational morale could be imagined!

In the terms of readiness for a given level of school work, a child is no less ready because of a history of cultural deprivation, chronic academic failure, and exposure to an unsuitable curriculum than because of deficient intellectual endowment. Hence, realistic recognition of this fact is not undemocratic, reactionary, or evidence of social class bias, of intellectual snobbery, of a "soft," patronizing approach, or a belief in the inherent uneducability of lower-class children. Neither is it indicative of a desire to surrender to the culturally deprived child's current intellectual level, to perpetuate the status quo, or to institute a double, class-oriented standard of education. It is merely a necessary first step in preparing him to cope with more advanced subject matter, and hence in eventually reducing existing social class differentials in academic achievement. To set the same *initial* standards and expectations for the academically retarded culturally deprived child as for the non-retarded middle- or lower-class child is automatically to insure the former's failure and to widen prevailing discrepancies between social class groups.

Consolidation.—By insisting on consolidation or mastery of ongoing lessons before new material is introduced, we make sure of continued readiness and success in sequentially organized learning. Abundant experimental research has confirmed the proposition that prior learnings are not transferable to new learning tasks unless they are first overlearned.[1] Overlearning, in turn, requires an adequate number of adequately spaced repetitions and reviews, sufficient intratask repetitiveness prior to intra- and intertask diversification,[2] and opportunity for differential practice of the more difficult components of a task. Frequent testing and provision of feedback, especially with test items demanding fine discrimination among alternatives varying in degrees of correctness, also enhance consolidation by confirming, clarifying, and correcting previous learnings. Lastly, in view of the fact that the culturally deprived child tends to learn more slowly than his non-deprived peers, self-pacing helps to facilitate consolidation.

Structured, sequential materials.—The principal advantage of programmed instruction, apart from the fact that it furthers consolidation, is its careful sequential arrangement and gradation of difficulty which insures that each attained increment in learning serves as an appropriate foundation and anchoring post for the learning and retention of subsequent items in the ordered sequence.[3] Adequate programming of materials also presupposes maximum attention to such matters as lucidity, organization, and the explanatory and integrative power of substantive content. It is helpful, for example, if sequential materials are so organized that they become progressively more differentiated in terms of generality and inclusiveness, and if similarities and differences between the current learning task and previous learnings are explicitly delineated.[4] Both of these aims can be accomplished by using an advance organizer or brief introductory passage before each new unit of material, which both makes available relevant explanatory principles at a high level of abstraction and increases discriminability. Programmed instruction can also be especially adapted to meet the greater needs of culturally deprived pupils for concrete-empirical props in learning relational propositions.

Although programmed instruction in general is particularly well suited to the needs of the culturally deprived child, I cannot recommend the small-frame format characteristic of teaching-machine programs and most programmed textbooks. In terms of both the logical requirements of meaningful learning and the actual size of the task that can be conveniently accommodated by the learner, the frame length typically used by teaching machines is artifically and unnecessarily abbreviated. It tends to fragment the ideas presented in the program so that their interrelationships are obscured and their logical structure is destroyed.[5] Hence it is relatively easy for less able students to master each granulated step of a given program without understanding the logical relationships and development of the concepts presented.[6] In my opinion, therefore, the traditional textbook format or oral didactic exposition that follows the programming principles outlined above, supplemented by frequent self-scoring and feedback-giving tests, is far superior to the teaching-machine approach for the actual presentation of subject-matter content.[7]

MOTIVATIONAL CONSIDERATIONS

Thus far I have considered various environmental factors that induce retardation in the culturally deprived child's intellectual growth, as well as different cognitive techniques of counteracting and reversing such retardation. These factors and techniques, however, do not operate in a motivational vacuum. Although it is possible separately to consider cognitive and motivational aspects of learning for purposes of theoretical analysis, they are nonetheless inseparably intertwined in any real-life learning situation. For example, school failure and loss of confidence resulting from an inappropriate curriculum further depress the culturally deprived pupil's motivation to learn and thereby increase his existing learning and intellectual deficit. Similarly, although a number of practice and task variables are potentially important for effective learning in a programmed instruction context, appropriate manipulation of these variables can, in the final analysis, only insure successful long-term learning of subject matter provided that the individual is adequately motivated.

Doing without being interested in what one is doing results in relatively little permanent learning, since it is reasonable to suppose that only those materials can be meaningfully incorporated on a long-term basis into an individual's structure of knowledge that are relevant to areas of concern in his psychological field. Learners who have little need to know and understand quite naturally expend little learning effort; manifest an insufficiently meaningful learning set; fail to develop precise meanings, to reconcile new ideas with existing concepts, and to formulate new propositions in their own words; and do not devote enough time and energy to practice and review. Material is therefore never sufficiently consolidated to form an adequate foundation for sequential learning.

The problem of reversibility exists in regard to the motivational as well as in regard to the cognitive status of the culturally deprived pupil, inasmuch as his environment typically stunts not only his intellectual development, but also the development of appropriate motivations for academic achievement. Motivations for learning, like cognitive abilities, are only potential rather than inherent or endogenous capacities in human beings; their actual development is invariably dependent upon adequate environmental stimulation. Cognitive drive or intrinsic motivation to learn, for example, is probably derived in a very general sense from curiosity tendencies and from related predispositions to explore, manipulate, and cope with the environment; but these tendencies and predispositions are only actualized as a result of successful exercise and the anticipation of future satisfying consequences from further exercise and as a result of internalization of the values of those significant persons in the family and subcultural community with whom the child identifies.

Intrinsic motivation.—The development of cognitive drive or of intrinsic motivation for learning, that is, the acquisition of knowledge as an end in itself or for its own sake, is, in my opinion, the most promising motivational strategy which we can adopt in relation to the culturally deprived child. It is true, of course, in view of the anti-intellectualism and pragmatic attitude toward education that is characteristic of lower-class ideology,[8] that a superficially better case can be made for the alternative strategy of appealing to the incentives to job acquisition, retention, and advancement that now apply so saliently to continuing education because of the rapid rate of technological change. Actually, however, intrinsic motivation for learning is more potent, relevant, durable, and easier to arouse than its extrinsic counterpart. Meaningful school learning, in contrast to most kinds of laboratory learning, requires relatively little effort or extrinsic incentive, and, when successful, furnishes its own reward. In most instances of school learning, cognitive drive is also the only immediately relevant motivation, since the greater part of school learning cannot be rationalized as necessary for meeting the demands of daily living. Furthermore, it does not lose its relevance or potency in later adult life when utilitarian and career advancement considerations are no longer applicable. Lastly, as we know from the high dropout rate among culturally deprived high-school youth, appeals to extrinsic motivation are not very effective. Among other reasons, the latter situation reflects a limited time perspective focused primarily on the present; a character structure that is oriented more to immediate than delayed gratification of needs; the lack of strong internalized needs for and anxiety about high academic and vocational achievement, as part of the prevailing family, peer group, and community ideology;[9] and the seeming unreality and impossibility of attaining the rewards of prolonged striving and self-denial in view of current living conditions and family circumstances, previous lack of school success, and the discriminatory attitudes of middle-class society.[10]

If we wish to develop the cognitive drive so that it remains viable during the school years and in adult life, it is necessary to move still further away from the educational doctrine of gearing the curriculum to the spontaneously expressed interests, current concerns, and life-adjustment problems of pupils. Although it is undoubtedly unrealistic and even undesirable in our culture to eschew entirely the utilitarian, ego-enhancement, and anxiety-reduction motivations for learning, we must place increasingly greater emphasis upon the value of knowing and understanding as goals in their own right, quite apart from any practical benefits they may confer. Instead of denigrating subject-matter knowledge, we must discover more efficient methods of fostering the long-term acquisition or meaningful and usable bodies of knowledge, and of developing appropriate intrinsic motivations for such learning.

It must be conceded at the outset that culturally deprived children typically manifest little intrinsic motivation to learn. They come from family and cultural environments in which the veneration of learning for its own sake is not a conspicuous value, and in which there is little or no tradition of scholarship. Moreover, they have not been notably successful in their previous learning efforts in school. Nevertheless we need not necessarily despair of motivating them to learn for intrinsic reasons. Psychologists have been emphasizing the motivation-learning and the interest-activity sequences of cause and effect for so long that they tend to overlook their reciprocal aspects. Since motivation is not an indispensable condition for short-term and limited-quantity learning, it is not necessary to postpone learning activities until appropriate interests and motivations have been developed. Frequently the best way of motivating an unmotivated pupil is to ignore his motivational state for the time being and concentrate on teaching him as effectively as possible. Much to his surprise and to his teacher's, he will learn despite his lack of motivation; and from the satisfaction of learning he will characteristically develop the motivation to learn more.

Paradoxically, therefore, we may discover that the most effective method of developing intrinsic motivation to learn is to focus on the cognitive rather than on the motivational aspects of learning, and to rely on the motivation that is developed retroactively from successful educational achievement. This is particularly true when a teacher is able to generate contagious excitement and enthusiasm about the subject he teaches, and when he is the kind of person with whom culturally deprived children can identify. Recruiting more men teachers and dramatizing the lives and exploits of cultural, intellectual, and scientific heroes can also enhance the process of identification. At the same time, of course, we can attempt to combat the anti-intellectualism and lack of cultural tradition in the home through programs of adult education and cultural enrichment.

Extrinsic motivation.—The emphasis I have placed on intrinsic motivation for learning should not be interpreted to mean that I deny the importance of developing extrinsic motivations. The need for ego enhancement, status, and prestige through achievement, the internalization of long-term vocational aspirations, and the development of such implementing traits as responsibility, initiative, self-denial, frustration tolerance, impulse control, and the ability to postpone immediate hedonistic gratification are, after all, traditional hallmarks of personality maturation in our culture; and educational aspirations and achievement are both necessary prerequisites for, and way-station prototypes of, their vocational counterparts. Hence, in addition to encouraging intrinsic motivation for learning, it is also necessary to foster ego-enhancement and career-advancement motivations for academic achievement.

As previously pointed out, however, the current situation with respect to developing adequate motivations for higher academic and vocational achievement among culturally deprived children is not very encouraging. But just as in the case of cognitive drive, much extrinsic motivation for academic success can be generated retroactively from the experience of current success in schoolwork. Intensive counseling can also compensate greatly for the absence of appropriate home, community, and peer-group support and expectations for the development of long-term vocational ambitions. In a sense counselors must be prepared to act *in loco parentis* in this situation. By identifying with a mature, stable, striving, and successful male adult figure, culturally deprived boys can be encouraged to internalize long-term and realistic aspirations, as well as to develop the mature personality traits necessary for their implementation. Hence, as a result of achieving current ego enhancement in the school setting, obtaining positive encouragement and practical guidance in the counseling relationship, and experiencing less rejection and discrimination at the hands of school personnel, higher vocational aspirations appear to lie more realistically within their grasp. Further encouragement to strive for more ambitious academic and vocational goals can be provided by making available abundant scholarship aid to universities, to community colleges, and to technical institutes; by eliminating the color, ethnic, and class bar in housing, education, and employment; by acquainting culturally deprived youth with examples of successful professional persons originating from their own racial, ethnic, and class backgrounds; and by involving parents sympathetically in the newly fostered ambitions of their children. The success of the Higher Horizons project indicates that an energetic program organized along the lines outlined above can do much to reverse the effects of cultural deprivation on the development of extrinsic motivations for academic and vocational achievement.

NOTES

1. See R. W. Bruce, "Conditions of Transfer of Training," *Journal of Experimental Psychology*, XVI (1933), 343–61; C. P. Duncan, "Transfer in Motor Learning as a Function of Degree of First-task Learning and Inter-task Similarity," *Journal of Experimental Psychology*, XLV (1953), 1–11, and his "Transfer after Training with Single versus Multiple Tasks," *Journal of Experimental Psychology*, LV (1958), 63–72; L. Morrisett and C. I. Hovland, "A Comparison of Three Varieties of Training in Human Problem Solving," *Journal of Experimental Psychology*, LV (1958), 52–55; and J. M. Sassenrath, "Learning without Awareness and Transfer of Learning Sets," *Journal of Educational Psychology*, L (1959), 202–12.

2. See Duncan, "Transfer after Training with Single versus Multiple Tasks," *op. cit.*; Morrisett and Hovland, *op. cit.*; and Sassenrath, *op. cit.*

3. D. P. Ausubel and D. Fitzgerald, "Organizer, General Background, and Antecedent Learning Variables in Sequential Verbal Learning," *Journal of Educational Psychology*, LIII (1962), 243–49.

4. D. P. Ausubel, "The Use of Advance Organizers in the Learning and Retention of Meaningful Verbal Learning," *Journal of Educational Psychology*, LI (1960), 267–72; D. P. Ausubel and D. Fitzgerald, "The Role of Discriminability in Meaningful Verbal Learning and Retention," *Journal of Educational Psychology*, LII (1961), 266–74, and their "Organizer, General Background, and Antecedent Learning Variables in Sequential Verbal Learning," *op. cit.*

5. S. L. Pressey, "Basic Unresolved Teaching-Machine Problems," *Theory into Practice*, I (1962), 30–37.

6. D. G. Beane, "A Comparison of Linear and Branching Techniques of Programed Instruction in Plane Geometry" ("Technical Report," No. 1 [Urbana: Training Research Laboratory, University of Illinois, July 1962]).

7. Pressey, *op. cit.*

8. F. Riessman, *The Culturally Deprived Child* (New York: Harper & Bros., 1962).

9. A. Davis, "Child Training and Social Class," *Child Behavior and Development*, ed. R. G. Barker, J. S. Kounin, and H. F. Wright (New York: McGraw-Hill Book Co., 1963), pp. 607–20.

10. *Ibid.*

Instructional Guidelines for Teachers of the Disadvantaged

Deborah Elkins

   Much has been written about the difficulties faced by children of the disadvantaged in the schools. But the schools have not as yet confronted either the complex causes of these difficulties or their own role in the perpetuation of them. Instead of effecting a confrontation with causes, we have permitted quick and easy "solutions" to be the order of the day: remedial reading, team teaching, and dividing the day into modules. Such solutions are hopefully but erroneously intended to fill the tremendous gaps in learning as well as the gaps in learning power with which the children come to school.

  The teaching strategies which the school devises must be founded in an intensive examination of those causes for gaps and not on the behaviors which are merely symptomatic. This we have never seriously undertaken. Inability to read, for example, is a symptom, not a cause. To fill the sixth-grade non-reader's day with drill in skills is to attack the symptom and not the causes. While the school did not cause and cannot cure the extensive social ills with which the child must contend, it can do much to counteract those ills. Certainly the school can do more than it has been doing; certainly the knowledge of what to do and how to do it is greater than that which is being put to use.

   Psycho-Social Factors Social conditions affect the school and dictate new models and strategies for teaching. A homogeneous group of academically able and highly motivated students has been characteristic of the population in the typical school of the past. Now it includes all the children of all the people and therefore encompasses great heterogeneity. This heterogeneity must be kept constantly in focus because it affects the strategies we must invent. The heterogeneous group includes alienated chil-

THE RECORD—TEACHERS COLLEGE, 1969, Vol. 70, pp. 593-615.

dren. With the speeding up of migration from rural areas to great industrial urban centers—Negroes from the rural South, Puerto Ricans from rural island communities, Mexicans and Indians in the Southwest—people have been catapulted from a simple, personal face-to-face culture into a highly complex, impersonal living pattern almost overnight. The resulting feeling of alienation is clear. Children describe this feeling in such terms as "I like my old place better," "We had enough to eat there," "There were places to swim and go fishing." They miss the personal contents that were a part of the simpler culture; here they are lost, children and adults alike.

Alienation is further accentuated by life in encapsulated communities; the symptoms of alienation are apparent in the hostility to school. The goals of the school are baffling; the content selected for learning is meaningless; and the practices, totally inappropriate. The goals, the content, the practices must be reexamined; for they, too, dictate new strategies. These strategies must be built with full awareness of the alienation and the heterogeneity involved. Uprooted children, those who are cut off from the mainstream of society which has created the school's goals, cannot learn from that society and cannot but be perplexed by these goals.

Alienation puts into motion a vicious cycle.[1] For one thing, it affects language facility so necessary for success in schools. Since children who live in segregated communities and who are cut off from larger culture cannot learn from it, they also cannot meet the school's expectations with respect to language facility. So begins the cycle of failure. Add to this the broken homes, and the large families which make it impossible for the remaining responsible adult to give the necessary personal attention needed for optimum growth, and the problem is compounded by deficit in cognitive functioning. The child of necessity is left on his own to explore his world with little interpretation or mediation by adults. It is that interpretation which helps him to develop not only language but also patterns of conceptualization. Adult mediation helps him make order out of his world and build concepts for understanding it. Cognitive functioning includes such processes as naming objects, identifying common elements in concrete objects and events, formulating concepts, and seeing relationships between cause and consequence, processes with which middle-class children grow up as a part of daily life, for their experiences include exploration of their daily environment which is accompanied by the interpretation of adults.

Not only does the disadvantaged child thus fail to learn concepts which are

1 Robert J. Havighurst and Lindley J. Stiles, "National Policy for Alienated Youth," in A. Harry Passow, Miriam Goldberg, and Abraham J. Tannenbaum, Eds. *Education of the Disadvantaged.* New York: Holt, Rinehart and Winston, Inc., 1967.

crucial for learning other things, but lack of attention from adults results in failure to develop the ego strength necessary to energize learning. There is no one to praise him for the tasks he does well, and the lack of ego strength creates the motivation and aspiration deficit. The label "lazy" or "apathetic" becomes attached to him and he is drawn deeper into the vortex of failure.

Cumulative Deficits   Because of these related language, cognitive and motivational deficits, the problems multiply. Teachers tend to consider the students natively unintelligent, even though the basic causes of the deficits in all of these areas are environmental. It is known that environment plays a tremendous role in the capacity to learn and in the development of intelligence. Piaget and his disciples make it clear that intelligence depends on a wealth of experience with manipulating concrete operations and that the experience must include adult help in interpretation of what is happening. Variety of stimulation is necessary for the development of flexible cognitive functioning as against rigidity of cognitive functioning. Further, variety of stimulation is closely associated with creating motivation: the more the child sees and hears and is helped to interpret, the more he will want to see and hear and interpret. Once he is motivated to do these things, once he wants to do them, he has energy to learn.

But the environment of the disadvantaged is limited. Systematic interpretation is lacking; rigid responses to situations are developed and motivation is restricted. A deficient development of flexible intellectual functioning must result. Children become accustomed to plunging from activity to activity with little organized attention given to any one thing. They survive with a bare minimum of experience with abstractions. When we consider that success in school depends on these very things—motivation, attention of an organized nature, ability to abstract, and facility with language—then the inevitability of failure for children with deficits in these areas is clear.

Nor does the cycle stop here. Deficits in the ingredients for success create a syndrome of behaviors which further retard the child's progress as he moves along in school. Low self-concept causes him to avoid uncomfortable competitive situations. Rather than confront the challenge which holds great possibility of more failure, he withdraws or becomes hostile. It is better to refuse to become involved than to appear "stupid" on yet another occasion; it is more comfortable to meet the challenging situation with hostility than to be on the losing side once more.

Nor are things improving. The problems of the children are multiplying far faster than the possible solutions. In New York City, for example, for the first time, the number of minority children who tend to live in encapsulated communities has passed the fifty percent mark.[2] The curriculum and teaching strategies which once suited the academically able minority are totally useless for the new majority of children entering the portals of our schools. Even the so-called experimental curricula with which we have been plaguing them are still founded on the principles appropriate for school populations of the 1920's and not for them. For example, in an effort to "upgrade" learning, one city's sixth-grade experimental curriculum includes knowledge of the work of Heinrich Schliemann, Arthur Evans, J. H. Breasted, Nelson Glueck, or "any other noted archaeologist of the teacher's choice."

The School's Share in Failure   As was pointed out above, the source of motivation for learning lies in the adult mediator. An adult has difficulty performing this function unless he can establish positive relationships with children. Who can deny that, all too often, the way teachers regard children has blocked the road to these positive relationships and thus deprived them of this source of motivation? The way teachers respond to what children say and write, even the way they correct or fail to correct a composition, has a crucial effect upon the relationship. An example is the composition of thirteen-year-old Maria who lives in East Harlem and her teacher's reaction to that composition.

"Stop, don't do it! Please stop them. Help." She screamed.

That was the words she pronounce when I was coming from the store. When I was coming up the stairs I saw blood down the stair and I look up I saw three policeman and two detective and I said what's wrong, were does blood come from? The detective said in a deep voice this blood come from the second floor two neighbors had a fight, and we are waiting for the ambulance. My heart stop for one second, and then I ran up the stairs and I said. "That is where I live." When I came up and saw Mr. Lopez with blood all over his shirt and I kneel down and said "Mr. Lopez what happen" and he said "That no good Luis he" he stop and then I said go on, but the policeman interb and said please young girl don't try to make him talk, then a policeman and a fat lady the lady was the nurse and she said take this man immediately! to the ambulance he is bleeding to much. The policeman took him to the ambulance. The other she put some bandage around his shoulders and then she said go to your home and report tomorrow at the hospital. Then the nurse call me over and said do you know the man

2 Fred M. Hechinger, "Negro and Puerto Rican Pupils in Majority Here for First Time," *The New York Times*, March 15, 1967.

that I sent in the ambulance? Yes nurse. "Then will you answer some questions." Yes. Will you please companion me to the hospital. Yes nurse.

Mr. Lopez die in the ambulance, I call Mrs. Lopez and gave her the bad news. She started to scream and cry. I came back from the hospital after I answer the question. The first thing that came in my mine was "why" "why" two neighbors fight. "Why" because they maybe don't understand each other or maybe one ask for a advice and the other said why come to me why don't you go to your family.

To be a neighbor is not necessary to be in the neighborhood, it can be country or city or the town anything. For example if you go to a country that you never gone before. All during your travels you would see people staring at your odd clothing, people who would not understand the language you spoke.

Then you would land in a strange country. Everything would be different. You would have to learn a strange language learn a new trade. Then you try to be kindful and helpful with people. The people will adore you truly. "Why" because you been not only a good neighbor but helpful and friendly with them. This is one of the simple ways to be kind with people, by helping them in anything they need your help today and tomorrow they help you. This composition is for the adolescent to give them an ideal to understand other persons. When a boy or girl comes into a classroom for the first time you try to make a conversation with him or her. Show the boy or girl around the school introduce the boy or girl to your friends so she don't feel lonely. In a way you are helping the boy or girl getting around.[3]

What was the teacher's reaction to Maria's composition? Maria knew only what she wrote at the end of it: "Too long!"

Secondly, teachers fail in their role as educators of disadvantaged children because they "teach" through the use of long verbal explanations. When such explanations are the process through which teaching is done, slum children "tune out."[4] They cannot attend to long explanations, for disordered home lives with choppy sequences of events have built in a short attention span. Let it not be denied that teaching is still done largely through verbal explanations; the research indicates this and a walk through the corridor of any school with

3 Leonard Kornberg, Ed. *Bridges to Slum Ghetto Children*, The Bridge Project, Publication No. 3. New York: Queens College, Department of Education, November, 1962.
4 Helen F. Storen *The First Semester: Beginning Teachers in Urban School.* New York: Project TRUE, Hunter College, 1965.

classes above the third grade reinforces research findings through a simple but repeated count of who happens to be talking in each classroom at the moment the observer passes.[5]

Furthermore, the conventional type of school work gives habits of inattention a chance to gain a stranglehold. The content is too often meaningless, having little to do with the lives of the children. An exerpt from almost any social studies textbook illustrates this.

Some Southern Neighbors

Because this is a history of the United States, we are most interested in the Indians of this area. The most civilized Indians in the Americas, however, lived south of what is now the United States. The Aztec and Mayan Indians lived in what is now Mexico, while the Incas lived in what is now Peru. By the time the Europeans discovered America, the Aztecs had conquered the Mayans and borrowed much of the Mayan culture for their own use.

City-dwelling Indians. The Aztec-Mayan culture in Mexico and the Inca culture in Peru were similar in several ways. In each case there was a large city surrounded by land controlled by the tribe. The Aztecs had a calendar —a system for counting days and years. In some respects the Aztec calendar was more accurate than the European calendar of that time. The Aztecs also had a form of picture writing and a system of numbers.[6]

To this kind of alien content we add new skills and thus further complicate their learning problems. For example, when a child can't read he is sent to the library to get a book. One of two things tends to happen. He wants so desperately to read what others can do that he secures a book far beyond his ability and refuses to give it up; or, he simply returns to school next day without having ever gone near that library. To strange content and new skills we add meaningless goals: committing facts to memory in order to pass the test. When all of these hurdles are piled on top of the language problem, it becomes impossible for him to function. So he stops. His behavior baffles the teacher who has not been able to analyze the school's role in causing the child's behavior. Frustration on the part of the teacher causes him to attach labels to the child which he regards as causes rather than as symptoms. There is little realization that for him to respond is to meet more failure and he has

5 Arno Bellack, *et al. The Language of the Classroom.* New York: Teachers College Press, 1963.
6 R. W. Patrick, J. K. Bettersworth, and R. W. Steen. *This Country of Ours.* Austin, Texas: The Steck Company, 1965.

had enough of that; there is little realization that the school system, including the teacher training institution, has played its role in that failure.

Consistently, educators have avoided a confrontation of the school with its failure to help the child learn. With the passing of years in school, the deficits multiply so that by the time the child reaches grade six, his self-image has been shattered to such an extent that hostility toward school is no longer hidden, and the general hopelessness is all-pervasive. The school has done little to eliminate the deficits with which children came to school, and yet it is in a uniquely favorable position to do something about those deficits. Fragmented solutions like remediation have been tried long enough and have been found wanting, for this is a negative approach to teaching and has proved itself unable to serve a positive function. Now we need curriculum and teaching strategies that have new and fresh vigor, untainted by such retarding factors as coverage of meaningless content.

In this task, the school has a powerful ally. As mentioned before, intellectual growth depends on the child's exploration of his environment and that exploration must include interpretation and variety of ingredients. It happens that the school is in a position to create such an environment, one with the quality necessary for mental growth. This is the clarion call to the schools; this is where we must concentrate our efforts: on the creation of the environment which nourishes the development of intelligence.

Charting the Course for Instructional Strategies
If schools are to adopt as one of their major goals the development of intelligence, there must be an acute awareness that acquiring knowledge and mastering skills, though important goals, are simply not enough. By placing the accent on acquiring information, we have deprived our pupils of the more important mental process of converting that information to ideas. By placing the emphasis on passive absorption, we have deprived them of needed mental growth that accompanies questioning, searching and discovering. By concerning ourselves with giving them the generalizations which they are forced to regurgitate on demand, we have deprived them of the power to make those generalizations themselves from the given data. By telling them which facts to study, we have deprived them of the power to select relevant facts and to discard the irrelevant. These are all thinking processes, and the children are the ones who need to engage in them if the school is to emphasize mental growth as a prime goal.

The school needs to create an environment in which searching, questioning and discovering are not only permitted but encouraged. Otherwise, the severe deficit in ability to abstract causes disaster to the child as he tries to function

216

in school. He finds difficulty seeing relationships and performing other cognitive processes. He needs systematic help in developing the ability to perform such tasks as categorization. Since he has no model for seeing consequence as related to cause, the environment must be conducive to learning this through such means as making hypotheses from given clues. Inability to see relationships and inability to abstract are key deficits and deter his progress in other kinds of learning tasks such as reading comprehension. But he can learn these cognitive skills[7] and the task of the school is to devise instructional strategies that will permit and encourage him to do so.

Sensitivity Training One area which encourages the learning of cognitive skills because it creates the environment which motivates learning is sensitivity training. It has the advantage of being a content area as well as one rich in potential for learning all kinds of skills, new attitudes, and important thinking processes simultaneously. Diagnostic devices used with students who are disadvantaged render undeniable evidence that sensitivity training is a needed and fruitful focus of study. In a number of situations answers to open-ended questions have been used as a diagnostic device. Students talked or wrote about "What makes me mad," "My wishes," "My worries," and revealed much about their feelings of loneliness and alienation, their constant and usually fruitless search for attention and affection, the lack of something as "common" as someone to talk to, the deep wounds caused by name-calling, especially in derogatory terms directed against mothers or racial and ethnic origins.

Sensitivity training must include attitudes toward oneself as well as others; diagnostic devices of more than one variety gave evidence of the need for development of such attitudes. Peers must be placed in situations where offering ego fulfillment in turn gives a feeling of satisfaction; insights into and solutions to interpersonal conflicts constitute important emphases; skills for coping with rebuff and criticism are necessary for ego development. Measures for preventing a sense of failure are of prime importance, and these must be an intrinsic part of the curriculum. All of these factors are included in the idea of sensitivity training.

However, if information gathering is the major objective, then sensitivity training tends to fall by the wayside. Thinking and attitudes are developed from an active process which is in no way the same type of learning experience as is used for acquiring facts. The learning of attitudes requires experiences

---

7 Hilda Taba and Deborah Elkins. *Teaching Strategies for the Culturally Disadvantaged.* Chicago: Rand McNally and Company, 1966.

which make an impact on emotions. These can be planned simultaneously with cognitive experiences as when the school helps students understand motivations of people, helps them gain insights into their own behavior including cause and effect, and concentrates on the development of human relations skills which energize other learnings because of the motivational power inherent in the mastery of those skills and insights. The motivational power is reinforced by the fact that students regard emphasis on "sensitivity content" and on preliminary diagnostic procedures which attend it as a personal concern for them and their welfare on the part of their teacher and the school. This is true only under one condition: that the rapport between teacher and students is a positive one. The teacher thus builds the first steps toward creating a climate for mediation as well as for motivation to learn. When results of the open-ended questions are tallied and given anonymously to the students under a heading such as "What our class thinks about punishments," this is a second step in the mediation process as well as in the motivational. Thus, multiple objectives are planned simultaneously.

Depth Study   Stress on coverage has been found wanting not only with respect to shortchanging students in sensitivity training and the development of thinking processes. Also it prevents the depth study which students need desperately for building significant concepts. This is attained if the student examines a few instances in depth rather then brushing by many instances ever so lightly. From careful analysis of a few instances illustrating an idea, the idea itself is more clearly and distinctly perceived. Enduring knowledge results from concentration on analysis of a small number of examples of an idea because such concentration permits time and energy for significant intellectual and social learnings. A limited number of details suffice to understand a complete idea if the illustrations are contrasting ones and are considered in depth. Contrast is important for perspective; perception becomes more precise, and cognitive functioning is thereby heightened.

The contrasting instances studied are the means to the end. Depth study is focused on the concept and thrusts the student into highly complex thinking processes such as hypothesizing, making inferences and perceiving relationships. For example, students can use information to hypothesize about why in one geographic area the animal served man in one capacity while in another the situation was altogether different. In such a study of the role of animals in the life of man, students need to see sharp effects, such as animals causing man to keep on the move, following the herd; but animals also helped man to settle the land and lead an entirely different kind of life. The concept that the same need—the drive for food—was met so differently by man because of one of a number of conditions gives an opportunity for studying a variety of contrasting situations. In this case the role of animals was one of the conditions. When students examine specific illustrations of men who follow the herd and relate their findings to the larger idea, they can make inferences about the kind of life that is led by families who follow the herd and contrast these with families who settle the land. Thus, they have opportunities for developing cognitive abilities with which the school must be concerned.

In all cases, learning must be initiated with concrete instances which are closely related to the experiences of the students. If the concept is "Animals affect the history of men," they must first pool ideas of what they already know about the roles animals play and in this way give to each other the beginnings of some perspective through their different experiences. Then they have something to which they can tie what they learn—when they see movies about the work animals do in helping men raise food in different parts of the world, when they read about scientific experiments performed through the use of animals, when they interview someone from the ASPCA, when they learn about laws regarding the keeping of certain animals as pets in a big city, and when they make systematic observation of the relationship between people they know and the animals they own. From all of these varied activities they gain an understanding of the idea that animals propel certain adjustments in the life of man; they have an opportunity to arrive at the same idea from several different perspectives.

Centering the study on concepts also permits the use of multiple skills including new cognitive skills. But to be effective, these must be natural parts of each learning experience. In other words, they must be needed in order to carry on a particular activity. For example, when students are composing a booklet on Animals in The Life of Man, it must be carried on in such a way that to achieve it requires language arts—skills of listening, reading and writing, the use of new models of thinking, and a feeling for the very real contribution of peers.

Providing for Heterogeneity   Plans for teaching strategies must give high priority to provisions for heterogeneity. It is necessary to do away with uniform materials, rigidly set pacing for everyone, and standards that leave little room for individuality. Too often individualization of instruction has been interpreted as individual pacing of coverage of the same material or topic. Individualization means not only more than this but something far different. It means that with respect to any one given topic, different students do different things.[8] It means a wide range of activities and

8 Deborah Elkins. *Reading Improvement in the Junior High School.* New York: Teachers College, Columbia University, 1963.

219

materials through which children can learn. One set of books cannot answer the need; reading alone cannot insure equal learning opportunity for everyone. A wide variety of books on different levels and for different interests can be found around given topics and can be read to find answers to common sets of questions. Observation, interview, experimentation offer still largely untapped resources for learning. Heterogeneity demands elimination of some old practices and substitution of as yet inadequately explored, but potentially fruitful ones. For example, tasks which encourage different ways of responding are in order. Questions which demand only one right answer must be eliminated. Rather, questions like, "What do you think causes people to want to own animals?" permit a variety of responses on many levels. Thus, children who are ordinarily cut off from responding in a group learning situation now can become participants.

The Need for Participation Participation is a critical factor in providing for motivation so necessary in children's learning. Rewards are often foreign to the experience of many disadvantaged children. Even simple compliments are all but unknown. One eighth-grade boy who was complimented by his teacher for a piece of work which showed genuine effort looked in wonderment at her and softly answered, "Once when I was in the second grade my teacher said, 'Good for you!' " It took six long years for another scrap of praise to be forthcoming. In the light of this, other devices must be used as motivation to supplement this kind of reward. One such device is to offer experiences which have strong emotional impact. Such experiences mobilize attention and energize learning. For example, a story which arouses feelings has the power to command attention and to supply energy for learning. The sheer drama of the sea of grasshoppers attacking the crops and animals and people in *Let The Hurricane Roar* by Lane is captivating, especially when read by the teacher to the class. The use of the familiar is also motivating; in this case, the children had all had unpleasant if not terrifying experiences with insects. The use of the novel and the unexpected has power to motivate: watching the behavior of live locusts in captivity if only to see how much they can consume; listening to a story recorded on tape and read to a background of music at a time when reading by themselves is resisted; seeing a real movie of themselves as they perform some group-learning activity. These introductory experiences must be close to their own concerns. Discussing what they do which makes parents angry or happy can serve to initiate a study of values we hold, how we learn them, and what effects they have on us and others. Such a discussion serves to catch attention.

Once attention is captured and learning is energized, other devices are needed to continue the energizing of learning. Introductory activities are necessary, but they will not sustain learning over long periods of time. Too often teachers rely on these introductory activities to do more than they are meant to do, to achieve more than their character enables them to achieve. The sustaining devices must be concrete, overt activities which keep curiosity alive and thus overcome the short attention span. Dramatizing, role-playing, and being authors of a "book" are examples of overt activities which have inherent in them motivating power for learning. Another important factor is the experience must allow for immediate success; this means success for everyone, not just a select few. A situation which is competitive and sets one student against the other is untenable in the early stages of overcoming short attention span; it serves merely to disrupt at a time when students need to learn to support each other. The result of overt activity must be tangibly rewarding. For example, a class booklet which they create, which they can see and touch, and which includes a contribution from every member of the class is a tangibly rewarding outcome. Ultimately, however, intrinsic motivation must take over. This lies in the feeling of mastery. Children do want that feeling; they can be intrigued with many intellectual processes such as making hypotheses from given clues and finding out how good a detective they'd make. Eventually the motivation must have its origins in the task itself and in the satisfaction that comes from mastery, from being able to cope with something one was not able to handle previously.

Literary Resources   Literature was mentioned earlier. It needs to be discussed again, for it is a powerful resource for creating a learning environment.[9] It is a motivating device to focus attention initially, but it also is equally useful for involving students in the study of intellectual problems, and for sustaining learning energy. It provides material that addresses the feelings and from this point on gives energy for learning difficult skills like reading and writing. Through it, knowledge can be gained for it can effectively build concepts like time and space which are difficult to learn. "Tuning up" feelings for differences in time and place is necessary before facts about them take on meaning, just as "tuning up the ear" is necessary for building a "sentence sense" before technical aspects of structure take on any meaning. These are long-term goals and take more than a month or a year. If students read about the roles of animals in *The Road to Agra* by Sommerfelt, *Old Yeller* by Gipson, and *Skip* by Aileen Fisher, they acquire a feeling for

9 D. Elkins, "Teaching and Learning Strategies for Educationally Disadvantaged Children and Youth," in A. Harry Passow, Ed. *Curriculum and Teaching in Urban Depressed Areas*. New York: Teachers College Press, 1968.

time and place because the same topic is dealt with in different times and different places and the contrasts in events due to these differences are sharp. Yet, they gain a feeling for the continuity of time and place in the affairs of men. Therefore, literature introduces new ideas and provides material for analysis, so that new concepts can emerge from analysis. It does these things even while it offers sensitivity training because it extends experience with human behavior beyond what everyday living can offer. Since social isolation of disadvantaged children is critical, since their concern about this is deep, literature offers the school an inexhaustible source of motivation for learning. It offers the school a means of achieving an important part of its task of acculturation, for it helps internalize values and identify with others. It gives perspective about their own problems and feelings as well as a sense of the universality of emotions and their causes and consequences.

All of this does not take place by the mere reading of a story. Activities surrounding the use of literature must be "balanced" for intake and output, as must all activities through which learning is intended to occur. Conventional school work was too concerned with intake of new information. Literature offers opportunities for expressive or output activities. When students dramatize a story, they practice tirelessly, because the play's the thing. Meantime, there is incentive for acquiring reading skills far more efficiently and in only a small portion of the time that it takes to achieve the same thing in a remedial reading session. Role-playing the ending of a story is an output activity which provides food for discussing the logic of events and of human motives. These very discussions held around the role-playing or the literature can be another output activity while achieving the discovery of the central idea of a story which in turn leads children to read with deeper insight and understanding. Output discussions are needed before and after the reading, each discussion serving its own specific purpose.

Other output activities are observation, interviewing, and scientific treatment of findings. Of course, in each of these there is a measure of intake of new information. But this is a secondary goal here. Systematic observation brings order to everyday events in the chaotic environment so often characteristic of the disadvantaged child. It focuses attention on important elements which are overlooked otherwise. Systematic observation produces content which lends itself to scientific treatment involved in tallying information to uncover patterns, comparing and contrasting various factors, formulating hypotheses and then testing them through further observation or other pertinent activities. For example, students observe things families do to teach their children; they compare findings, and draw conclusions. All families do some things which teach, but different members may assume the same roles in different families. Students who return to school with the conclusion that their families don't do anything that educates soon change their minds and appreciate the opportunity to have a new look at their "hypothesis." Observation has still another function: it helps students see the relationship between school and out-of-school life. The latter is brought into the schoolroom systematically as the school itself reaches out to make more meaningful what goes on elsewhere. Observing younger siblings makes them take on an aura of something genuinely interesting; interviewing adults gives to those adults a significance they did not have before, as when children ask about tales that were told to them "when they were young" in order to discover universal emotions even in tales that are handed down from generation to generation, so enduring are they. Emotions, whether expressed by adults or adolescents, take on more meaning and thus become more tolerable. Further, observation brings to stories the meaning of everyday life so that while literature helps interpret life, daily experiences in turn help interpret literature. Finally, observations and interviews can be written up and tallied and used for purposes of comparison as the study progresses, thus putting into focus new and less concrete experiences that are offered.

Model of A Learning Sequence: Human Hands

The above guidelines cannot be put to use without diagnosis of specific needs which dictate how they shall be used. Open-ended questions were mentioned as one diagnostic device. Role-playing, sociograms, sociometric interviews, diaries, systematic observation of children all bear fruit in furnishing details which are needed to decide on concepts, content, learning activities and learning sequences. For example, with one group of students it was discovered that they needed a feeling of self-worth, that they were intensely interested in anything to do with the physical aspects of the human being, that they had few notions of what results teamwork could produce, were unable to listen to each other, were unable to express themselves adequately or to conceptualize about many everyday events around them, and had developed inadequate relationships with people around them. These findings gave helpful direction to the planning. On occasion a paradox was uncovered which dictated certain characteristics of teaching models. For example, disadvantaged children need time for depth study, but their short attention span demands short sequences. This meant that teachers had to do long-term planning for a theme and, within it, a series of short sequences that were vital parts of it and that provided for the study in depth.

The Family of Man was chosen as a long-term theme because it is the kind of topic which is important for understanding of self as well as of the larger society. It permits a study of concepts such as human beings everywhere have the same basic needs and emotions, and all human beings aim for something important to them. It permits a variety of activities that are productive and that are needed to achieve multiple goals such as development of cognitive powers and mastery of skills. It was the kind of topic that lent itself to several shorter sequences, each closely related to the other and each contributing to the larger one. Inherent in it were many concrete topics, intimately related to children's previous experiences. These topics were also inherently true illustrations of the concepts planned for the long-term unit. The central value of each of these topics was significant enough to bear rather thorough exploration.

Human Hands was chosen as the first sequence and proved to be a good one because children were concerned with the physical, because it lent itself to needed experiences, permitted movement from the concrete to the abstract, and helped build concepts outlined for the unit. Not all teachers chose the same initial sequence because the needs of their students were different. Some chose Sound in Our Lives; others preferred Growing Up while a fourth group selected Who's Afraid?

Those who studied Human Hands began by having the children draw an outline of their own hands on a piece of paper. This involved them immediately in an overt, concrete, engaging activity. When later the drawings of all students were posted with stories which accompanied them written right in the outline of the hands themselves, peers were observed time after time trying to measure their own hands against the outline of others. There was quiet talk around that bulletin board for days to follow. Then, with the teacher, they discussed the beauty of human hands and the similarity. Three things were achieved here: the beginnings of the concept of a common humanity, the beginnings of a conversation in which at least one or two children actually responded to each other, and the initiation of new attitudes about their own persons. When they next wrote about "Important Things My Hands Can Do," they offered none of the usual resistance to writing because they now had something to say, because they enjoyed the novelty of entering their story within the outline of their own hands, and they took readily to the notion that even their hands were worthy of note. Typically they mentioned eating and dressing, but there were always implications for the teacher to ponder. Hands pray, they said; and hands give people things.

As they talked about what they wrote, the teacher quickly listed the categories "work" and "play" on the board, so that each child's offering was listed under at least one of these. This was their first experience with categorization, a crucial thinking process. The "simple" act of deciding in which category certain events fell offered an opportunity to introduce the notion that not all events can be rigidly pigeonholed. The tally was completed by a committee to save time and to initiate them into the experience of a few working in the service of the many. The tally was rexographed and distributed to everyone for immediate use next day. This served two functions: early gratification and building the notion that what they do has purpose. The tally of their own experiences was to be used to compare with experiences of people outside their own lives, people in books.

They listened to a chapter from *Big Doc's Girl* about punishment of a child by an older sibling. The experience was close to them and therefore emotionally involving, but it was not theirs. It was one step removed. Because it was involving and yet not their own, they could gain perspective that would not otherwise be possible. During the discussion which followed the reading, they compared their findings with their own original tally and added items, thus making use of the work they had done the previous day and building upon it. Discussion centered around sharp emotional reactions: Did Sis have the right to spank the children? The issues must be sharp in order to force attention to what peers have to say, to sustain involvement, and to learn to resolve issues verbally rather than with the fists. Discussions were very brief at the outset, and increased in length as children were able to handle longer conversations. Even while this was slowly being achieved, other goals were being attained as teachers became aware of them. Once children became involved, they all wanted to talk, yet they were unable to sustain a conversation. So the teacher used this occasion to begin to build faith that tomorrow will bring new opportunities. She did this by listing names of those who still wanted to talk, gave them time to jot down what they wanted to say so they would not forget, and promised that tomorrow the discussion would be continued. A third goal was being achieved too: slowly the teacher was moving their attention from student-centered issues to less personal ones.

Then they observed for one-half hour what adults or babies or adolescents do with their hands, and they took notes on observations. Note-taking for this purpose needed previous preparation which was achieved through role-playing. Not only did the children learn how to take notes, but the teacher learned a great deal about the soul-saving sense of humor they possessed, the wit and the sarcasm and the very real insights that were revealed through their mimicry.

The results of their observations were shared in class next day. They found that adults shook their index fingers at others, while teenagers did not; mothers cuddled babies but fathers did not. This time, when categories were selected for tallying, the students supplied one or two. Again, they wrote about their observations and did so willingly because their productions were to constitute a rexographed book of which they would be the authors, and because they discovered that the teacher gave ready help. The paragraphs were corrected, rewritten over and over again to be rexographed and bound the very next day. Once more, gratification must be within a very short time.

The next day they insisted on hearing every single person's creation, even though the teacher was ready to settle for five or six. The earlier tally became the summary sheet, thus putting their own previous work to good use again. Now came their first genuine acquaintance with a table of contents. After all, a book needs a table of contents. Here, the set of textbooks came in handy for the first time; children examined the format of the table of contents and set up their own. Seeing their names there, seeing others turn to the page to find a particular story, they enriched their self-images. Adults at home added to the good feeling, as in wonderment they regarded the accomplishments of the child. Not in all homes did this happen, however. Some children did not share life with such adults. These could experience the feeling of a boosted ego when the class decided that one copy of their book should be placed in their church so that others could have something to read and could see what they had to say.

Findings needed further interpretation in order that more perspective be gained. "What is the relationship between emotions and what hands do?" The teacher read a chapter from *Caddie Woodlawn* about the punishment meted out to her. Students had to infer the function of hands, their first experience in formally and consciously making inferences. This activity involved going from the concrete to the abstract. Inferential thinking could be introduced because students identified with the characters. Hands showed anger and pleaded forgiveness. They cried out in loneliness as when Ruth drew the picture of her mother on the wall of her room.

A variety of "Help Wanted" ads which the teacher rexographed was examined to see the jobs that needed hands most, from clerk typist to floor-walker. At first they rejected all but the obvious ones, but closer examination through discussion pushed forward the inference-making. They attempted rank-order of jobs using the criterion of importance of hands, and concluded that it was possible to rank them only if quantity alone and not type of use were considered. It is this kind of high level conclusion which offers significant evidence that children can learn to make abstractions even when they begin with a deficiency in this ability.

Pictures offered another aid to moving them outside of their own environment. They discussed a soldier in Vietnam holding a baby in one arm and a gun in another, and talked of what he was doing, and what we were doing there, good and bad. Magazines were distributed to find pictures of good things and bad which we were doing in other parts of the world. Children worked together in pairs for moral support on a new task requiring that they defend the category in which they placed their picture. The defense again gave very important evidence of the school's ability to teach children to make generalizations, and of the children's ability to learn this important thinking process. They concluded that few things we did with other people were all good or all bad. This discussion also demonstrated their ability to make the transition from what people do to their motivations for doing these things. The ability to perform these thinking processes can be developed if the curriculum provides step by step procedures through which this learning can take place. Not all students made these strides at this moment. Many more experiences, and many varied experiences, all consciously planned, would be needed before this could happen. The abstractions which pictures encouraged were on a relatively low level, but they were abstractions nevertheless.

From low-level abstractions using pictures, students moved to an examination of news items of "human interest" and made inferences about the roles of hands. The consequences of floods, forest fires and crime to millions of people could be inferred from such materials for they were on a level at which children could operate. Some students could even extract from these materials the notion that people must help each other build a new life when disaster strikes.

They examined what happened in history, moving still farther away in time and space but building on what had been learned previously. What did people do to make these historic events occur? How do these acts affect us now? Social studies textbooks were not used; rather biographies told about people and what they did. Each student selected his own biography and read it to discover answers to the three questions. During the discussions which followed they compared these three ideas as they occurred in different times and places. This procedure helped them "tune up" their sense of time and place as well as develop concepts about particular human activities. They also read fiction, with school time allotted for reading until they became emotionally involved in their book and then "reported" by conversing informally about what people were doing, how hands helped, and how the acts affected other people or how they showed emotions. Many children finished "skinny" books in two days and begged for more. Most important of all, the kinds of conclusions children drew from their independent reading showed the results of the previous step-by-step learning experiences through which students gained power to see relationships, draw inferences, make generalizations and abstractions.

The following outline of the learning sequence described above will serve to pinpoint a number of critical guideposts: the importance of planning activities, each of which builds on the learnings provided by the previous ones; the way in which multiple objectives are achieved simultaneously; the variety of activities that must be used around one large idea in order to achieve depth study, provide for heterogeneity, and permit balance of input and output. It takes all of these things, and more, to help children feel free to learn, to help them achieve over and over again until they gain the emotional energy to keep on learning.

MODEL OF A SEQUENCE
THE FAMILY OF MAN: HUMAN HANDS

ACTIVITY	SOME PSYCHOLOGICAL AND INSTRUCTIONAL CHARACTERISTICS AND FUNCTIONS
Draw outline of hands	Overt, concrete activity Offers motivation through involvement Recognizes student concern about the physical
Discuss similarities and beauty of hands	Beginnings of concept of universality Builds self-image Beginnings of conversation; listening to each other
Write "Important Things My Hands Can Do"	Development of skills Builds self-image Opportunity for diagnosis of values by teacher
Categorize students' contributions	Development of thinking processes: discrimination, finding common elements Pooling ideas and gaining perspective Introduces notion of small group in the service of the large (Committee completes tally begun by class)
Rexograph copy of tally for all	Seeing "immediate" results of work achieved Making early use of work previously done

Discuss observations about final tally	Development of thinking process: making generalizations
Listen to story: chapter from *Big Doc's Girl*	Emotional involvement
	Beginnings of concept development through concrete instance
	Movement from student-centered issue to less personal aspect
	Seeing relationships between cause and consequence
	Sensitivity training: understanding human behavior
Discuss issue of punishment	Involvement in concept development through issue of close concern evoking sharp emotional reaction
	Rudiments of conversation; listening to others' opinions
	Examination of values in story and expressed by peers
	Open-ended issue to permit all levels of response
Observe adult, child, or adolescent *Take notes* on observation	Develop notion of order within a chaotic environment
	Introduce new quality of interest in people around them rather than mere emotional reaction
	Relate school to out-of-school life to enrich meaning of both
	Skill development
	Sensitivity training
	Engage in learning process of questioning, searching, discovering
Share observations	Offers new perspective as findings are pooled
	Opportunity for concept development and drawing of generalizations
Select categories and tally	Students themselves select at least one or two categories: thinking processes

229

	of deciding common elements and making discriminations
	Participation by all; involvement of all
Write observations—to be rexographed as booklet	Building self-concept through pride in achievement and taking a task seriously
	Mastery; skill development
Read peer stories in booklet	Early gratification
	Give meaning to student effort since product is useful and enjoyable
	Self-image development through appreciation of peer effort and contributions
	Skill building
Discuss and *use* tally above as summary sheet in booklet	Previous work serves new function
	Giving meaning to school work
	Re-examination of conclusions previously made
Making table of contents for booklet	Use of textbooks available to seek model for table of contents
	Gaining information
	Skill development
	Self-image: seeing own name and work listed in table of contents
Read chapter from *Caddie Woodlawn* *Compare* with *Big Doc's Girl*	Discovering sequence of events and rationale for sequence
	Thinking processes of comparing and contrasting
	Skill development
Discuss relationship between emotions and what hands do	Introduction of inferential thinking at a higher level made possible through identification with situation and characters
	Moving from concrete to abstract
Examine "Help Wanted" ads for occupations in	Offers concrete "handle" for making inferences

which hands are important	Opportunity to evaluate, discriminate, compare, and contrast Movement to the more impersonal
Rank order jobs advertised	Thinking processes of evaluation, making differentiations, drawing conclusions, generalizing
Select pictures of work of hands	Thinking process of evaluation, making inferences, finding common elements Moving from concrete to abstract Moving outside own environment
Defend selection	Working in pairs to give energy for new task Moving from concrete to abstract, from what people do to motivation for doing Assuming responsibility for decisions made
Select news items	Thinking processes of making inferences, relating cause and consequence, generalizing Developing attitudes and values in sensitivity training: roles of people in helping each other during periods of disaster such as floods, war, crime
Read historical events through biography	Gaining information Skill in seeking and finding answers to specific questions
Discuss findings; *Compare*	Compare, contrast same ideas in different times and places
Read self-selected fiction; *Discuss*	Providing for heterogeneity Making use of new concepts gained Sharing and pooling ideas to gain perspective Skill development Providing for emotional involvement to sustain interest in mastery

Examining values and attitudes: sensitivity training
Listening to each other
Searching and discovering through
reading

The type of strategy described here has no semblance of what is usually regarded as "compensatory education." What is called for now is a complete
overhauling of the curriculum so that the school can perform its function of
increasing the ability to learn.

WALDORF EDUCATION FOR THE DISADVANTAGED CHILD

Earl J. Ogletree

John A. Rackauskas

Theo Buergen

The objective of this paper is to discuss the applicability of Waldorf methods for the education of culturally disadvantaged children at the elementary level. The authors believe that the Waldorf teaching methods and the administrative organization of the schools would be highly suitable for solving some of the problems posed by the education of children from the lower socio-economic group. Some of the reasons for the poor scholastic achievement of these children are believed to be the following:

1. Inadequate language skills (both listening and hearing).
2. Inadequate model figures at home and in the community.
3. School teaching staff unstable.
4. Poor work habits.
5. Lack of drive for achievement and lack of encouragement.
6. Frequent tardiness and/or absenteism.
7. Unfamiliar content in textbooks.
8. Lack of sensory stimuli at home.
9. Psychological problems at home which are peculiar to the socio-economic background.
10. Class size too large.
11. School tests inadequate; damage severly confidence and basic self-esteem.

THE WESTERN CAROLINA UNIVERSITY JOURNAL OF EDUCATION, Fall 1971, pp. 33-43.

12. Poor physical health.
13. Substandard school facilities.
14. Initial school failure caused by the above factors damages self-esteem and self-confidence.

Part Two of this paper gives a brief history and description of the salient features of Waldorf Education, while Part Three contains a point for point discussion of the stated problems together with possible solutions offered through Waldorf methods. This paper is meant to be of a strictly descriptive and suggestive nature, and the suggestions would have to be tried in actual practice. Therefore no conclusions have been made.

THE WALDORF SCHOOL MOVEMENT

The Waldorf School Movement is the second largest independent, non-denominational school movement in the world. Founded in 1919 by the Austrian philosopher Rudolf Steiner, the movement derives its name from the Waldorf Asteria Company whose general director, Emil Malt, had been the sponsor of the first school, located in Stuttgart, Germany. The success of Steiner's educational philosophy, as practiced at the Waldorf School in Stuttgart, soon received wide recognition. The number of Waldorf Schools (often called Rudolf Steiner Schools) rapidly increased throughout Europe. When Hitler came to power the Waldorf Schools in Germany were closed. They were reopened with the help of the American Government after the war. Today, there are over 70 such schools throughout the world (including nine in the United States), educating some 35,000 children.

Philosophy and Methodology of Waldorf Education

Rudolf Steiner, the founder of the Waldorf School Movement, claims that for a child before the age of twelve, the steps in the learning process which lead to the formation of knowledge and

234

skills are reversed when compared to those of an adult. Typically an adult in a learning situation starts out with a set of definitions or concepts. He digests them cognitively (he applies his thinking to them) and then assimilates them or integrates them into his personality. At this point he becomes emotionally involved and possibly "motivated," and this motivation can lead to action. For example, consider an adult who wants to learn about the stock market. He will first try to get some information about it (conceptual stage), which may or may not motivate him, If it does, he may gradually engage in financial transactions with stock, gradually gain experience and become more expert. The sequence of events that in this case has led to learning has been the following: (1) conceptual stage (cognition), (2) emotional involvement stage (motivation), and (3) action stage.

In the young child the sequence of events is clearly reversed: He watches the gardner plant out cabbages and imitates him, possibly using little sticks instead of the plants. In the process of this action he gets emotionally involved and motivated to know more about what is going on. He asks the gardner questions and gets information. Here the sequence of events is: (1) Action by imitation, (2) emotional involvement, (3) cognition (maybe now, maybe years later).

Consequently, Waldorf teachers at the elementary level use a kinesthetic, action-loaded approach to intellectual subjects which involves the child first in the realm of impulse and emotion, and then gradually leads over to knowledge and skill. An important teaching aid for this type of teaching is the use of art. Young children have primarily an imaginative consciousness and their thinking takes place in pictorial mental representations. For this reason every effort is made to present the subject matter artistically. In this sense art is not an isolated subject but becomes a pervasive factor which gives meaning to every subject and provides intrinsic motivation. How these principles can be used for the teaching of reading and writing is shown in the third part of this paper.

A significant feature of the Waldorf approach is the student-teacher relationship. The class teacher, who takes over the class in first grade, follows the class throughout the elementary grades. This gives him the opportunity to form a personal relationship with each student to the order of a "third parent." It also makes him personally responsible for the scholastic achievement of each single student, since he can provide very few reasons for failure. However, the class teacher is not the only teacher with whom the class comes into contact. Certain special subjects, such as music, foreign languages, physical education, are often taught by specialists.

Another special feature of the Waldorf School program is the "main lesson." This name has been given to a period of study which takes place at the beginning of each day for two hours. It is devoted to one subject for three weeks or longer. Typical main lesson subjects are mathematics, language arts, social studies, and science. The other subjects (physical education, foreign languages, art, etc.) are taught in a regular rhythmic distribution. The main lesson approach allows the student to give his undivided attention to each subject in succession. He lives with his studies more intensively. The brighter student deepens his interest and is stimulated to intensified creative work. The slower student, whose interest may be hardly touched in 50 minute periods, has time to develop his interest in the subject and to effectively deal with it.

LEARNING PROBLEMS OF THE CULTURALLY DIS-ADVANTAGED AND THE SOLUTIONS CONTAINED IN WALDORF EDUCATION

1. Language Skills

The children of the lower socio-economic groups are said to have inadequate language skills for the ordinary curriculum which is geared toward the language background of the middle classes. This refers to both listening and speaking, that is, the children are neither used to listening to adult "talks" given to them, nor to having lengthy conversations with adults.[1]

In this respect the culturally disadvantaged children obviously need compensation through the school, and here Waldorf method has much to offer. Waldorf Education is not book-oriented. In first grade hardly any text books are used. The children make their own textbooks in the form of handprinted and self-illustrated notebooks. They read only that which they first have written or printed with their own hands. Thus reading is developed from writing which conforms to the fundamental Steiner principle: first action, then affective involvement, and then only cognitive activity. Visual discrimination is achieved by drawing ribbon patterns which teach at the same time the left-to-right sequence. Auditory discrimination comes from simple poetry and alliterative verse for which the following verse may serve as an example:

> Freckled fishes, flirting flitting.
> Flashing fast, or floating free
> Flicking filmy fins, like feathers,
> Feeding from the flowing sea.[2]

It is immaterial whether the children understand all of the words at the outset. The main thing is that they enjoy them, which means that they learn to enjoy human speech as such. This in turn will act as a motivation for understanding. But the teacher may tell them perhaps the story of a little fish in the lake, and then, from a colorful chalk drawing on the board, derive a letter "F". In this fashion most of the letters can be developed from pictures and stories, and with each letter the children will have been personally involved. The stories will allow the discussion of action, of feelings, and of concepts, and the poetry and alliterative verse will gradually develop articulation, enunciation, and speech in general. Thus the basal readers with their "unfamiliar" content can be avoided, and to, the children of the lower socio-economic class will be confronted with proper human language. Riessman points out that the culturally disadvantaged children do enjoy speech and demonstrate a language which is often rich in simile and analogy.[3] The point is to reach them at their own speech level and then to raise it, not through any pre-conceived idea of what good language is, but through the inherent charm of any living language, no matter whether "hip" or Shakespearean. In particular, modern poetry has become very free of formality, and this could be suggestive for the development of the language skills of the culturally disadvantaged.

2. Model Figures

Inadequate model figures produce inadequate model figures in the next generation. This is a vicious circle. It can only be broken if the school can provide model figures that have a strong and lasting influence and appeal as personalities upon the individual child.[4]

Under the given circumstances, even if the school has adequate model figures, they will be of little influence. The children stay with one teacher for one year only and then are "passed on". Moreover, in many school systems teaching is completely departmentalized even in the intermediate elementary grades. The child then "parades" every day five to six different teachers, who sometimes hardly know his name. But to become a model figure, an intimate personal contact is essential.

In a Waldorf School the class teacher stays with the class for the first six to eight years. Every year he will write a personal, verbal report about each child, he will meet the parents, and discuss the child at faculty meetings. It is inevitable that he will become a "third parent" and, therefore, a strong model figure. It has already been mentioned that the class teacher is not the only teacher of the class.

3. Stability of Teaching Staff

It is a well known fact that the faculty turn-over in the inner city schools is considerably higher than in the suburbs, whereby the higher turn-over is indicative of lower quality education.[5] The authors believe that if the class teacher would stay with "his class" for a number of years, that a certain feeling of responsibility would develop between class teacher and class, which would stabilize the faculty. There is reason to believe that teachers would find teaching culturally disadvantaged children even more rewarding than teaching middle-class children, providing that the culturally disadvantaged children show progress.

4. Work Habits

The work habits of the culturally disadvantaged are said to be poor in general. This is attributed to a lack of order, discipline and example in the home environment. The school can compensate for this by providing order, discipline, and example. To make this effective, however, some **intrinsic** motivation has to be build in. The Waldorf Schools use art and ceremony to help children acquire order and discipline and through them better work habits.[6] The start of a lesson, and the end of a lesson is a ceremony, as is the distribution of pencils and paper. To write out an arithmetic problem, for instance, is an art. It is done very carefully with **colored** pencil into a white notebook, and it will be adorned with individual ornaments and pictures. All earlier civilizations have known that art and ceremony are self-motivating; they knew that artistic experiences and the religious act (more than the belief) has an educating and personality transforming influence.

5. Drive for Achievement

The drive for achievement must come from intrinsic motivation, since extrinsic motivation (deferred gratification syndrom, etc.) has proved to be ineffective for the culturally disadvantaged children.

How intrinsic motivation can be built into the **form** of the teaching process has been touched upon in the previous section. To build it also into the **content** the teacher has to bring the subject matter **alive** before the class. He can only do this if he becomes completely independent of textbooks. Textbook knowledge at the elementary level is passive knowledge. Only individualized, assimilated, spontaneously presented, enacted, and experienced knowledge can carry the spark of enthusiasm which springs over to the child and kindles motivation and drive. The textbook comes after, as reinforcement only. Waldorf teachers are especially trained in the artistic and lively presentation of subject matter.

6.   Regular School Attendance

Frequent tardiness and absenteism can be overcome on the one hand through close cooperation between class teacher and home, and on the other by motivating the children in such a way that they like to come to school. Both of these points were discussed in previous sections.

7.   Content of Textbooks

The content of the usual textbooks, in particular of the basal readers is unfamiliar to a large degree to the culturally disadvantaged child.

It has already been mentioned that the Waldorf method is not book-oriented, but that the teacher is the core and the key to the learning-teaching situation. Whenever books are used they are chosen from original literature. In first and second grade, for example, short fairy tales, and other stories in simple but uncontrolled vocabulary would be used as readers. The important point is that the child is thouroughly acquainted with the content of the story through telling, before he reads it. The children like to read over and over again those stories which they already know. This procedure also protects the slow learner from exposure, since it is in the teacher's control to let him read passages with which he is more or less familiar.

8.   Sensory Stimuli

Sensory stimuli are connected with concept formation and development. Their lack is an important factor in the learning difficulties of disadvantaged children.[7] Some researchers even believe that lack of sensory stimuli before the age of four cannot be compensated at a later age.

The richness of the Waldorf curriculum and the extraordinary position that art has as a teaching vehicle, should offer much compensation in this area. Two foreign languages are introduced in first and second grade in an informal way, which gives the children an opportunity to experience new songs, new games, and also to learn foreign customs. By comparison and analogy foreign languages teaching also enriches and deepens the knowledge and mastery of the native language. Each child learns a musical instrument from first grade on, usually the wooden recorder, and a special art of movement, called eurhythmy, is used to train physical and psychic coordination.

9. Class Size

Most teachers of inner city schools complain about overcrowded classes, which makes it difficult to reach all children.

This problem can be tackled from two sides: (1) to reduce class size or (2) teach the staff to use the group effectively as a teaching vehicle. It seems that success would come from a combination of both. Waldorf schools have developed effective group exercises for the formation of language, counting,[8] and other skills. Such experiences also have a socializing and harmonizing effect on the children.

10. Tests

It has been said that the school tests are inadequate; that they severly damage confidence and basic self-esteem.[9]

The Waldorf schools do not use any tests, except occasionally teacher made tests in mathematics and spelling. All other evaluation is performed from the original, creative work of the children, that is, from compositions, essays, and from the class participation. The evaluation is always verbal, and so are the reports given to the parents. Through this, competition between children is kept to a reasonable minimum. The Waldorf ideal is that each child should compete with himself, with the best in him.

11. Physical Health

The health program could be met by the weekly visit of a school physician. If each teacher could send one child per week to the physician and then discuss the case with the doctor, many academic and behavioral problems which are due to physical causes could be solved. This is the procedure followed in the Waldorf schools.

12. School Facilities

Substandard school facilities can only be met with dollars and not with Waldorf methods. However, imaginative teaching can help to overcome or to alleviate the handicap of inadequate school facilities.

13. Self-Esteem and Self-Confidence

It is commonly held that school failure caused by the above factors can damage self-esteem and self-confidence, which in turn lowers scholastic achievement. This is again a vicious circle which has to be broken.

Waldorf Education reckons with a very broad conception of achievement. This allows the teacher to let all children succeed within the range of positive, constructive criticism. It is often the intellectually slow child who, for instance, does the most beautiful drawings in geometry. If the teaching of the subject is arranged in such a way that he can show his manual skill and get praise for it, it may well motivate him to come to grips also with the conceptual content of the subject.

These preliminary considerations of Waldorf Education as it could be applied in the education of culturally disadvantaged children are in need of further study and evaluation. No claim is being made that Waldorf Educational methodology is the cure for the learning problems of the disadvantaged, but serious and close study of the methodology and the philosophy of Rudolf Steiner may be warranted. The remarkable success of Waldorf Schools in developing the child's cognitive and affective domains should not be overlooked in the planning of programs for the culturally disadvantaged.

References

1. Riessman, F. *The Culturally Deprived Child.* New York: Harper and Row, 1962. pp. 75, 84.

2. De Havas. *Singing Words,* Surrey, G.B.: The Forerunner Publications, 1951. p. 28.

3. Riessman, **op. cit.**

4. Davis, A. "Teaching Reading and Language to Disadvantaged Negro Children,"*Elementary English.* Vol. 42, 1965. pp. 791, 793.

5. Smith, M.B. "Curriculum Innovations for Disadvantaged Elementary Children—What They Should Be." *Teachers College Journal.* Vol. 37, 1965. p. 7.

6. Hayes, H. "Some Ways to Teach Culturally Deprived Children," *Chicago Schools Journal.* Vol. 2, 1964. p. 228.

7. Berlin, I. "Special Learning Problems of Deprived Children," *NEA Journal.* Vol. 55, 1966. p. 23.

8. Ogletree, E.J., Rackauskas, J.A., and Burgin, T.F. "Teaching Number Sense Through Rhythmical Counting." *Elementary School Journal.* Vol. 71, 1970. pp. 11-17.

9. Davis, **op. cit.**

ISSUES IN URBAN EDUCATION

WHY GHETTO SCHOOLS FAIL

by HENRY M. LEVIN

Urban schools have been failing disadvantaged students for a long time. This failure has been a fact despite its not having been widely recognized by a society that acknowledges Southern problems but not those found in the cities of the North. We are now facing a problem that is complex, pervasive, and of longstanding duration. Not only does the present method of financing place most large-city school districts at a severe disadvantage in supporting needed services, but the distributions of those finances systematically shortchange those children drawn from poor and powerless constituencies. But, most importantly, much of the money that finally filters down to schools attended by the urban disadvantaged is wasted on traditional approaches that are not appropriate for inner-city schools.

The inequities of the present system of financing schools through local property taxes and state aid constitute a by now familiar litany. Greater pupil needs, higher costs, municipal overburden, and smaller resources to draw upon mean that the present system of financing schools places a city at a severe disadvantage relative to its suburbs. It is more difficult for a city to raise equal dollars; equal dollars do not buy equal educational services because of higher costs in the city, and the educational services that a city must provide are far more massive than those that must be provided by suburban neighbors.

At the same time, there is evidence that many cities receive fewer dollars from the state for each pupil than do their wealthier suburbs. Although some states provide additional financial support to their cities for educating children from low-income families, the supplemental aid is so nominal that the pattern does not change appreciably. Even the effect of federal aid for schooling the disadvantaged, such as that allocated under Title I of the Elementary and Secondary Education Act of 1965, makes but a small alteration in the basic system of support, which is unequal to begin with.

But the financial stringencies faced by the large-city school districts are not the only such factors hindering the improvement of inner-city schools. The school districts themselves systematically shortchange those schools attended by disadvantaged populations. Few school superintendents or other high officials will admit that such disparities exist since to do so would be politically dangerous. Nevertheless, internal audit studies of the school-by-school funding patterns within cities have consistently found that fewer dollars are spent in schools educating poor children and black children than in schools attended by their white middle-class counterparts. Not only have these differences been tolerated (and perhaps promoted in the past), but it appears that even the monies for compensatory education are often used to support district-wide services instead of being applied to

SATURDAY REVIEW, March 21, 1970, pp. 68-82.

the disadvantaged populations for whom they were intended. If the inner-city schools are shortchanged under the existing distribution of funds, there is no reason to believe that funds from higher levels of government for the disadvantaged will reach their mark. Traditional administrative devices, an accounting system that masks school-by-school discrepancies, and uneven distribution of political power all augur the financial shortchanging of schools attended by the disadvantaged.

But perhaps the greatest tragedy in the financial chain is that, when additional dollars finally filter down to the inner-city schools, they are often squandered on traditional approaches that have consistently failed the inner-city youngster. The record of spending on compensatory education is an outstanding testimony to the futility of doing more of the same things that have not worked in the past.

Indeed, the inability of compensatory education programs to produce significant results is traceable directly to the questionable ideology on which they are tacitly based. Inherent in compensatory education programs is the condescending view that the urban minority child is somehow inferior to the middle-class child. The schools assume that his cultural differences represent inferiorities that must be eliminated. "Remediation" is considered the key to the minority child's emancipation. Inherent in this approach is a total disregard for the cultures and experiences of black and other minority children. Yet, to a minority youngster, his experience is certainly as valid as that of his white counterpart.

There is no reason that he must deny or deprecate his background in order to "learn." Indeed, such forced self-denunciation can only guarantee the development of a serious and widening breach between the school and the child. Unfortunately, the large urban school systems have shown themselves to be incapable of building educational programs that will capitalize on the cultural attributes of minority children. This fact becomes quite clear when one examines the way in which so-called compensatory education programs have been formulated. Most money has been spent on such traditional routes as reducing class size, increasing the number of counselors and remedial specialists, and buying more library volumes. That is, more money has been spent on the same remedies that have not worked well in the past. The inevitable result is that a larger budget purchasing more of the same ingredients will make a larger version of the same dismal cake. There must be qualitative changes in the recipe in order to improve the quality of education for minority children.

Comparing dollar inputs between schools attended by minority students and those attended by middle-class whites is an erroneous way of measuring school resource endowments between races. To the degree that money is spent in both cases on teachers, curriculum, and other inputs that are more effective for white children than for black or Spanish-speaking students, dollar expenditures tend to overstate vastly the relative resources available to the latter groups. Rather, nominal resources devoted to the two groups of schools must be weighed by their effectiveness in order to ascertain their true value.

The ludicrous nature of comparing schools attended by majority and minority children on the basis of physical checklists of characteristics or on dollar expenditures is reflected in the following illustration. If black schools and white schools have the same number of teachers with the same preparation and experience, the two sets of schools are considered to be equal according to conventional criteria. Now what if all of the teachers have white racist views? Clearly, if black schools and white schools have equal numbers of white racist teachers, the two sets of schools are not equal even though the actual numbers of teachers are. This example raises additional questions about the present definition of remediation and compensatory education. If we double the number of white racist teachers in black schools, class size will be reduced by 50 per cent; yet, it is difficult to argue that healthy increases in educational output will take place. Such a situation, however, is perfectly consistent with the conventional arithmetic of spending on compensatory education. Attention is heavily focused on the amount of traditional resources available to minority children with almost no consideration of the appropriateness or the efficacy of those resources.

It follows that such a simple cure as merely obtaining more money for the cities will hardly guarantee solving all or even most of the infirmities of urban education. Rather, the solution requires a tripartite response. First, how can we increase the financial resources available to large-city school districts? Second, how can we assure that an appropriately large share of the additional resources will be devoted to the inner-city schools? And finally, how can we increase the probability that this support will be used on educational programs that will produce results?

Strangely enough, obtaining more dollars for the large-city school districts is the problem most likely to be solved in the near future, because present financing arrangements for schools appear to violate the "equal protection" clause of the Fourteenth Amendment of the U.S. Constitution. Simply stated, the states are responsible for financing the schools. Whether school taxes are collected by the state or by local school districts, they are considered to be state taxes; and if disparities exist in the revenue resources available to school districts, then such differences exist as a consequence of the state's discretion. By basing school support for any student on such fortuitous circumstances as where he lives, the wealth of his community, or the community's concern for education, it is contended that the states are not granting equal protection of the law to all residents.

On this premise many cities have begun to sue their respective states with the goal of requiring the states to foster a true measure of equality of educational opportunity. While some of the suits argue for equal expenditures among schools, others assert that equal protection under the law requires unequal expenditures based upon the higher costs and greater student needs in urban schools. In practical terms, the states would be required to undertake a far larger share of the educational burden, one that would shift substantial financial resources to the city schools.

Unfortunately, more money for the city schools will not be enough in itself to overcome the particular problems of the inner-city schools. Under the present accounting system, where school-by-school expenditures are not reported, the central school administration can continue to discriminate against inner-city schools with virtual impunity. The states can make a salutary move toward ensuring that cities make fair allocations to the inner-city schools by requiring school-by-school reporting of budgetary allocations. That is, each state should require expenditure information for individual schools from all of its school districts. The visibility of school-by-school budgets would provide a relatively simple method of seeing that monies for compensatory education are spent in the schools for which they were intended.

The reporting of expenditures and other information by cities on a school-by-school basis would have additional advantages. Since aid from higher levels of government is often given according to the socio-economic level (degree of disadvantage) of the student population, it is easiest to assess this criterion for each school. In a feasibility study for New York State, it was found that a measure of educational need for disadvantaged children could be constructed from information provided by school principals. Using various combinations of data on student race and social class—generally available for each school— a useful measure of need for resources could be computed. The authors of this study also suggested ways in which a measure of school resource need could be woven into the state school finance formula. Accounting for expenditures on a school-by-school basis is mandatory, if we are to obtain equity for the inner-city schools.

Obtaining more money for city school districts and ensuring that inner-city schools receive adequate shares of those finances requires fairly specific mechanical changes in any state's finance and accounting procedures. Given the recommended changes that we have specified in these two areas, the impact of the new arrangements is fairly predictable, and both goals can be achieved with rather straightforward departures from existing state policies. The third problem, that of spending dollars more effectively in the inner-city schools, is more elusive, for, although financial and accounting arrangements can be mandated, school effectiveness cannot. Indeed, this is the weakest link in the financial chain, for it is the one over which the bankers of the public schools have the least measure of control.

The basic flaw that characterizes an educational system (as well as most public enterprises) is that there are no incentives built into the system to satisfy social goals. If students are not learning to read in a particular school, there are no direct incentives to change the situation. Principals and teachers get pay increases on schedule, whether they fail or succeed. A teacher has only to live long enough to rise to the top of the salary scale. Nowhere in the present organization of schools do we have financial or nonfinancial incentives for making schools succeed. The reward structure is systematically divorced from educational effectiveness.

This fundamental weakness of the schools must be remedied by an approach that rewards success and penalizes failure, just as other organizations do. The kinds of appropriate incentives appear to be ones that would reward educational responsiveness in terms of the needs of the students and families served. Two kinds of models have been posited that would pursue these goals: the market approach to schooling and the political or community control approach.

The market approach is based upon a plan suggested by Professor Milton Friedman of the University of Chicago. Schools are essentially monopolistic in that they provide services for a captive audience. Since most children and their parents have little choice but to attend their local schools—no matter how poor the performance of such institutions—the students are locked into a system which does not have to satisfy their educational needs. The proponents of the market approach believe that by giving students and their families a choice of schools, and by requiring schools to compete for students, substantial increases in educational effectiveness would result. For, if schools had to compete for students in order to survive, they would likely be much more responsive to the particular needs of their potential clientele.

What are the mechanics of such an arrangement? The state would provide tuition vouchers to parents for a specified maximum sum per year for each child. Parents would be free to use these vouchers at any approved institution of their choice. Institutions would be encouraged to enter the marketplace to compete for students, and any school that met minimal requirements in such areas as curriculum and personnel would be eligible to participate. Thus, a system of nonpublic schools would compete with the public ones for students.

Data on school costs, programs, strategies, effectiveness, and student populations might be required of all approved schools in order to keep parents and potential educational sellers informed of available alternatives. Such an arrangement would induce innovation and experimentation in that each school would try to obtain competitive advantages over the others. Only those public schools that would be responsive to the needs of their students could survive such competition; so a healthy infusion of nonpublic schools into the market would also tend to keep the remaining public schools on their toes.

In addition to the basic Friedman plan, there are many other ways of using an educational marketplace to fulfill the social goals set for inner-city schools. In an excellent discussion on the subject, Anthony Downs has suggested that the cities merge several existing attendance areas so that all students within a given section of the city can attend any of a number of schools within that boundary. Schools within the merged area would compete for students, and teachers and other resources would be shifted from the less successful schools — those whose enrollments decline—to those attracting new enrollments. Portable classrooms could also be added to the latter schools, if necessary. Thus, principals would have an incentive to maximize the important educational outputs desired by the residents of the merged attendance areas, or face a loss of clientele and resources.

In a similar vein, James S. Coleman, author of the Office of Education's report *Equality of Educational Opportunity*, has suggested contracting out such services as reading and arithmetic, and paying educational contractors only on the basis of their students' results on standardized tests. There are many ways to create competition within the inner-city schools, and virtually all of them would provide market-type incentives for utilizing educational resources far more effectively than they have been in the past.

Yet, the market schema is not the only means of providing incentives for ensuring that schools in the inner city will fulfill the needs of their clientele. It is also possible to redirect the efforts of such institutions through revamping the political processes by which decisions are made. Good educational strategies are made on the basis of the particular characteristics and needs of the children being served. They cannot be set out at a highly centralized, abstract, and depersonalized level just to satisfy an administrative compulsion for order.

Decentralized school districts could be formed in the inner city based upon proximity and commonality of needs among schools. Each decentralized or community school district would elect a representative school board to govern its constituent schools. Financial accounts and accountability would remain in the hands of the central school authority, but the actual disbursements for each school would be authorized only by the local governing board for that school. On the basis of this decision-making power, the local governing boards, in conjunction with administrators and teachers (and perhaps student representatives), would construct their programs and purchase the necessary components to implement them — a course of action not permitted under existing regulations. Political decentralization would then enable schools to reflect more closely the educational needs of their constituents. The inner-city schools would be pressured to break out of the pattern of ineptitude fostered by the mindless universalism of traditional big-city school administration.

Both political and market incentives could be combined to make the inner-city schools more effective. Under a system of decentralized schools, students should be given a choice of attending a school in their own community or in any other community. Moreover, the central school board would continue to operate a few schools as alternatives open both to individual students and parents via market choice, and to groups of students and parents via political action within the community.

Further, the decentralized school districts might find it desirable to purchase some services from private contractors. The community school board would plan its educational requirements and compare these with its capabilities. The school board would then solicit bids from industry, universities, and nonprofit groups for fulfilling objectives in those areas where the local district had the least proficiencies. Educational contractors would compete for the particular services the community wished to buy, and remuneration might be based on the success of the programs.

All these suggestions are possibilities for the reform of inner-city schools. The point is that it is imperative to recognize that an increase in city, state, or federal dollars will make little difference to the inner-city school if nothing is done to improve educational effectiveness. Some system must be adopted that will reward schools that are excelling while penalizing those that are failing, differences that are ignored by present financial arrangements. The use of market and political incentives both show promise in this respect. Without substantial moves in this direction, much of the additional financial support for the inner-city schools will be wasted through the same inept and insensitive schooling processes that have not worked in the past.

James C. Harvey and Charles H. Holmes

BUSING AND SCHOOL DESEGREGATION

A review of the court cases since 1968 which have brought us to the present impasse

There is now little question that "law and order," the dominant emotional domestic political issue in 1968, has been replaced by "busing" in 1972. In the recent Florida presidential primary, "forced busing" was overwhelmingly repudiated by the voters while, at the same time, most of them claimed to favor equal opportunity in education. The issue was a major factor in George Wallace's victory in Florida.

Some political leaders have proposed new federal laws and constitutional amendments to halt busing. Even President Nixon has reacted by proposing a moratorium on busing to Congress; he has also called for compensatory funding for so-called inferior schools in the inner cities and rural areas. Moreover, the President has directed the Justice Department to "intervene in selected cases where the lower courts have gone beyond the Supreme Court's requirements in ordering busing." Acting Attorney General Richard Kleindienst has mentioned that his department would probably intervene in the Richmond and Denver suits.

We believe that in order to understand this public policy area it is essential to examine some recent major court decisions on the subject. In May, 1968, the "freedom of choice" approach to school desegregation followed by a rural Virginia county school board was struck down in *Green* et al. v. *County*

PHI DELTA KAPPAN, 1972, Vol. 53, pp. 540-543.

School Board of New Kent County, Va., et al.[1] The U.S. Supreme Court held in effect that continued delays were no longer acceptable in those Southern and border states still having legally sanctioned dual school systems. Freedom of choice methods were declared to be inadequate if they did not end school segregation as rapidly as other methods would. The school authorities were charged with the affirmative duty to do whatever was necessary to eliminate racial discrimination "root and branch."[2] Although not all freedom of choice plans were ruled unconstitutional per se by this decision, nevertheless, as they had generally been drawn, such plans were invalidated. Northern de facto segregation was not covered by the decision.[3]

It soon became evident that at least one major tool available for school desegregation was the busing of white and black children. Ironically, this tool had often been used in the past to perpetuate segregation, as would be documented in the Richmond and Charlotte decisions. As one writer recently pointed out:

> Deep problems are involved in busing children to achieve desegregation — particularly when inordinately long distances are involved, or when students are shifted from a perfectly good school to one that may be inferior. But until such things as housing patterns are radically modified, busing — within reasonable limits — remains one of the few tools immediately available for desegregating America's schools. And we would do well to remember that nearly 20 million pupils are now being bused to schools without apparent harm.[4]

Busing as a tool for desegregation was at issue in *Swann* v. *Charlotte-Mecklenburg Board of Education*.[5] In this case the Nixon Administration and the Justice Department intervened on the side of the defendants in support of the neighborhood school concept. The Supreme Court unanimously upheld the constitutionality of busing as a method by which dual school systems could be dismantled. The justices also ruled that this decision did not apply to de facto segregation based on neighborhood patterns in the North.

The court concurred with the conclusion of the federal district court that the assignment of children to the school nearest their residence would not produce an end to the dual system. Therefore, school desegregation could not be limited to the "walk-in" school. The Supreme Court pointed out that:

> All things being equal, with no history of discrimination, it might be desirable to assign pupils to schools nearest their homes. But all things are not equal in a system that has been deliberately constructed and maintained to enforce racial segregation.[6]

At the same time, the judges held that busing was a proper method unless "the time or distance is so great as to risk either the health of the children or significantly impinge on the educational process."[7]

In upholding the district court, the Supreme Court did not require any particular degree of racial balance or mixing and did not eliminate all-black schools per se. However, the Court did rule that the existence of all-black schools created a presumption of discrimination and that federal district courts might resort to racial quotas as a guide in preparing school desegregation decrees (as a starting point toward shaping a remedy). Moreover, pairings and noncontiguous school zones were held to be permissible tools for desegregation.

There is little doubt, however, that:

> Despite the promise of the occasion, the Court fell far short of pronouncing definite standards for school desegregation. The approach taken in Chief Justice Burger's opinion was to vest considerable discretion in district court judges, without providing them with any explicit guidelines as to when or how to use it. While more definite standards may be implied in the Court holding, the opinion's language leaves several questions unanswered.[8]

Although busing was upheld as a viable tool in *Swann* for dismantling dual systems in the South, a number of matters remained, including enforcement. The Department of Health, Education, and

Welfare had rarely required "busing" to achieve desegregation in the past. After *Swann*, HEW's Office of Civil Rights began to review plans which called for all-black schools. However, the U.S. Commission on Civil Rights recently charged that few changes have been required which adequately reflect the *Swann* rulings.[9] In addition, there is the problem of the flight of whites to the suburbs from the cities. The effect of the population shift has been to lessen chances for racially mixed schools, as the suburbs generally have their own school districts. Inner cities are becoming increasingly black, suburbs predominantly white. This population shift has occurred in the South as well as the North. Moreover, school segregation still exists on a major scale inside Northern and Western cities.

A significant decision was made by a federal district judge in February, 1970, affecting the schools in Pontiac, Michigan. In *Davis* v. *School District of the City of Pontiac, Inc.*[10] the court held that

> ... the Pontiac Board of Education has intentionally utilized the power at their disposal to locate new schools and arranged boundaries in such a way as to perpetuate the pattern of segregation within the city and thereby, deliberately, in contradiction of their announced policies of achieving a racial mixture in the schools, prevented integration.[11]

The lower court ordered the Pontiac board to integrate the students, faculties, and administrators by September of 1970. Boundary lines for attendance purposes were to be revised and busing was to be carried out in order to achieve maximum integration.

The Pontiac decision was delayed and was appealed first to the U.S. Court of Appeals in Cincinnati. There the lower court was upheld. The district court finally issued an order (August 10, 1971) for busing to go into effect for the fall term. Opposition to this decree quickly mounted in the white community. Nevertheless, in October, 1971, the U.S. Supreme Court declined to review the court order calling for busing. That action had the effect of validating the district court's order.[12]

In the meantime, in *Keyes* v. *School District One, Denver, Colorado,*[13] a federal district judge held that while the school system did not have a de jure segregation policy except in three schools, nevertheless it was following some practices similar to de facto segregation with respect to black and Hispano children in others. The judge decreed that:

> The evidence . . . establishes, and we do find and conclude, that an equal educational opportunity is not being provided at the subject segregated schools within the district. The evidence establishes this beyond doubt. Many factors contribute to the inferior status of these schools, but the predominant one appears to be the enforced isolation imposed in the name of neighborhood schools and housing patterns.[14]

The board failed to come up with an acceptable plan and in May, 1970, the federal district judge ruled that Denver must desegregate 15 minority schools by 1972 and make changes at two others (all 17 schools had at least 70% black or Spanish-American students). There would be open enrollment and free transfers, with space guaranteed and compensatory education programs provided for minority children. He also declared that mandatory busing to the extent possible should be avoided, but held that it "may well be necessary to effectuate much of the court's plan."[15]

The Denver school board appealed the decision to the U.S. Court of Appeals for the Tenth Circuit. This court upheld the lower court only in the case of three schools shown to be segregated as a result of official actions. This decree caused the invalidation of the order pertaining to the other schools.

The Denver case was scheduled for U.S. Supreme Court hearing in April and a decision is anticipated by this fall. Apparently the Court has decided to come to grips with the question of whether or not a community is obligated to end segregation caused by housing patterns. Moreover, the Court will consider once more the discriminatory actions of public officials.[16]

In the meantime, on January 10, 1972, a district judge in Richmond, Virginia, issued what could become a landmark decision in *Carolyn Bradley* et al. v. *The School Board of the City of Richmond, Virginia* et al.[17] Interestingly enough, the Richmond school board joined with the black plaintiffs in the midst of the court hearings. The court decided that before September, 1972, the city of Richmond public schools and those of Henrico and Chesterfield counties in the suburbs must be merged into a single metropolitan school district.

The federal judge declared

> ... that the duty to take whatever steps are necessary to achieve the greatest degree of desegregation in formerly dual school districts by the elimination of racially identifiable schools is not circumscribed by school district boundaries created and maintained by the cooperative efforts of local and state officials. The court also concludes that meaningful integration in a biracial community, as in the instant case, is essential to equality of education, and the failure to provide it is violative of the Constitution of the United States.[18]

As in *Swann,* implementing the *Bradley* decision will require a large amount of busing. The lawyers who won the case claimed that the Richmond decree would have a nationwide impact, particularly in Northern cities.[19] If the decree were upheld by the U.S. Supreme Court (and barring possible constitutional and/or statutory changes), it might serve to curtail the white flight to the suburbs, since they would no longer offer a haven from integrated schools. In addition, the Richmond decree seemed to reinforce decisions by other courts calling for an equalization of expenditures per child for public education in affluent and low-income school districts.

Needless to say, the *Bradley* decision has been unpopular in some quarters, especially in the white community in the Richmond suburbs. This decree, along with others (including the ones mentioned earlier) has brought widespread repercussions. It is too early to predict just what effect the Administration's efforts will have. Busing, like school desegregation itself, will require sometimes tedious and difficult negotiations in the days ahead. In fact, these two facets of the school problem cannot be fully separated. The effort to halt busing could also lead to a curb on school desegregation itself. The National Association for the Advancement of Colored People's leadership fears that there is an attempt under way to turn back the clock and reverse hard-won gains. Governor George Wallace is calling for a return to "freedom of choice," which meant token desegregation in the past.

---

1. 88 S. Ct., 1689 (1968).
2. *Ibid.*, 1694.
3. *The New York Times,* May 28, 1968, p. 33.
4. Robert P. Kriss, "The Split-Level Presidency," *Saturday Review,* March 11, 1972, p. 32.
5. 91 S. Ct. 1267 (1971).
6. *Ibid.,* 1282.
7. *Ibid.*
8. "The Supreme Court, 1970 Term," *Harvard Law Review,* November, 1971, p. 75.
9. "School Desegregation," *Civil Rights Digest,* December, 1971, p. 9.
10. 309 F. Supp. 734 (1970).
11. *Ibid.,* 741.
12. See *The New York Times,* October 27, 1971, p. 1.
13. 313 F. Supp. 61 (1970).
14. *Ibid.,* 83.
15. *Ibid.,* 96-98.
16. Editorial, *Phi Delta Kappan,* March, 1972, p. 402.
17. Xerox copy of the decision.
18. *Ibid.,* 21.
19. *The New York Times,* January 13, 1972, p. 32.

DESEGREGATION AND MINORITY GROUP PERFORMANCE

NANCY H. ST. JOHN*

Harvard University

The 1954 Supreme Court desegregation decision was based on fine legal and moral argument, but on rather slim social science evidence (Deutscher and Chein, 1948; Clark, 1953). In view of the clear challenge to the caste system that the decision represented and the extent of the changes called for, it is singular that so few empirical tests of the dictum that segregation *per se* is harmful to children were undertaken in the decade that followed. Then came the Equality of Educational Opportunity Survey (Coleman, 1966). The magnitude of this study and its unexpected findings suggest that research on the education of minority children should be labeled "before Coleman" or "after Coleman." The insights afforded by the survey and its methodological limitations propel social scientists to more definitive research. To date no longitudinal studies with adequate samples and controls have been published, but reports on an increasing number of small-scale bussing experiments are becoming available. Pieced together, such bits of evidence help define the shape of the larger puzzle and identify what is known and what is not known.

This chapter reviews Pre-Coleman, Coleman, and Post-Coleman empirical evidence on the relation of school racial composition to the acadamic performance of black children. The independent variable is called "racial composition" advisedly; neither scholars nor schoolmen agree on the definitions of *racial balance, desegregation, non-segregation,* or *integration.* Some use these words interchangeably, while others distinguish between them according to whether or not the school ethnic mix matches that of its community, whether or not a uni-racial school has become bi-racial, whether or not the process was planned, and whether or not the minority group is accepted into the social life of the school. I am interested in school racial mixture of any type, although I recognize that surrounding circumstances may condition its relationship to academic performance.

Many possible outcomes of schooling-creativity, curiosity, civic responsibility, moral judgment, artistic taste, human sensitivity—are im-

---

*Dr. David Cohen, Harvard University, served as a consultant to Dr. St. John on the preparation of this chapter. Support for the preparation of this manuscript was supplied in part by U.S.O.E. contract #6-10-240 with Yeshiva University.

REVIEW OF EDUCATIONAL RESEARCH, 1970, Vol. 40, No. 1, pp. 17-27.

portant, but they typically go unmeasured in social research. Therefore, although the subject of this chapter could be the relation of school racial composition to children's total intellectual, emotional and moral development, for the most part I review research in which achievement *test scores* were the criterion variable.

Choice of Research Design

The experimental model is a convenient way of organizing the evidence I am interested in. To establish a causal relationship between classroom ethnic composition and academic performance, a researcher should employ the classic pre-test, post-test model with subjects randomly selected and assigned to experimental and control groups. Both groups are tested before the experimental group is subjected to the test condition (desegregation), all other conditions must remain the same for both groups, and later both groups are tested again. A greater change between Time 1 and Time 2 for the experimental than for the control group can presumably be attributed to the effect of desegregation (Stouffer, 1962; Campbell and Stanley, 1963; Pettigrew and Pajonas, 1964).

Such experimental research in the area of desegregation is very difficult to achieve. The random assignment to control and experimental conditions usually seems politically and morally questionable, and the loss of cases through migration or school leaving is apt to jeopardize the randomness of the sample. Therefore one finds frequent use of a longitudinal design without a control group, of a cross-sectional design without a Time 1 measurement, or of quasi-experiments with statistical rather than actual control of other variables, even though any correlation between key variables can not be taken as evidence of a causal relation between them.

Two rival independent variables, school quality and family background, are especially likely to contaminate research on the effect of ethnic segregation on the performance of children. In pre-Coleman Report days probably few people doubted that school quality varied with racial composition or that predominantly black schools were by and large inferior to predominantly white ones in physical plant, equipment, curricular offerings and teacher qualifications. Comparisons of Negro and white schools in the South (McCauley and Ball, 1969; Miller, 1960) or ghetto and non-ghetto schools in the North (Public Education Association, 1955; Conant, 1961; Sexton, 1961; Wolff, 1963; Katzman, 1966) certainly supported this conclusion. There have also been repeated reports that teachers in ghetto schools have low morale, a low opinion of their pupils, and an eagerness to transfer to more middle class (or white) settings (Becker, 1952; Gottlieb, 1964; Clark, 1965; Herriott and St. John, 1966). Coleman

(1966) found many differences within regions between schools attended by majority and minority children, to the advantage of the former, though most of these were surprisingly slight. Critics of the Coleman Report argued that various methodological limitations of the study mask the true relation between race and school quality (Nichols, 1966; Bowles and Levin, 1968; Dyer, 1968). Thus, any superiority in the performance of integrated over segregated children could in part be due to a difference in school quality.

The issue of school equality is raised in a different form by the recent introduction of compensatory programs into most Northern city school systems. To the extent that such programs tend to remove former inequities and to equalize education across schools, they act as a control in studies comparing performance in segregated and integrated settings. To the extent that they go beyond equalization and offer *extra* services to minority group children—newer buildings, smaller classes, greater per pupil expenditure, better prepared teachers—they in theory make it more rather than less difficult to test the effect of ethnic composition *per se* (Gordon and Wilkerson, 1966; U. S. Commission on Civil Rights, 1967).

The second variable most likely to contaminate research on the effect of school desegregation on pupil performance is the social and economic level of home or neighborhood. Most researchers find that socioeconomic status (SES) predicts achievement for Negroes, though less well than for whites (for example, McGurk, 1953; Klineberg, 1963; Kennedy, Van de Riet and White, 1963; Pettigrew, 1964; Stodolsky and Lesser, 1967). In an attempt to isolate other measures of a child's home environment that would predict his school achievement better than the usual indices of SES, Peterson and Debord (1966) interviewed 11 year-old Negroes in a Southern city; they found a set of 11 home variables that had a multiple correlation of .82 with achievement scores. In a similar endeavor, Whiteman, Brown, and Deutsch (1966) developed a Deprivation Index (measuring housing dilapidation, number of siblings, kindergarten attendance, educational aspiration of parent for the child, dinner conversation, and family cultural experiences) which contributed significantly to the verbal test performance of Negro children in New York. The Coleman (1966) and U. S. Commission on Civil Rights (1967) reports corroborated such evidence on the relationship between aspects of home background and the verbal achievement of minority group children. If school quality and the family background are positively related to the achievement of minority pupils and to their schools racial composition, it is crucial to control them in any study of the influence of ethnic composition.

Longitudinal One-Group Studies

The merit of the longitudinal study is that selection bias is partly ruled out if the same subjects are tested before (or at the beginning of) a period of non-segregated schooling and again after some months or years in the desegregated situation. The weakness of such a design is that with‿ut a control group, there is no assurance that any observed effect is not due to the influence of previous testing, to normal maturation, to extraneous events, or especially to a change in the quality of schooling.

Desegregation of School Systems

Two studies often referred to as evidence of the beneficial effect of the desegregation of a school system are Hansen's report on Washington, D. C. (1960) and Stallings's report on Louisville, Kentucky (1959). Hansen reported that in the five years following consolidation of the separate school systems in the District of Columbia, median city-wide achievement improved at all grade levels and in most subject areas. Unfortunately, for a number of reasons this finding is not evidence that desegregation was causally related to improved minority group performance. 1) No testing of black children was done before desegregation, and no separation of black and white scores was made after desegregation. 2) The scores of the same children were not traced through the years; instead successive third grade (etc.) classes were compared. 3) Actual racial composition of schools and classrooms was not considered, and the simultaneous establishment of the track system probably resulted in considerable classroom segregation in those schools that were technically desegregated. 4) With desegregation came major improvements in the quality of education— lowered teacher-pupil ratios, increased budget, more remedial services; these furnish plausible alternative explanations of the improved performance.

Schools in Louisville were desegregated by court order in 1956. Stallings (1959) reported that the academic achievement of Negro and white students was significantly higher after than before desegregation and that the Negro students made greater gains than the white students did. But again there is evidence that most schools remained segregated. The gains of black pupils were greatest when they remained with black teachers, i.e., in all-black schools (United States Commission on Civil Rights, 1962, p. 34). Stallings suggested that one factor may have been increased motivation resulting from legal desegregation.

Desegregation of Individuals

In studies of the effect of Northern residence on the intelligence test scores of Negro children, the investigators regularly found that migrants from the South score higher in proportion to their length of residence in the North (Klineberg, 1953; Lee, 1951; Moriber, 1961). Unfortunately in these migration studies, the racial mix of the Northern schools was not reported and the effects of three variables are confounded: community with school desegregation and school desegregation with school quality. Researchers can more successfully test the unique effect of school desegregation when individuals enter a mixed school, especially if those individuals do not change residence to a mixed neighborhood.

A large longitudinal study of the impact of desegregation on pupil attitudes and performances is in process in Riverside, California. In the fall of 1965 the Riverside Board of Education decided to close three buildings and bus their Negro and Mexican-American pupils to other buildings in the system (Purl, 1967, 1969). Since *de facto* segregation was thereby eliminated, no control group will be available. To date the only progress reports indicate that two years of integration have had "not much effect" on achievement, but since neither social class nor other variables were controlled, even this conclusion seems unwarranted.

Katzenmeyer (1963) studied all pupils who entered the public kindergartens of 16 Jackson, Michigan schools in the year 1957 and 1958. The 192 Negro children, who thus represented the full socio-economic range in the city, were distributed among 11 integrated schools; one school was 66% black and the rest were below 40% black. Children were given the Lorge-Thorndike IQ test at the beginning of Kindergarten and second grade. The two-year gain for white children was 1.87 points, for Negro children 6.68—a difference significant at the .001 level. It is regrettable for research purposes that no matched group of black children spent those years in segregated Jackson schools.

A recently completed evaluation of Project ABC, a scholarship program which brings disadvantaged high-school students to independent boarding schools, followed an entering class of 82 boys (70% Negro, 10% American Indian, 9% Puerto Rican, 2% Oriental, and 9% white) who entered 39 different schools in the Fall of 1965 (Wessman, 1969). Faculty reported scholastic gains for half the group, but test-retest showed no significant change on mean Otis IQ or Cooperative English Achievement tests.

Clark and Plotkin (1963) surveyed Negro students at integrated colleges. The sample consisted of the 509 students who returned questionnaires out of the 1519 who received aid or counseling from the National Scholarship and Service Fund, 1952-1956. College grades were found to be higher than could have been predicted on the basis of pre-college scholastic aptitude test scores. The net dropout rate of 10% was one-fourth the national rate and far below the rate for segregated Negro colleges. This study would have been strengthened by more random sampling, by post-tests and by the testing of a control group of similar students at segregated colleges, since it seems probable that many students who applied to the NSSFNS were especially able, motivated and likely to succeed wherever they enrolled. Even so, there would be no way of knowing whether any differences found were due to the integration or to the quality of the college experience. These criticisms, especially of the lack of control on other variables, apply not only to the Clark and Plotkin study but to all one-group "before and after" studies that have been reviewed here.

Cross-Sectional Studies

The major weakness of cross-sectional studies, in which segregated and integrated subjects are compared without either group having been tested before the introduction of desegregation, is that there is no guarantee that the two groups were originally equivalent. Systematic differences are found by researchers who compare the characteristics of families living in integrated and segregated neighborhoods (Duncan and Duncan, 1957; Stetler, 1957; Hughes and Watts, 1964) or of families who do and do not volunteer for bussing experiments (Crockett, 1957; Luchterhand and Weller, 1965; Weinstein and Geisel, 1962). It is therefore quite likely that the integrated subjects are a selected group, in terms of social class and/or ability.

Pre-Coleman Studies

As early as 1930, Crowley studied Stanford Achievement Test scores of Negro fourth to sixth grade pupils in two segregated and four mixed schools in Cincinnati. Of 110 children equated on grade, age, and Stanford Binet IQ, half had experienced only segregated and half only integrated schools. The two groups were said to be comparable also on "Physical condition, family history and social status". No statistically significant differences were found on 11 of 13 achievement tests. Spelling and writing were the exceptions; differences in these skills favored mixed schools (Crowley, 1932).

Radin (1966) studied the black pupils of two neighboring elementary schools (45% and 100% Negro) in Ypsilanti, Michigan. The schools were said by Radin to be alike in financial support and curriculum and in the IQ and SES of pupils, but the original equivalence of pupils in the two schools was not satisfactorily demonstrated. No statistically significant differences were found in mean scores on IQ or Iowa Test of Basic Skills, though the direction of the difference was uniformly in favor of the integrated school. When the performance of very high or very low achievers was examined, however, the differences were in favor of the segregated school.

In a similar study of naturally segregated and non-segregated elementary school children in New York, Jessup (1967) compared a) Negro and Puerto Rican second and fifth graders in a traditional, middle-class school

(75% white) with b) students in a comparable, low SES, project school (96% Negro and Puerto Rican) and with c) students in a new, Higher Horizons school (93% Negro). Since social class (measured by residential census tract data) was found to be so highly related to achievement, subsamples of 18 integrated and 80 segregated low SES children were compared on IQ, math and reading. This comparison revealed a distinct disadvantage for the segregated children, even for those in the Higher Horizon school with superior facilities and remedial services. The lowest SES children in the integrated school showed higher achievement than middle SES children in the segregated school. This study is handicapped by small sample size, inadequate control on individual SES, and lack of any "before" measurement.

In four recent dissertations, the investigators used roughly the same design. Meketon (1966) gave a battery of tests to Negro fifth and sixth graders in three schools in Kentucky: school A, *de facto* segregated; school B, peacefully integrated; and school C, integrated under "anxiety arousing circumstances". In schools A and B samples of children were matched on age, grade, sex, Otis Quick Scoring IQ and SES. In school C all children were included; though not matched with the other children they were reported to be generally similar in background but of somewhat higher IQ (on the California Test of Mental Maturity). Contrary to prediction children in school C had significantly higher scores than pupils in school A on the Digit Span Backward and Verbal Meaning Tests, and higher than school B pupils on these and a Space Ability Test. Unfortunately, the initial difference in IQ could explain the superior performance of school C pupils.

In a New York State community, Lockwood (1966) compared 217 sixth grade black students attending balanced and unbalanced (over 50% Negro) schools for two years or longer. Contemporaneous scores on Iowa Tests of Basic Skills and the California Test of Mental Maturity indicated that the students in the balanced schools were significantly higher at all IQ levels. When IQ was not controlled or when students had been less than two years in balanced schools, the differences were in the same direction but not statistically significant. The absence of control on individual SES and the evidence presented of higher mean SES in the balanced schools render the findings inconclusive. Samuels (1958) matched Indiana students on IQ and SES and found that at the first and second grade levels, Negroes in a segregated school had higher achievement scores, but in the third through sixth grades the achievement was higher in a racially mixed school.

The most statistically sophisticated study in this group is Matzen's (1965) correlational analysis of the fifth and seventh grade achievement scores of 1,065 Negro and white children in 39 segregated and integrated classrooms in one California community. Zero order correlations indicated that per cent of Negroes in the classroom was significantly and negatively related to Negro achievement, especially at the higher grade level (presumably because there was grouping by ability for seventh graders but not for fifth graders). However, when IQ and SES were controlled, second-order partial correlation showed the relationship to be no longer statistically significant.

Thus, of six recent cross-sectional comparisons of black children's performance in segregated and integrated elementary schools in six different communities and in five states, all found that without controls, achievement was higher in integrated schools. Several of the studies then controlled on IQ, but since they used a score more or less contemporaneous with that of achievement, they naturally found that the differences between segregated and desegregated children tended to disappear. IQ as well as achievement is malleable and the two tend to co-vary. A more valid procedure would be to test ability at the outset of pupils' careers in segregated or integrated settings. But none of these investigators did so. Moreover the controls on social class were rough. The suspicion remains, therefore, that self-selection may have biased their findings.

There have been a number of quasi-longitudinal cross-sectional studies in which investigators compared the secondary or college performance of students from segregated and integrated earlier schools. Wolff (1962) examined the high school records of black students in Plainfield, New Jersey; he found fewer dropouts, higher reading achievement, higher rank in the graduating class and higher enrollment in further education for the 20 graduates of an all-Negro school. No SES data and no significance tests on their differences were reported. Vane (1966) compared the high-school records of 52 black children from predominantly white schools in a large suburban community with those of 19 black children from an 89% Negro school. The average IQ was 100 for students from both types of school. She equated 17 pairs on IQ and SES and found no significant differences in achievement at any level. St. John (1962, 1964) reported that with SES controlled there was a non-significant trend toward higher high school test scores for those New Haven blacks who had attended more integrated elementary schools.

Johnson, Wyer and Gilbert (1967) tabulated first term grades of 121 Negro freshmen at one University of Illinois campus according to the racial composition of their Chicago high schools. A curvilinear relation was found; students from schools less than 50% or more than 90% black did better than those from schools 50-89% black. Further examinations indicated that students from one group of schools more than 90% black attained considerably higher grades than those from another group of schools of the same racial composition. The authors speculated that individual or school social class probably explained the difference, but they gave no data with which to test their assumption.

St. John and Smith (1969) analyzed the achievement of two-thirds of the black ninth graders in the city of Pittsburgh in 1966 (1388 pupils). When the effects of individual and neighborhood SES and sex had been removed through regression analysis, arithmetic achievement was significantly and negatively related to the average racial composition of a pupil's school in grades 1-9.

Thus, the balance of evidence of pre-Coleman cross-sectional studies is that, at the very least, integration had little negative effect on minority group performance and that it apparently had a positive effect, though it is hard to be sure, since other variables could account for the observed trends. (See Weinberg, 1968, for reports on other cross-sectional studies.)

Coleman and Commission Reports

In the Equality of Educational Opportunity Servey (EEOS), the investigators administered a series of achievement tests and questionnaires to more than 600,000 students in some 4,000 elementary and secondary schools (Coleman, 1966). Verbal ability scores showed more variation than other test scores and were selected as the chief measure of academic achievement.

Only a small part (10-20%) of the variance in achievement was found to be *between* rather than *within* schools (see Table 3.221.2 in Coleman et al., 1966). For Negroes, up to 30% of the between-school variance was accounted for by differences in family background (see Table 2.221.2). With the effect of family background removed, school characteristics accounted for little of the remaining achievement variance, but of these, characteristics of fellow students accounted for more than other school attributes (see Table 3.23.1). For this review the most important findings of the report concerns the effect of racial segregation: when students' own background, characteristics of the school, and characteristics of the student body were controlled, school per cent white accounted for almost no verbal ability variance for Negroes (see Table 3.23.4).

The U. S. Commission on Civil Rights (1967) reanalyzed the Coleman data in tabular form; they concentrated on twelfth grade Negro students in the metropolitan Northeast and on ninth grade Negro students in eight regions. The analysis showed that classroom racial composition (in the previous year) made a difference in verbal achievement, beyond the social class of either the pupil or his fellow students or of teacher quality. (See Appendix Tables 4.1 to 8.12.) Moreover, the earlier the grades at which Negroes reported first having had white schoolmates, the higher their achievement. There are three probable reasons why classroom per cent white "last year" should be more related to achievement than school per cent "this year": 1) At the ninth grade many pupils move from segregated elementary schools to desegregated secondary schools. "Last year's" experience may be a proxy for eight years' experience and, therefore, more influential than a few weeks' experience "this year." (The EEOS tests were administered in September.); 2) Within desegregated schools, considerable segregation often results from the practice of assignment to classrooms on the basis of test scores: i.e., ability influences classroom per cent white. (It may also influence school per cent white but less strongly.); 3) Classroom per cent white influences ability and has a stronger effect than school per cent white. The authors of the Commission Report stressed this last point, but either of the other two may also be operative.

Further analyses of the EEOS data (McPartland, 1968) supported the Commission's conclusion on the relation between classroom composition and achievement. McPartland showed that school desegregation was associated with higher achievement for black pupils only if they were in predominantly white classrooms, but classroom desegregation was favorable irrespective of school per cent white. He claimed that the classroom racial composition effect was not entirely explained by selection into track or curriculum.

The evidence that the Equality of Educational Opportunity survey made available on the *extent* of ethnic segregation and academic retardation for minority group children is invaluable. The evidence of the *relation between* segregation and retardation is not completely convincing, since it is subject to a number of methodological criticisms: 1) The representativeness of the sample was compromised by the non-cooperation of a number of large cities. 2) The measures of social class are unconvincing. There is no measure of family income. The item measuring parental occupation proved uncodable. Eighteen per cent of the ninth graders left blank or did not know their parents' educational level. Other researchers have found that children tend to upgrade their parents' education or occupation on a precoded questionnaire (Colfax, 1967. St. John, 1969). Self-reports on items in the home may also be biased and in any case, only the quantity not the quality of these items was told. The reliability study conducted by Coleman's staff in two school districts in Tennessee found 64% to 100% agreement between children and their teachers depending on grade level and nature of item. It should be noted, however, that teachers' and children's responses were not necessarily independent and that blanks and *I don't know*'s were counted as agreement, a questionable procedure. In short, it is difficult to have confidence that the effect of social class was entirely removed. 3) Part of the apparent effect of the background of fellow students may be due to unmeasured variation in a pupil's own background. Smith's (1969) reanalysis of the EEOS data indicated that two errors made in the original analyses led to underestimation of the effect of home background and an exaggeration of the effect of student characteristics. 4) The percentage of white schoolmates in the current year or of white classmates in the previous year may be less important than the per cent of white schoolmates or classmates over a number of years. Particularly at the ninth grade level *present* school racial experience is a poor estimate of *past* school racial experience. (See St. John and Smith, 1969.) 5) A cross-sectional analysis with no estimates of original ability or of the original equivalence of segregated and nonsegregated students can not conclusively demonstrate a causal relation between segregation and achievement or attitude.

Experimental or Quasi-Experimental (Four-Celled) Studies

A few studies have employed an experimental or quasi-experimental model, in that they provide Time 1 and Time 2 measurement of segregated and desegregated children matched on key variables. Two dissertation studies in the border South are four-celled in this sense. Fortenberry (1959) studied the mean achievement gains made in three subject areas during eighth and ninth grades of black pupils of similar IQ who attended mixed and nonmixed classes in Oklahoma City. Those in mixed classes made greater gains in arithmetic and language, but less gain in reading than did segregated pupils. No controls on social class were reported. Anderson (1966) found that 75 black fourth, fifth and sixth graders in five Tennessee desegregated (8 to 33% Negro) schools achieved significantly higher scores on Metropolitan Achievement Tests than did 75 black students from three segregated schools. The segregated and desegregated schools were judged "equivalent with respect to tangible factors" and their pupils were matched on age, intactness of family, third grade IQ scores and second grade achievement. The younger the age at which children had entered the desegregation schools, the greater was the apparent benefit.

Bussing Experiments

With increasing frequency in the last few years, school systems have issued reports of bussing experiments in which ghetto children are transported to predominantly white schools. In most cases the bussed children were tested before the program began and again one or two years thereafter, and their gains were compared with those of children who remained in segregated schools. The validity of the comparison as a test of the effect of racial composition on pupil performance hinges on 1) the equivalence of the bussed and non-bussed children at the outset, 2) the holding power of the two programs, and 3) the equality of schooling in every way except racial composition. Therefore, evaluation of bussing studies should note a) whether there is random assignment to experimental and control groups, or at least matching on key variables, b) whether there is mortality of cases through withdrawal from either program or failure to appear for tests, and c) whether children are bussed to another school in the same system or to schools in a presumably superior system.

New York state was the scene of a number of desegregation experiments and of the first five studies reviewed here. An early study of the effect of bussing in New Rochelle does not really belong in this group of 4-celled studies since it lacks measurement of pre-desegregation achievement (Wolman, 1964). Except at the kindergarten level, no statistically significant differences were found between those who transferred to integrated, middle class schools and those who stayed in a *de facto* segregated school, perhaps because as another study indicated (Luchterhand and Weller, 1965) more lower class families elected to transfer. It is also reported that in the year of the study the segregated school had the benefit of extra services (Kaplan, 1962).

In 1964 the White Plains school board initiated a racial balance plan which involved closing one elementary school and bussing about 900 black pupils from two sending schools to six receiving schools (White Plains Board of Education, 1967). Participation was mandatory. A three-year study was made of the IQ and Stanford Reading and Arithmetic Test scores of 33 of these black pupils (who entered grade 3 in 1964) in predominantly white schools. Since segregated schools no longer existed in the city, the 33 were compared with 36 black pupils who in 1960 had entered the third grade in the segregated school. The newly desegregated children gained slightly more in paragraph meaning and arithmetic than the earlier central city children. However, in word meaning the segregated children gained more. The findings remain inconclusive due to a number of methodological limitations, especially the small number of students tested and the lack of a contemporaneous control group.

Another small program involved bussing 75 pupils from central Rochester to a suburb, West Irondiquoit (Rock et al., 1966, 1967, 1968). Each year from 1965 to 1967, kindergarten teachers selected a pool of above-average pupils from which fifty names were drawn and assigned randomly, half to the experimental and half to the control group. Parental objections resulted in some shifts, and testing mortality was high. In 13 of 27 comparisons on Metropolitan Achievement Tests over three years, there were significant differences between the bussed and non-bussed black children; in each instance the difference was in favor of the bussed children. It should be noted that the receiving schools were in a high quality school system.

Beker (1967) reported on an experiment in Syracuse in which 60 of the 125 Negro elementary children bussed in the year 1964-1965 to a predominantly white school (Experimental Group) were compared with

270

35 children whose parents requested transfer but for whom places were not available (Control Group 1) and with 36 children whose parents refused transfer (Control Group 2). After the first year there was no significant differences in achievement gain among the three groups. This contradicts the U. S. Commission's (1967) Report for Syracuse of greater gains for 24 bussed children in comparison with an unspecified number of non-bussed children who had the benefit of a compensatory program. The latter gain may have been a Hawthorne effect in the first year of the program. Nevertheless, the small numbers involved and the lack of any control of SES make the Syracuse findings quite inconclusive.

In Buffalo, New York in 1965, there was mandatory bussing of 560 Negro pupils from closed and overcrowded schools to predominantly white schools in the same city (Dressler, 1967). Of these, 54 in grade 3 were tested and compared with 60 in a sending school. The author did not specify how these were selected. Comparison on reading showed greater gain over the year for bussed students. No controls on SES or other variables and no significance tests were reported. A later report from Buffalo (Banks and DiPasquale, 1969) described a 1967-1968 study of 1200 fifth to seventh grade Negro pupils bussed from 6 segregated inner city schools to 22 integrated schools. Whole classes were selected for the transfer. Though there was no difference in control test scores, the main growth for the year for the integrated pupils was .83 and for the segregated pupils .56 (grade equivalence scores). There was, however, no assurance that the integrated children or those with available test scores did not have more favorable background or higher native ability than the segregated.

There are two sources of information on the results of a bussing experiment in Philadelphia. The U. S. Commission (1967) reported that bussed Negro children of the same social class and reading grade level as Negroes in segregated schools with compensatory education (EIP) had by the third grade surpassed EIP children and equaled students of slightly higher SES in non-EIP schools. Laird and Weeks (1966) may have referred to the same experiment; in any case they make more details available. Ninety-nine pupils in grades 4-6 were bussed from one segregated school to two integrated schools and compared with the 420 pupils who remained in the segregated school. The bussed pupils performed better on reading and arithmetic tests than their IQ's predicted, especially at the fourth and fifth grade levels. When a smaller sub-sample of control and experimental children were matched on grade, sex and IQ, the bussed children made significant gains only on reading.

The Berkeley, California experiment reported by the U. S. Commission on Civil Rights (1967, p. 131) for the 1965-1966 year is corroborated by an evaluation of the following year's bussing project (Jonsson, 1967).

Two hundred and fifty Negro students transported from segregated low SES schools in the Flats to integrated middle-class schools in the Hills made higher average gains than in previous years and higher gains than non-bussed students receiving compensatory education. Though SES data were not available on individuals, the students bussed to Hill schools were presumably lower class, since they came from a lower-class area of Berkeley (Sullivan, 1968). However, the Negro children selected for bussing were those "who were predicted to adjust well emotionally and academically to the new school" and parental consent was required (Jonsson, 1966). In other words, the children bussed to the Hills might well have been initially superior to their neighbors who remained behind. (See also Wilson, 1963.)

Under the auspices of the Metropolitan Council for Educational Opportunity (METCO), over 700 Negro students from Boston are being bussed at their parents' request to schools in suburban communities. During the first year of the program pre- and post-Metropolitan Achievement Test scores, available for 66 children in grades 3-8 in three school systems, showed significant improvement on reading, word, and spelling tests, but not on arithmetic. No control group was possible, since the Boston school system did not supply records on its students (Archibald, 1967). In his recent evaluation of the same program, Walberg (1969) solved the control group problem in an ingenious fashion by using siblings of the bussed children matched as closely as possible to them on age. As Walberg pointed out, the design does not guarantee the equality of groups, since there may be bias in the family's choice of child to be bussed, but at least the family and neighborhood environments of siblings are similar. Further bias was introduced because only 47% of the 737 eligible METCO children and 25% of the 352 eligible siblings were tested in both October 1968 and May 1969. Except that METCO children gained significantly less on mathematics at grades 5-6, there were no significant differences in achievement between the two groups from grades 2-12. Neither sex, nor year in program (1-3), nor initial achievement level interacted with bussing status.

Project Concern, which involves bussing Central Hartford, Connecticut Negro and Puerto Rican students to several suburbs in the metropolitan area, was more carefully designed (Mahan, 1967, 1968). Intact classes were randomly selected from eight eligible (85% or more nonwhite) elementary schools in the low SES North End. All 300 children in these classes with an IQ of 80 or above were bussed, except 12 whose parents refused and a random 22 for whom no places were available. A control group of 305 children drawn from the same schools proved to be like the experimental group in grade distribution (K-5) but to have more girls. In the course of the two-year study, 25% of the experimental and 20% of the control group were lost through moves from the target area, dropping out of the project or missing tests. A unique feature of this project is that, by selecting whole classes, central city teachers were released to accompany the pupils to their new schools and supply extra remedial and guidance services. Since not all bussed students received this supportive team assistance, it was possible to compare bussed students with and without compensatory education in their segregated schools.

In his two-year evaluation the project director concluded that 1) "Youngsters placed in suburban classroom at grades K-3 have a significantly greater tendency to show growth in mental ability (WISC and Test of Primary Mental Abilities) than those remaining in inner city classrooms"; 2) In measures of school achievement differences in lower grades are significantly in favor of the experimental group, but in the upper grades in favor of the control group; 3) Suburban placement with special supportive assistance proved more effective than suburban placement without such assistance; and 4) "There is no evidence that special supportive assistance is an effective intervention within inner city schools."

The final bussing study reviewed here is the largest—the New York Open Enrollment Study (Fox, 1966, 1967; Fox et al., 1968). Since 1960 some 22,300 pupils have, on their parents' initiative, transferred from predominantly Negro and Puerto Rican "sending" schools to predominantly white "receiving" schools. Fox (1968, p. 27) concluded: "When children who entered O. E. in 1962 were matched in initial reading ability with children who remained in the sending school, data from the 1965-66 study indicated no difference between them in reading ability. The 1966-67 study found that unmatched, randomly selected samples of O. E. children were reading at higher levels than randomly selected samples of sending school children. These findings suggested to the investigator that the O. E. children did not reflect the full range of ability in the sending schools and that academically more able children entered the O. E. programs."

Investigators in five of the nine bussing studies here reviewed found greater gains for desegregated children than for segregated children, but the case for the beneficial effect of desegregation is marred by several methodological shortcomings. The numbers involved were not large, and (more serious) in all cases the number tested is considerably smaller than the number bussed. This alone would jeopardize the randomness of the sample, even if the experimental and control groups were randomly drawn from the same pool, but in no case is there assurance on this point. Staff selection or parental self-selection always played a part, even in Hartford, where assignment was most nearly random. Therefore, it is possible and likely that more favorable home background and "achievement press" explains the somewhat better performance of bussed pupils. In none of the studies was there a careful attempt to evaluate the equality of education in integrated and segregated classrooms. In the Boston, Rochester, and

273

Hartford experiments there was the further complication of bussing out of a central school district into suburban districts where schools have benefits that ampler budgets provide. Therefore, there is no way of comparing the effects of the rival independent variables of school quality and school ethnic or economic composition. The short duration of most of the programs—too short to offset the stimulation or trauma of transfer—is another reason for concluding that the over-all effectiveness of desegregation via bussing programs has not yet been demonstrated and must await further evidence. (For more details on bussing experiments, see Matthai, 1968.)

The Wilson Study

Of all the studies on the relation of school ethnic composition to minority group performance, the one with the most adequate design was Alan Wilson's (1967) survey, reported in an appendix to the Civil Rights Commission Report. The sample was a stratified random sample of more than 4,000 junior and senior high school students in the San Francisco Bay area. The design is a cross-sectional comparison of verbal test scores, according to the racial and social class composition of neighborhoods and schools, but longitudinal control is introduced by the data on school racial and social class composition at each grade level and first grade individual mental maturity test scores. Wilson argued that controlling on these test scores equates children on the effects of genetic differences and preschool home environment, so changes can be attributed to new (school?) experiences and not to uncontrolled initial differences.

Although the sample is large (over 2,400 Negroes), analysis of the separate effects of neighborhood and school segregation or of racial and social class segregation is hampered for Negroes by the confounding of these variables, and the fact that few Negroes live in integrated neighborhoods. Nevertheless, Wilson showed by regression analysis that after controlling for variation in first grade IQ, the social class of the primary school had a significant effect on sixth grade reading level and the social class of the intermediate school had a significant effect on eighth grade verbal reasoning scores. School racial composition, however, had no significant effect on achievement over and above school social class (pp. 180-84).

Other than the small size of the numbers in some of the cells, there are further limitations to this study. First grade scores were presumably available only for the most stable members of the sample, and its representatives may have been affected by attrition. Children were matched only by father's occupation and primary mental maturity scores; in other respects segregated and integrated children could have been quite different. Parental and school social class assignment based on the questionnaire replies of students are potentially inaccurate. No evidence is offered as to the equality of segregated and integrated schools in Richmond. But in spite of these quibbles, the study is impressive in design and quite convincing that in this community, at least, racial integration *per se* was not significantly related to the academic performance of Negroes.

Conclusion

The literature reviewed offered some evidence as to the relation between school racial composition and academic achievement, but much more evidence as to the difficulties of research in this area.

The "before and after" studies of the desegregation of school systems or individuals suggest that following desegregation, of whatever type or at whatever academic level, subjects generally perform no worse, and in most instances better. Those studies in which the same individuals were measured at Time 1 and Time 2 (Lee, 1951; Katzenmeyer, 1963; Wessman, 1969; and Clark and Plotkin, 1963) have thus largely ruled out the enduring characteristics of the subjects and factors in their past (SES, IQ) as explanation of the change. But interaction between desegregation and quality of schooling has not been ruled out as the explanation of the difference. In fact, desegregation in Washington, D. C. reportedly brought an upgrading of education and in Louisville gave a psychological boost to teachers. Such changes could well explain the gain in achievement in those cities and in situations involving more classroom desegregation.

The general finding of the pre-Coleman cross-sectional studies reviewed is that achievement levels are higher for desegregation than for segregated pupils. Several of these studies were so small-scale and statistically limited that researchers would have little confidence in the generalizability of their findings, if they were not in agreement with studies such as those by Matzen or St. John and Smith which with larger samples and better controls also found higher achievement for the desegregated. However, for all these studies the unresolved question is: Were the desegregated students a select group to start with?

The Coleman data are extensive and have been analyzed with statistical finesse. However, the attempt to draw conclusions from the data is handicapped by the cross-sectional design, the unconvincing measures of social class, the failure to separate the effects of neighborhood SES and of school quality, the imprecise and non-longitudinal measure of school ethnic composition. In spite of such limitations, the survey provides fairly convincing evidence for the existence of a powerful relation between social class integration and achievement. The evidence is less clear for a residual relation between racial integration and achievement. The effect appears to be small, but could be either exaggerated or masked by inadequate control of school quality and home background characteristics.

In theory, investigators using four-celled studies can avoid most of the weaknesses of both panel and cross-sectional research. But no investigation to date has been able to meet all the canons of pure or quasi-experimentation. The matching problem plagues all attempts to equate naturally segregated and non-segregated populations. Wilson (1967) achieved a *post facto* "before" measurement by controlling on primary grade mental maturity, but this procedure did not control on all variables and may have masked the effect of racial segregation.

If, in bussing studies, subjects could be randomly assigned to experimental and control groups, the matching problem would be avoided; but politics and parental preferences seem invariably to bias the selection. Further bias is introduced by differential subsequent dropout from experimental or control groups as some children leave town, leave the program or are not tested. The small number of children involved in most bussing experiments not only handicaps statistical tests of their effectiveness, but also may add to the Hawthorne effect for those involved. The stimulation or embarrassment of being a guinea pig or a newcomer is probably short-run and can be discounted if the experiment is of long enough duration. But the effect of riding a bus to a community other than one's own might be continuing and could only be controlled if students were bussed both to segregated and to integrated schools.

The laboratory experiments of Katz (1964, 1968) and the lessons he draws from them are very convincing as to the "threats" and "facilitations" involved in the process of desegregation. Though as yet unsupported by adequate field research, the most plausible hypothesis is that the relation between integration and achievement is a conditional one: the academic performance of minority group children will be higher in integrated than in equivalent segregated schools, providing they are supported by staff and accepted by peers. As evidence for the first condition there is the report from Hartford that bussed students who received staff support in their new schools showed greatest gains (Mahan, 1968). As evidence for the second condition, there is the findings of the U. S. Commission on Civil Rights (1967) on the importance of interracial friendship to achievement in an integrated setting. In this review, I have perforce ignored the growing and important literature on the relation of ethnic integration and self-concept on one side and of self-concept and achievement on the other. As Wilson (1967) and Pettigrew (1968) suggest, researchers must assume a very complicated, two-way process in which the three variables interact. Support by staff and acceptance by peers undoubtedly contribute to both.

In rapidly changing times the nature of variables and their interrelationship may change. This review has revealed rather inconclusive evidence of a relation between ethnic integration and achievement. But the research examined refers to the immediate or distant past. The meaning of integration may be changing, and the conditions under which it is implemented can be made different in the future. One good reason that there has been no adequate research to date on the effect of integration is that there have been no adequate real-life tests—no large-scale, long-run instances of top-quality schooling in segregated minority-group schools. Until our society tries such experiments, researchers will not be able to evaluate them.

Bibliography

Anderson, Louis V. *The Effects of Desegregation on the Achievement and Personality Patterns of Negro Children.* Doctor's thesis. Nashville, Tenn.: George Peabody College for Teachers, Univ. Microfilm No. 66-11, 237; 1966. Abstract: *Dissertation Abstracts* 27: 1529A-30A, No. 6A; 1966.

Archibald, David K. *Report on Change in Academic Achievement for a Sample of Elementary School Children: Progress Report on METCO.* Roxbury, Mass.: METCO Education Program (178 Humboldt Ave.), 1967. (Mimeo.)

Banks, Ronald and Di Pasquale, Mary E. *A Study of the Educational Effectiveness of Integration.* Buffalo, N. Y.: Buffalo Public Schools, Jan. 1969.

Becker, Howard S. The Career of the Chicago Public School Teacher. *American Journal of Sociology* 57: 470-77; 1952.

Beker, Jerome. *Final Report: A Study of Integration in Racially Imbalanced Urban Public Schools.* Syracuse, N. Y.: Syracuse Univ. Youth Development Center, May 1967. (Mimeo.)

Bowles, Samuel and Levin, Henry. The Determinants of Scholastic Achievement: An Appraisal of Some Recent Evidence. *Journal of Human Resources* 3: 1-24; Winter 1968.

Campbell, Donald T. and Stanley, Julian C. Experimental and Quasi-Experimental Designs for Research on Teaching. *Handbook of Research on Teaching.* (Edited by N. L. Gage.) Chicago: Rand-McNally, 1963. Pp. 171-246.

Clark, Kenneth. B. Desegregation: An Appraisal of the Evidence. *Journal of Social Issues* 9: 1-76; 1953.

Clark, Kenneth B. *Dark Ghetto: Dilemmas of Social Power.* New York: Harper and Row, 1965.

Clark, Kenneth B. and Plotkin, Lawrence. *The Negro Student at Integrated Colleges.* New York: National Scholarship Service and Fund for Negro Students, 1963.

Coleman, James S. et al. *Equality of Educational Opportunity.* U. S. Dept. of Health, Education, and Welfare, Office of Education. Washington, D. C.: Superintendent of Documents, Government Printing Office, 1966.

Colfax, Allen. Pre-Coded versus Open Ended Items and Children's Reports of Father's Occupation. *Sociology of Education* 40: 96-98; 1967.

Conant, James B. *Slums and Suburbs: A Commentary on Schools in Metropolitan Areas.* New York: McGraw-Hill, 1961.

Crockett, Harry J. A Study of Some Factors Affecting the Decision of Negro High School Students to Enroll in Previously All-White High Schools in St. Louis, 1955. *Social Forces* 35: 351-56; 1957. Microfilm No. 181.

Crowley, Mary R. Cincinnati's Experiment in Negro Education: A Comparative Study of the Segregated and Mixed Schools. *Journal of Negro Education* 1: 25-33; 1932.

Deutscher, Max and Chein, Isidor. The Psychological Effects of Enforced Segregation: A Survey of Social Science Opinion. *Journal of Psychology* 26: 259-87; 1948.

Dressler, Frank J. *Study of Achievement in Reading of Pupils Transferred from Schools 15 and 37 to Peripheral Schools to Eliminate Overcrowding to Abandon an Obsolete School, and to Achieve a More Desirable Racial Balance in City Schools.* Buffalo, N. Y.: Board of Education, Division of Curriculum Evaluation and Development, Mar. 1967. (Mimeo.)

Duncan, Otis D. and Duncan, Beverly. *The Negro Population of Chicago.* Chicago: Univ. of Chicago Press, 1957.

Dyer, Henry S. School Factors and Equal Educational Opportunity. *Harvard Educational Review* 38: 38-56; 1968.

Fortenberry, James H. *The Achievement of Negro Pupils in Mixed and Non-Mixed Schools.* Doctor's thesis. Bloomington: Univ. of Ind., Univ. Microfilm No. 59-5492, 1959. Abstract: *Dissertation Abstracts* 20: 2643; 1960.

Fox, David J. *Free Choice Open Enrollment—Elementary Schools.* New York: Center for Urban Education, Aug. 31, 1966. (Mimeo.)

Fox, David J. *Evaluation of the New York City Title I Educational Projects 1966-1967: Expansion of the Free Choice Open Enrollment Program.* New York: Center for Urban Education, Sept. 1967. (Mimeo.)

Fox, David J. et al. *Services to Children in Open Enrollment Receiving Schools: Evaluation of ESEA Title I Projects in New York City, 1967-1968.* New York: Center for Urban Education, Nov. 1968. (Mimeo.)

Gordon, Edmund W. and Wilkerson, Doxey A. *Compensatory Education for the Disadvantaged: Programs and Practices Preschool through College.* New York: College Entrance Examination Board, 1966. Chapter 7, A Critique of Compensatory Education, pp. 156-89. ERIC: ED 011 274, MF $0.45; HC $12.36.

Gottlieb, David. Teaching and Students: The Views of Negro and White Teachers. *Sociology of Education* 37: 345-53; 1964.

Hansen, Carl F. The Scholastic Performances of Negro and White Pupils in the Integrated Public Schools of the District of Columbia. *Harvard Educational Review* 30: 216-36; 1960.

Herriott, Robert E. and St. John, Nancy H. *Social Class and the Urban School.* New York: John Wiley and Sons, 1966.

Hughes, Helen and Watts, Lewis G. Portrait of the Self-Integrator. *The Journal of Social Issues* 20: 103-15; 1964.

Jessup, Dorothy K. School Integration and Minority Group Achievement. *The Urban R's.* (Edited by Dentler, Mackler and Warshauer.) New York: Frederick Praeger, 1967.

Johnson, Norma J.; Wyer, Robert; and Gilbert, Neil. Quality Education and Integration: An Exploratory Study. *Phylon* 28, Fall 1967.

Jonnson, Harold A. *Attitudes Towards Bussing and Integration Expressed by Berkeley Mothers, Teachers, and Children: A Summary of 1966 Survey Findings.* Berkeley, Calif.: Berkeley Unified School District. Nov. 1966. (Mimeo.)

Kaplan, John. *New Rochelle: Civil Rights U.S.A. Public Schools. Cities in the North and West: A Report to the United States Commission on Civil Rights.* Washington, D. C.: Superintendent of Documents, Government Printing Office, 1962.

Katzenmeyer, William Gilbert. *Social Interaction and Differences in Intelligence Test Performance of Negro and White Elementary School Pupils.* Doctor's thesis. Durham, N. C.: Duke Univ., Univ. Microfilm No. 63-2227, 1962. Abstract: *Dissertation Abstracts* 24: 1904-1905, No. 5; 1963.

Katz, Irwin. Review of Evidence Relating to Effects of Desegregation on the Intellectual Performance of Negroes. *American Psychologist* 19: 381-99; 1964.

Katz, Irwin. Academic Motivation and Equal Educational Opportunity. *Harvard Educational Review* 38: 57-65; 1968.

Katzman, Martin T. Distribution and Production in a Big City Elementary School System. *Yale Economic Essays,* No. 8. New Haven, Conn.: Yale Univ., Spring 1968. Pp. 201-56.

Kennedy, A.; Van De Riet, V.; and White, J. C. A Normative Sample of Intelligence and Achievement of Negro Elementary School Children in the Southeastern U. S. *Monographs of the Society for Research in Child Development* 28: 6; 1963.

Klineberg, Otto. *Negro Intelligence and Selective Migration.* New York: Columbia Univ. Press, 1935.

Klineberg, Otto. Negro-White Differences in Intelligence Test Performance: A New Look at an Old Problem. *American Psychologist* 18: 198-203; 1963.

Laird, Mary Alice and Weeks, Grace. *The Effects of Bussing on Achievement in Reading and Arithmetic in Three Philadelphia Schools.* Philadelphia: Board of Education, Division of Research, Dec. 1966. (Mimeo.)

Lee, Everett S. Negro Intelligence and Selective Migration: A Philadelphia Test of Klineberg's Hypothesis. *American Sociological Review* 16: 227-33; 1951.

Lockwood, Jane Durand. *An Examination of Scholastic Achievement, Attitudes and Home Background Factors of 6th Grade Negro Students in Balanced and Unbalanced Schools.* Doctor's thesis. Ann Arbor: Univ. of Mich., Univ. Microfilm No. 67-8303, 1966. Abstract: *Dissertation Abstracts* 28: 54A, 1967.

Luchterhand, Elmer and Weller, Leonard. Social Class and the Desegregation Movement: A Study of Parents' Decisions in a Negro Ghetto. *Social Problems* 13: 83-88; Summer 1965.

Mahan, Thomas W. *Project Concern: An Interim Report on an Educational Exploration.* Hartford, Conn.: Board of Education, Sept. 1967. (Mimeo.)

Mahan, Thomas W. *Project Concern—1966-1968: A Report on the Effectiveness of Suburban School Placement for Inner-City Youth.* Hartford, Conn.: Board of Education, Aug. 1968.

Matthai, Robert Arthur. *The Academic Performance of Negro Students: An Analysis of the Research Findings from Several Bussing Programs.* Qualifying Paper. Cambridge, Mass.: Harvard Graduate School of Education, June 1968.

Matzen, Stanley Paul. *The Relationship between Racial Composition and Scholastic Achievement in Elementary School Classrooms.* Doctor's thesis. Stanford, Calif.: Stanford Univ., Univ. Microfilm No. 66-2518, 1965. Abstract: *Dissertation Abstracts* 26: 6475-76, No. 11; 1966.

McCauley, Patrick and Ball, Edward D. (editors). *Southern Schools: Progress and Problems.* Nashville, Tenn.: Southern Education Reporting Service, 1959.

McGurk, F. C. J. On White and Negro Test Performance and Socioeconomic Factors. *Journal of Abnormal and Social Psychology* 48: 448-50; 1953.

McPartland, James. *The Segregated Student in Desegregated Schools.* Final Report to the Center for the Study of Social Organization of Schools. Baltimore, Md.: Johns Hopkins Univ., June 1968.

Meketon, Betty Field. *The Effects of Integration Upon the Negro Child's Response to Various Tasks and Upon His Level of Self-Esteem.* Doctor's thesis. Lexington: Univ. of Ky., 1966.

Miller, Carroll L. Educational Opportunities and the Negro Child in the South. *Harvard Educational Review* 30: 195-208; 1960.

Moriber, Leonard. *School Functioning of Pupils Born in Other Areas and in New York City.* Publication No. 168. New York: Board of Education, May 1961.

Nichols, Robert C. Schools and the Disadvantaged. *Science* 154: 1312-14; 1966.

Peterson, R. A. and DeBord, L. *Educational Supportiveness of the Home and Academic Performance of Disadvantaged Boys. IMRID, Behavioral Science Monographs,* No. 3. Nashville, Tenn.: George Peabody College, 1966.

Pettigrew, Thomas F. Negro American Personality: Why Isn't More Known? *Journal of Social Issues* 20: 4-23; Apr. 1964.

Pettigrew, Thomas F. Race and Equal Educational Opportunity. *Harvard Educational Review* 38: 67-76; 1968.

Pettigrew, Thomas F. and Pajonas, Patricia J. Social Psychological Consideration of Racially Imbalanced Schools. Paper presented at New York Educational Dept. Conference, Mar. 1964. *Report of the Advisory Committee on Racial Imbalance and Education of the Massachusetts State Board of Education.* Boston, Mass.: Board of Education, Apr. 1965.

Public Education Association. *The Status of the Public School: Education of Negro and Puerto Rican Children in New York City.* New York: Public Education Assoc., Oct. 1955.

Purl, Mabel C. *The Effect of Integration on the Achievement of Elementary Pupils.* Riverside, Calif.: Dept. of Research and Evaluation, Riverside Unified Schools, Nov. 1967 and Mar. 1969.

Radin, Norma. *A Comparison of the Test Performance of Negro Students Attending All-Negro and Integrated Elementary Schools in One Community.* Ypsilanti, Mich.: Board of Education, Apr. 1966.

Rock, William C. et al. *An Interim Report on a Cooperative Program Between a City*

School District and a Sub-urban School District. Rochester, N. Y.: Board of Education, July 20, 1966. (Mimeo.)

Rock, William C. et al. *An Interim Report on a Cooperative Program Between a City School District and a Suburban School District.* Rochester, N. Y.: Board of Education, July 25, 1967. (Mimeo.)

Rock, William C. et al. *A Report on a Cooperative Program Between a City School District and a Suburban School District.* Rochester, N. Y.: Board of Education, June 28, 1968. (Mimeo.)

St. John, Nancy Hoyt. *The Relation of Racial Segregation in Early Schooling to the Level of Aspiration and Academic Achievement of Negro Students in a Northern High School.* Doctor's thesis. Cambridge, Mass.: Harvard Univ., 1962.

St. John, Nancy H. *Measuring the Social Class Background of School Children.* Cambridge, Mass.: Harvard Univ., School of Education, 1969. (Mimeo.)

St. John, Nancy Hoyt and Smith, Marshall S. *School Racial Composition, Aspiration and Achievement.* Cambridge, Mass.: School of Education, Harvard Univ., June 1969. (Mimeo.)

Samuels, Ivan G. *Desegregated Education and Differences in Academic Achievement.* Doctor's thesis. Bloomington: Ind. Univ., Univ. Microfilm No. 58-2934, 1958. Abstract: *Dissertation Abstracts* 19: 1293-94, No. 6; 1958.

Sexton, Patricia. *Education and Income: Inequalities of Education in Our Public Schools.* New York: Viking Press, 1961.

Smith, Marshall S. *A Replication of the EEOS Report's Regression Analysis.* Cambridge, Mass.: Harvard Univ., School of Education, 1969.

Stallings, Frank H. A Study of the Immediate Effects of Integration on Scholastic Achievement in the Louisville Public Schools. *Journal of Negro Education* 28: 439-44; 1959.

Stetler, Henry G. *Private Interracial Neighborhoods in Connecticut.* Hartford, Conn.: Commission on Civil Rights, 1957.

Stodolsky, Susan and Lesser, Gerald. Learning Patterns in the Disadvantaged. *Harvard Educational Review* 37: 546-93; 1967.

Stouffer, Samuel A. Some Observations on Study Design. *Social Research to Test Ideas.* Glencoe, Ill.: Free Press, 1962. Pp. 290-99.

Sullivan, Neil V. Discussion: Implementing Equal Educational Opportunity. *Harvard Educational Review* 38: 148-55; 1968.

United States Commission on Civil Rights. *Public Schools Southern States.* U.S. Dept. of Health, Education, and Welfare; Office of Education. Washington, D. C.: Superintendent of Documents, Government Printing Office, 1962.

United States Commission on Civil Rights. *Racial Isolation in the Public Schools.* U.S. Dept. of Health, Education, and Welfare; Office of Education. Washington, D. C.: Superintendent of Documents, Government Printing Office, 1967.

Vane, Julia R. Relation of Early School Achievement to High School Achievement when Race, Intelligence and Socioeconomic Factors are Equated. *Psychology in the Schools* 3: 124-29; 1966.

Walberg, Herbert J. *An Evaluation of an Urban-Suburban School Bussing Program: Student Achievement and Perception of Class Learning Environments.* Draft of Report to METCO. Roxbury, Mass.: METCO Education Program (178 Humboldt Ave.), July 1, 1969. (Mimeo.)

Weinberg, Meyer. *Desegregation Research: An Appraisal.* Bloomington, Ind.: Phi Delta Kappa, Summer 1968.

Weinstein, Eugene A. and Geisel, Paul N. Family Decision-Making over Desegregation. *Sociometry* 25: 21-29; 1962.

Wessman, Alden E. *Evaluation of Project ABC (A Better Chance): An Evaluation of Dartmouth College Independent Schools Scholarship Program for Disadvantaged High School Students.* U. S. Dept. of Health, Education and Welfare; Office of Education. Washington, D. C.: Superintendent of Documents, Government Printing Office, Apr. 1969.

Whiteman, Martin; Brown, Bert; and Deutsch, Martin. *Some Effects of Social Class and Race on Children's Language and Intellectual Abilities.* Presented at the Biennial Meeting of the Society for Research in Child Development, Minneapolis, Minn.,

Mar. 1965. New York: New York Medical College, Institute for Developmental Studies, Dept. of Psychiatry.

White Plains Public Schools. *A Three-Year Evaluation of the White Plains Racial Balance Plan.* White Plains, N. Y.: Board of Education; Oct. 16, 1967.

Wilson, Alan B. Social Stratification and Academic Achievement. *Education in Depressed Areas.* (Edited by A. Harry Passow.) New York: Bureau of Publications, Teachers College, Columbia Univ., 1963.

Wilson, Alan B. Educational Consequences of Segregation in a California Community. *Racial Isolation in the Public Schools.* Vol. II. Washington, D. C.: U. S. Commission on Civil Rights, 1967. Pp. 165-206.

Wolff, Max. *Racial Imbalance in Plainfield Public Schools. Annex Special High School Study.* Plainfield, N. J.: Board of Education, July 1962. (Mimeo.)

Wolff, Max. Segregation in the Schools of Gary, Indiana. *Journal of Educational Sociology* 36: 251-61; 1963.

Wolman, T. G. Learning Effects of Integration in New Rochelle. *Integrated Education* 2: 30-31; Dec. 1964, Jan. 1965.

EARL OGLETREE and VILMA E. UJLAKI

The Effects of Ability Grouping
on Inner-City Children

Ability grouping of children is a widely accepted instructional practice in the elementary schools of our country. The purpose of such grouping is to provide better instruction on the children's own levels of need and ability. With more effective instruction, the schools hope to achieve one of the most cherished ideals of American education— the opportunity for each individual to develop to his fullest potential. The achievement of this goal through the practice of ability grouping, however, has fallen far short, and its usefulness is being challenged by many serious educators who claim that grouping practices have had harmful and damaging effects on children in the inner-city schools.

Professional educators have long debated the values of ability grouping. Those who favor their use claim that the pace of learning is accelerated and that the number of failures is reduced. Those who object to it argue that while bright children do gain academically, the gain is at the expense of the less able children. They reason that students of average and slow abilities are denied the intellectual and social stimulation which groups of wider ability differences provide. The slower groups also lack the aura of high expectations by their teachers. This lack of aura acts as an operative self-fulfilling prophecy, as it were.

Research findings too are inconsistent. It is possible to support either stand with findings from equally painstaking research. The argument

ILLINOIS SCHOOLS JOURNAL, Spring 1970, Vol. 50, pp. 63-70.

seems to focus on which objective of ability grouping is considered most important: academic achievement or social adjustment. The protagonists claim that ability grouping, when properly handled, will permit students to be with others with whom they feel free to interact and to find common interests and purposes. The opposition contends that classifying children by levels of ability calls attention to other differences of which they had hitherto been unaware. It tends to encourage and perpetuate a kind of academic caste system in the school. This tendency finds support in studies which have shown the existence of a positive relationship between social class and school achievement. Ability grouping then becomes for the children just another system of de facto segregation based on social class distinctions.

Recent studies on the streaming system (ability grouping) in England show that children from middle class families are generally found to be in the top streams while children from working class families are in the lower streams.[1] Studies in our country by Robert J. Havighurst and Bernice Neugarten suggest that not only are children grouped by social class or status for academic purposes but that schools also tend to treat children of higher social status differently from children of lower class status.[2]

It becomes apparent, then, that children's attitudes both toward themselves and toward their school work must be affected by their group placements. Here, too, research findings are inconsistent. In separate studies by Borg and by Goldberg, Passow, and Justin, the results show no adverse effects on children's attitudes because of ability grouping.[3]

It is important to note, however, that in both of these studies the groups were organized for the research study. In addition, Goldberg's study included children with high I.Q.'s only. Neither study included children from the inner city.

Other studies by Luchins and Luchins and by Mann conducted under school-instituted grouping practices revealed a type of intra-school caste system in which low-ability group children appeared to

[1] *Children in the Primary Schools: A Report of the Central Advisory Council for Education*, Vol. II, (London: Her Majesty's Stationary Office, 1967), pp. 589-91.

[2] *School and Society* (Boston: Allyn and Bacon, 1957), p. 230.

[3] Walter R. Borg, "Ability Grouping in the Public Schools," *The Journal of Educational Psychology*, XXIV (Winter 1966), 89-90; Miriam Goldberg, A. Harry Passow, and Joseph Justin, *The Effects of Ability Grouping* (New York: Teachers College Press, Columbia University, 1966), pp. 167-70.

have feelings of inferiority and ostracization.[4] The brighter children, on the other hand, were generally snobbish and felt superior toward their less able peers. A decided stigma was attached to the members of low ability groups.

What are the effects of ability grouping on inner-city children, especially Black children? Kenneth Clark, critic of big-city schools, stated some of the implications in the following statement:

> Homogeneous ability grouping burdens children with resentment and humiliation, while masking significant differences in aptitude, interest and ability among children of the same I.Q. range. . . . It may create as many problems and stigmas as segregating by race.[5]

Educators have been warned by psychologists and others of the possible dangers of maladjustment resulting from ability grouping practices, but no study to date has dealt with their possible effects on the attitudes of children in the inner-city schools.

One of the writers, while teaching in the public elementary schools in Chicago and Detroit, studied the practice of grouping children on the basis of I.Q. and previous scholastic achievement. A simple questionnaire was designed of twenty-four objective-type questions, which required answers of Yes-No-Sometimes-Don't Know. Two open-ended questions also were included to which the children could respond freely. The questionnaire was given to 172 fifth and sixth grade pupils, ages eleven and twelve. The children were in ability groups designated by A for high, B for average, and C for low abilities. The school was a public elementary school in a lower socio-economic Black community in Detroit. The respondents were asked to express their true feelings and did not have to sign their names to the questionnaire.

The results indicated that a larger percentage of children in groups B and C desired to stay away from school than those in the A group in response to the question: "Do you feel like staying away from school often?" Only one percent of the A group wished to stay away as opposed to 21 and 18 percents from the B and C groups respectively. The replies of the high ability group showed they had more pride

---

[4] Abraham Luchins and Edith Luchins, "Children's Attitudes toward Homogeneous Ability Grouping," *Journal of Genetic Psychology*, LXXII (January 1948), 3-9; Maxine Mann, "What Does Ability Grouping Do to the Self-Concept?" *Childhood Education*, XXXVI (April 1960), 357-60.

[5] "Educational Stimulations of Racially Disadvantaged Children," *Education in Depressed Areas*, ed. A. Harry Passow (New York: Teacher's College Press, Columbia University, 1965), p. 152.

in their school than those of the two lower groups. There also was more absenteeism among group B and C pupils as reported by their teachers.

A series of questions on children's attitudes toward grouping and their relationships to their particular groups was also asked. Their responses are shown in Table I:

Questions	Responses in Percentage					
	Yes			No		
	A	B	C	A	B	C
Do you like being in this group?	76	45	26	7	28	50
Are you proud of this group?	53	26	24	15	34	37
Do you think this is a smart group?	48	6	10	2	48	38
Do you think this is a dumb group?	1	24	21	72	48	38
Would you be happier in another group?	5	48	55	52	36	18
Are you happier because you are in this group?	62	44	29	16	40	45
Would you do better work in another group?	22	54	61	35	15	16

Each of the groups had the same teachers for the basic subjects of English, arithmetic, social studies, and science. The groups moved from subject teacher to subject teacher. The responses indicated that the two lower groups were dissatisfied. The teachers too commented that the B and C groups had to be "ruled with an iron hand" while the A group was subject to considerably less rigid discipline. However, even the A group expressed some dissatisfaction as indicated by their selection of more preferable groups as shown in Table II:

In which group would you like to be?

Groups	Groups Preferred and Selected—Percentage			
	A	B	C	Heterogeneous
A	39	26	0	43
B	48	30	7	15
C	52	37	0	3

The responses indicated that all pupils were aware of the status and the stigma associated with each level of grouping. This is especially notable by the fact that none of the A and C groups and only seven percent of the B group chose the C group while most of the C group pupils chose a higher group.

A further conflict is indicated between group placement and desire for status in the paradoxical relationship between the relatively positive attitudes of the A group and the high percentage of members of the A group who wished to be placed in the B group or a heterogeneous class. One interpretation of this is that by moving to a lower or different group, competition might be lessened, and they would be restored to their former higher positions in the class and to their own elevated self-images.

Awareness of status was also shown in responses to questions about how their friends viewed them in regard to certain group memberships. Those in the A group whose friends saw them as bright students gave a much larger percentage of positive responses than those from the two lower groups. Peer relationships and group placement also were affected with the A group showing the highest number of positive responses concerning their liking of other children in their group and having close friends in it.

The findings also showed that as a result of particular group memberships, those in the A group lost fewer friends than those in the other two groups. The comparatively poorer social relationships in the two lower groups may also account for their more negative attitudes toward school and group placement. Or conversely, since children learn about themselves through interaction with others, the status stigma that becomes attached to certain groups may have adversely affected the children's attitudes toward themselves and toward school.

The responses given by the children to open-ended questions are indicative of attitudes toward grouping practices, too. They also show the desperateness of those in the C group in seeking a way out.

Question: How do you feel about being placed in this group?

Group A responses:
"This is a smart group."
"Everyone thinks I am bright."
"My parents are proud of me."
"They (parents) want me to get ahead."
"I would like to be with my section." (heterogeneous group)
"I don't want to be with dumbells."
"I'm not stupid, like some people."
"Group B and C are dumb groups."
"I like it here."
Group B responses:
"It is not a dumb group like group C."
"I don't feel like I'm in the right group. I should like to be in the A group."

"It makes me sick."

"Give me A group."

"I like this group."

"I don't want to be in the dumb group (C)."

"I'm smarter than some people."

Group C responses:

"Please, I don't like it."

"I would feel so good in the smart group."

"I'm dumb."

"People tell me I'm dumb."

"This class is bad."

"I'm too smart for this class."

"This class makes me sick."

Question: Why were you placed in this group?

Group A responses:

"I'm smart, what else?"

"Because I got most of my answers right."

"Naturally I belong here."

"It is an honor to be in this class."

"I'm not dumb."

"I do good work."

Group B responses:

"I don't really know. I guess they don't know my work."

"I'm half smart and half dumb."

"Because I don't have my tests right."

"I'm not dumb like the C group."

"Don't make no difference to me."

"The teacher thinks my work is good."

Group C responses:

"I'm not a hard worker."

"Because I'm not smart."

"Don't know."

"I work hard, but nobody sees it."

"This is a backward class."

"I never was good at books."

"I hate school."

Supporters of ability grouping claim that slower children do not suffer as much from feelings of inferiority and frustration and that bright children are not as complacent about their abilities as might be the case in a random group. This was not supported by the findings in this study. As one can see, many of the pupils in the C group har-

287

bored feelings of inferiority while the children in the other two groups felt snobbish and self-satisfied with their elevated status positions, which created a kind of intellectual caste system in the school.

Teachers in addition reported that it was rare for pupils to be moved to a higher group, but when children were changed to a lower group, it was a traumatic experience both for the pupils and for the class. Pupils literally pleaded to be allowed to remain with the original group. It is obvious that they were aware of the status and the stigma attached to each level.

Although these findings speak clearly enough for themselves of the effects ability grouping may have on children's self-concepts and their feelings about group structures, caution must be exercised in the interpretation of these results. That is, the attitudes of the children toward themselves and toward grouping practices cannot be attributed entirely to the practice itself. Other factors, such as the attitudes of teachers and administrators and the general milieu of the school and its philosophy must be taken into consideration. One can safely assume that it did contribute to an already undesirable situation. It is not the intent of the writers to cast aspersions on the school or school system used in this study, but it is a generally known fact that big-city school systems do utilize ability grouping in some form or other to try to meet the pressing demands for improving academic achievement and for standardization of instruction in the inner-city schools. Thus the findings of this study could be descriptive of other inner-city schools, regardless of their locations.

These results do point out the disparate and subtle implications of a one-sided philosophical view of the educational process. This view assumes the major role of the teacher to be that of a facts and informational purveyor. This seems to preclude the role of the teacher also as the purveyor of values and attitudes. This view is based on the premise that certain people have more educational potential than do others and that what is to be taught has to be adjusted accordingly.

A recent but much criticized study by Robert Rosenthal and L. Jacobson showed that people tend to perform at the level expected of them.[6] This finding is not hard to accept, however, when one considers the many fixed and group-oriented teaching methods of today and the attitudes of teachers that seem to accompany them. If attitudes affect the quality of learning, one wonders where the equality of opportunity for learning is? It seems to the writers that any organizational plan for instruction which convinces one out of three pupils, whether intentionally or not, that he is stupid is a waste of human resources and

6 "Institutionalization of Expectancy," *Urban Renewal*, III (September 1968), 16.

talents. It is especially devastating for inner-city children for whom the school is often the only institution in which they can gain the necessary skills and experiences, attitudes and values needed for healthy concepts of self and of the society in which they live and work.

Is ability grouping worth it? This becomes a question of utmost importance. Since the practice cannot be recommended either on the basis of accelerated learning or on the basis of positive attitudinal development, the answer seems that it is not.

Ability grouping is not a panacea for complex educational ills. Rather, it is like an untested antibiotic, hopefully curing one illness but also creating serious after-effects that must be considered. These too educators must consider with great urgency.

Poverty Research in the Seventies

S. M. Miller

The sixties have been a terrifying decade for this nation. Consensus, pluralism, affluence, and good-will—all have proven slogans rather than descriptions; panaceas, not strategies; blinding, not mind-opening. Instead of consensus, we have deep conflict; pluralism decomposes to reveal profound differences in power; affluence turns out to be maldistributed and inadequate for our needs, unless we constrict wants; the attempts to overcome racial and class discriminations encounter deep antagonisms rather than a reservoir of good will.

The Sixties—A Decade of Scorching Revelations

Social scientists have not escaped similarly scorching revelations. As the nation learned about poverty, social scientists learned about themselves. First, was the wry dismay that it took non-academics to introduce this nation to the facts and the scandal of poverty amid affluence. Second, was the much more disturbing discovery that our data were skimpy, our theory inadequate, and our perspectives not sharpened by the North light of pure objectivity but molded by our convictions.

As this volume demonstrates, the data upon which generalizations are wrought are indeed very scanty. Not only do they often collide with each other, but they are based on studies of restricted, constricted situations—which should impede extending their

JOURNAL OF SOCIAL ISSUES, 1970, Vol. 26, pp. 169-174.

sovereignty to life as it is lived rather than experimented upon in the laboratory. The experience of the sixties should have chastened us to realize how little we know about the root facts of human existence—whether economic, political, social, or psychological. Ignorance, not codified knowledge, is our state—hopefully, not our destiny.

The inadequacy of theory has been the recurring theme of this volume in its reassertion of the significance of the situation, rather than only the psyche, in behavior. Fashions in social science and in politics one-sidedly emphasize one or the other of these elements of the human condition. The theme of the culture of poverty became the theoretical support for a political program of motivation for jobs without the assurance of jobs for trainees. Despite the awareness that academic disciplines are conveniences rather than universalities or moral imperatives, we continue to generalize in terms of limited sets of variables which have been packaged within a particular discipline. (In this volume some healthy departures from this practice are visible.)

Perhaps most striking in the sixties was the attack upon the presumed objectivity and neutrality of social scientists and other academicians and professionals. Universities and their faculties were charged with serving as the guardians of the (liberal) establishment. Expertness was seen as mainly at the service of power elites; advocacy planning, where experts openly and consciously commit themselves to working in the interests of disadvantaged groups, emerged as a repudiation of neutrality. Where one stood in terms of political attitudes affected where one could make studies—low-income communities were dubious about researchers researching them unless they had some confidence in the outlook of the researchers. Social scientists are not impermeable and insulated; their genius as well as their failure comes from their permeability with the world around them. Acting as though this were not the case distorts us.

The questioning of the goal of integration—no longer regarded as the high ground on which one could move, both black and white, as both researcher and citizen—made us aware that our perceptions, feelings, and desires affected our "scientific outlook." The heady moment before Vietnam and before Black Power when our scientific and citizen roles coincided, when we could believe that we could improve the society as we performed our flourishing scientific work, was short indeed. Divisions in political aims unfolded, the ease of change proved illusory, money became tight, and our social concerns as intellectual issues were poorly absorbed through the toughened hides of the academic disciplines. (Even in this issue, social psychologists seem to have to prove themselves worthy of that title by writing articles in the systematic vein of their discipline, though they are highly critical of the work and perspectives that they review.)

Looking Toward the Seventies

I write this harsh postmortem only partly because of my feelings of despair and rage at the sixties. (I do not share the fashionable view of the sixties as having no positive importance; no indeed.) I feel that we social scientists can/should do better in the seventies. I will not attempt what is needed—a full-scale analysis of what the seventies are likely to be and the issues that are raised for social scientists who recognize their aim is to change the society as well as to understand it. (At the end of the sixties, I have come back to Marx's formulation; during the hopeful mid-sixties, I used to say that now that we are changing society, we also had better learn to understand it. Some of that understanding became more painful than I thought it would.) Rather, I will pick up several issues of perspectives which should affect research in the seventies.

The Issue—Not Poverty but Inequality

First, I would repeat what I and many others have tirelessly (but with little effectiveness) said through the sixties. The issue is inequality, not poverty. To say poverty implies a fairly fixed line, defined by some pretentiously scientific standards, to which all families should be brought. Inequality asserts that the issue is the relative position of individuals. Therefore, it forces attention to the relationships and relativities of different groups in society. We can discuss poverty by discussing the poor alone; we cannot discuss inequality without discussing the better-off. I cannot pinpoint the consequences of the shift in terms, but I have the very strong feeling that if one is concerned with inequality rather than poverty, different issues and different ways of studying old issues emerge.[1]

It should not be necessary to say to social psychologists that inequality is not an economic issue. But there does seem to be little research on the interaction of high and low groups in real life situations. Are they changing? For some reason, psychologists seem to believe that historical change is of no importance in their work. In a devotion to the universals of psyche and behavior, academic psychologists have been uninterested in how and why behavior changes over relatively long time-periods (a decade) as a

[1]Pamela Roby and I have tried to develop an analysis of the dimensions and facts of inequality in our *The Future of Inequality*, New York: Basic Books, 1970.

result, at least in part, of large social changes. Psychologists are little interested in time series of human behavior because of an excessive concern with the non-time (and non-cultural?) bound. That is at least how one non-psychologist sees the field.

I hope that a concern with inequality would lead to efforts to study changes in social interactions over time and to discern the factors involved in making for changes. There is some little ground between Erik Erikson and Robert Lifton, on one hand, and "history is bunk," on the other; academic psychologists should search for a place to plunk their flag.

A Mobility Model Downgrades the Poor

Second, the goals of national efforts are in conflict and this conflict extends to social scientists. Is the goal "changing opportunity" or "changing conditions"? Much of the anti-poverty effort of the sixties was aimed at increasing opportunity, especially for the young, particularly through education. The promotion of individual social mobility was the objective. A much higher rate of movement out of poverty ranks would be acceptable even if those left behind were as poorly off as before. Opening doors is the objective, not lifting floors so that no one is in dire circumstances.

Many of us have accepted the mobility motif without evaluating it. This perspective accepts the society fundamentally and seeks to get the disprivileged into the higher economic levels of it at a more rapid rate. A counter perspective accentuates the importance of improving the conditions of those at the bottom, those left behind in the social mobility race, and even sometimes argues for the importance of changing the values of society rather than trying to give more people a better start in the race to affluence.

My strong suspicion is that many of us have absorbed the mobility model and that it affects the kind of research that we do and the way we go about it. My guess is that the mobility model encouraged social scientists to downgrade the strengths and flexibility of the poor. I may be wrong about this, but I am convinced in any case that social scientists have to become more aware of what their own perspectives are and how they are being used by others.

Recognizing Limits of Remediation Policies

Third, we have to be willing to recognize the limits of the remediation policies of this country. The so-called "welfare state" policies and education, as the major vehicle of social mobility and as the mid-wife of a meritocracy where merit achieves its just reward, may not be as effective in producing redistribution and lessened inequality as was commonly thought to be the situation in the sixties. Since the kinds of policy implications that the researcher thinks about effect the nature of his research (choice of problems, angle of analysis), it is important to be open to a wider range of action implications than we have been.

Reallocating Academic Disciplines

Fourth, should we not begin to think seriously about the recutting of academic disciplines? Is social psychology best developed by thinking of it as intrinsically connected to academic psychology rather than to sociology or economics? Or, as part of a new discipline that is struggling to emerge—which is about urban studies and political economy? Or as part of action fields, like education, in which the core is a concern with a set of social problems or issues rather than with a methodology? My suspicion is that deep changes are taking place in the field of social psychology but that these changes in practice have not permeated the training and location of social psychologists.

In the sixties, social scientists apparently jumped from the laboratory and the clipboard to the corridors of power. The whiff of the top was intoxicating—at least until we learned how long those corridors were and how difficult to influence those at the end of the passageway. We should also have learned the limits of what we had to offer and how in turn we were often manipulated.

In the seventies, we should refrain from providing a rationale for, nor a beautifying of, programs that cannot work. We should help uncover and refine the important values for society. We should assess the possibilities and the limits of governmental policies and actions. We should alert ourselves and the nation to the things that government cannot do and which we as a nation yet must do for ourselves.

Examining Ourselves

The seventies will require more complicated perspectives from social scientists than they exhibited in the sixties. For it is now clear that the issues are not only those of integrating the poor and the discriminated into society but changing that society at the same time. Our unclarity about our own perspectives aggravates the faulty data and limited generalizations which plague social science. But better data and generalizations will not alone solve our problems. We have also to examine ourselves.